Hastings

Symmetries of Culture

Above, bronze *yu* (Fig. 6.9); *facing,* wood
figurine, Yombe (Fig. 5.291)

Symmetries of Culture

Theory and Practice
of Plane Pattern Analysis

Dorothy K. Washburn
Donald W. Crowe

University of Washington Press   *Seattle and London*

Copyright © 1988 by the University of
 Washington Press
Second printing (pbk.), 1992
Designed by Veronica Seyd
Printed and bound in Japan

The paper used in this publication meets
the minimum requirements of American
National Standard for Information
Sciences—Permanence of Paper for Printed
Library Materials, ANSI Z39.48–1984. ∞

Publication of this book was made possible
in part by the assistance of the J. Paul
Getty Trust, and by a grant from the
Division of Research Programs of the
National Endowment for the Humanities.

Library of Congress
Cataloging-in-Publication Data
Washburn, Dorothy Koster.
Symmetries of culture.
    Bibliography: p.
    Includes index.
    1. Repetitive patterns (Decorative arts).
2. Pattern perception.   3. Symmetry (Art).
I. Crowe, Donald W. (Donald Warren),
1927– .   II. Title
NK1570.W34   1987   745.4   87–27924
ISBN 0–295–97084–7

Endsheet illustrations: front, tapa, Samoa
(Fig. 7.5); *back,* burial mantle, Paracas
(Fig. 7.17, detail)

Stirrup, Edo (Fig. 5.286)

Contents

Loincloth, Chancay style (Fig. 5.1, detail)

Acknowledgments

THE AUTHORS began this endeavor separately, Washburn in her 1977a monograph and Crowe in his several articles (1971, 1975, 1982). We joined forces realizing that we could contribute substantially to each other's knowledge and understanding of cultural and mathematical aspects from our respective disciplines. Washburn gratefully thanks the Miller Institute for Basic Research in Science, University of California, Berkeley, for an unrestricted two-year Fellowship (1976–78) which supported the developmental phases of this work. Crowe is indebted to Claudia Zaslavsky, whose invitation to contribute to her book *Africa Counts* led to his first study of symmetry in cultural objects; to the 1978 article by Doris Schattschneider, which was the inspiration for the flow charts; and to California State University, Chico, for a Visiting Professorship which gave him the time to dig in Ghana and begin his collaboration with Washburn. We also thank Branko Grünbaum and G. C. Shephard, pioneers in the analysis of patterns, who kindly made available sections of their work, *Tilings and Patterns* (1987), before its publication.

An endeavor of this magnitude could not have been successful without the assistance of many people. We thank especially all the museums that made available photographs of objects from their collections. These are acknowledged separately with each illustration. Photographs of the many objects from the California Academy of Sciences were taken by Christopher Thomas. Copy photographs from books were made by Susan Middleton and Judith Steiner. Coleen Sudekum and Amy Pertschuk redrew objects for which photographs were unobtainable. The computer-generated schematic drawings of the two-dimensional motion classes were made by Mike Case of Beloit College. Melanie Herzog-Stockwell of the Cartographic Laboratory of the University of Wisconsin added the reflection lines and centers of rotation. Funding for the purchase of museum photographs and the preparation of illustrations was provided by the Irving Fund and research funds of the California Academy of Sciences, and the College of Letters and Sciences, University of Wisconsin, Madison. Finally, we are especially grateful to Marian Bock and Veronica Seyd of the University of Washington Press for their careful attention to the difficult task of polishing the rough spots in the manuscript while preparing it for final publication.

Introduction

THE USE of the geometric principles of symmetry for the description and understanding of decorated forms represents the union of two normally separate disciplines—mathematics and design. The only limitation to the types of designs which can be described by these principles is that they must consist of regularly repeated patterns. That is, they must be designs with parts moved by rigid geometric motions.

In this book we demonstrate how to use the geometric principles of crystallography to develop a descriptive classification of patterned design. Just as specific chemical assays permit objective analysis and comparison of objects, so too the description of designs by their geometric symmetries makes possible systematic study of their function and meaning within cultural contexts.

This particular type of analysis classifies the underlying structure of decorated forms; that is, the way the parts (elements, motifs, design units) are arranged in the whole design by the geometrical symmetries which repeat them. The classification emphasizes the way the design elements are repeated, not the nature of the elements themselves. The symmetry classes which this method yields, also called motion classes, can be used to describe any design whose parts are repeated in a regular fashion. On most decorated forms such repeated design, properly called pattern, is either planar or can be flattened (e.g., unrolled), so that these repeated designs can be described either as bands or strips (one-dimensional infinite) or as overall patterns (two-dimensional infinite) in a plane.

This is essentially a handbook for the nonmathematician. There are a number of geometry textbooks which derive the pattern classes, but they usually offer more detail than is needed by a user in the humanities. Conversely, there have been a number of articles and monographs written by and for social scientists, but these are usually specific to one body of data. We have attempted to offer a more comprehensive survey of patterns occurring on decorated objects from cultures all over the world and to systematically show how to classify the finite, one-dimensional, and two-dimensional one- and two-color designs with the use of flow charts and other detailed descriptions of the symmetry motions and colors present.

Chapter 1 presents a short historical review of the discovery and enumeration of the plane pattern classes, the importance of symmetry for form identification and classification, and theoretical issues in the application of this type of analysis to designs found on cultural material. Chapters 2 through 6 show how to classify patterned design with the aid of flow charts, schematic drawings of each class, and photographs and drawings of actual objects decorated with such patterns. These chapters treat the one- and two-color, one- and two-dimensional patterns, and the common finite designs, because these are the most frequently encountered.

The mathematical background needed to understand and perform symmetry analysis is summarized in Chapters 2 and 3. The reader must be conversant with these principles before reading Chapters 4, 5, and 6, which describe the one-dimensional, two-dimensional, and finite designs respectively. Each of the chapters on one- and two-dimensional designs begins with a section which describes the flow charts and leads the reader through the use of the charts with an example from each motion class. The last section of each of these two chapters presents a more detailed explanation of each motion class and shows actual examples of this class. Chapter 7 discusses special problems which may be encountered in symmetry classification. Three Appendixes present in detail the mathematical proofs for the existence of the four motions and the seven one-dimensional designs, and correlate the several other nomenclatures with the standard crystallographic nomenclature which we use in this book.

We suggest that the user first grasp the principles of geometry outlined in Chapters 2 and 3 and become familiar with the flow charts, before embarking on a study of a specific body of data. Then, in order to classify any particular pattern, use the flow charts in Sections 4.2 and 5.1 and the schematic drawings in 4.3 and 5.2 to key out the pattern. As a final check, turn to the examples shown in 4.3 and 5.2 for comparison with patterns already identified.

There are computer-generated schematic drawings of every one- and two-color, one- and two-dimensional design. Indicated in each drawing are the mirror (solid) and glide (dashed) lines and centers of rotation: ◑ , ○ for twofold rotation, with and without color reversal; ▽ for threefold rotation; ◪ , □ for fourfold rotation, with and without color reversal; and ✦ , ○ for sixfold rotation, with and without color reversal. In these drawings, right triangles or trapezoids represent the asymmetrical fundamental building blocks of repeated patterns.

A number of patterns have been illustrated for classes where the symmetry is particularly difficult to see, where it frequently occurs on a number of different kinds of media, or where there are problems and deviations from the symmetry which must be considered. Further discussion of problem situations which repeatedly occur is contained in Chapter 7.

Symmetries of Culture

Plate, Deruta, Italy, A.D. 1520–25 (Fine Arts
Museum of San Francisco, no. 54.45.3)

1 History and Theory of Plane Pattern Analysis

1.1 Introduction

IN THIS CHAPTER we first present a short mathematical history (1.2) of the plane pattern crystallographic motion classes and their initial applications to non-mathematical fields (1.3) as a preliminary to our discussion (1.4) of the appropriateness of this methodology, in terms of the perceptual process of pattern recognition and the theoretical needs of style analysis, for the study of designs in material culture.

1.2 Crystallographic and Mathematical History

In his brief prehistory of group theory, A. Speiser (1927) suggested that the origin of higher mathematics (at that time thought to be in Greece about 500 B.C.) should be pushed back a thousand years to the Egyptian use of one-dimensional and two-dimensional patterns (see Jones 1856 for illustration of such designs). In his view, the creation of certain of these two-dimensional patterns, with many complicated symmetries, was a mathematical discovery of the first magnitude.

In contrast to these Egyptians, the later Greeks, who otherwise studied geometry in a most profound way, seem to have had less interest in such infinite patterns. However, they developed the theory of finite designs—in the form of regular polygons, especially the equilateral triangle, square, regular pentagon, and regular hexagon—to a high level. This theory included, in Euclid, a detailed analysis of the five regular polyhedra and, later, the thirteen Archimedean polyhedra. Both of these classes of polyhedra can be interpreted as patterns on the surface of a sphere. However, the Greeks apparently did not emphasize the analogous (infinite) patterns in the plane: the three regular tessellations, and the eight semiregular tessellations.

Following these Greek constructions there is little record of purely mathematical studies for hundreds of years. But the work of Byzantine artisans of Ravenna and Constantinople and their successors in Venice, and the Islamic pattern makers throughout the Mediterranean and east to India, carried on what we must think of as mathematical work. Although they did not call themselves mathematicians, in retrospect (cf. Müller 1944) we see their methods and results as having important geometric content.

During the Renaissance, Italian artists and architects made much use of finite designs. It is thought that Leonardo da Vinci consciously studied the symmetries of finite designs and determined all of them so as to be able to attach chapels and niches without destroying the symmetry of the whole. His conclusion, now called Leonardo's Theorem (Martin 1982:66), was that the only possible (one-color) finite designs are those which have rotational symmetry alone, like a swastika (Figure 1.1a), and those which have both rotational and reflection symmetry, like a Greek cross (Figure 1.1b) or a square.

We will use the symbol $c4$ to denote designs with fourfold rotational symmetry but no reflection symmetry, like the swastika. More generally, cn denotes any design having only n-fold rotational symmetry, such as a swastika

1.1a Swastika with rotation symmetry

1.1b Cross with rotation and reflection symmetry

with n arms. For the corresponding designs with reflection symmetry, we use the symbol dn. Thus a Greek cross and a square have type $d4$ symmetry and a regular hexagon has type $d6$ symmetry.

Other regular polygons, in the form of fountains, are ubiquitous in Italy. A typical example, the Maggiore fountain in Perugia, has two tiers, the upper one having 12-fold (i.e., $d12$) rotational symmetry and the lower one 25-fold rotational symmetry. The rose window of Santa Chiara in Assisi has 15-fold and 30-fold symmetry (Munari 1966:63). The pulpit of St. Stephen's in Vienna alternates threefold ($c3$) and fourfold ($c4$) symmetries (Weyl 1952:67). An unusual assemblage of examples of $c3$, $c4$, $c5$, $c6$, and $c7$ symmetries, carved in wood to imitate Gothic windows, is found in the St. Johannes church in Lüneburg.

Dürer's book on geometry (1525) carried this and other information about regular polygons to Germany for the use of artists. A hundred years later, Kepler made careful studies of regular polyhedra, and in 1611 wrote a monograph on the snowflake in which he considered the packing of circles in a plane and spheres in space. Kepler's work can be thought of as the forerunner of crystallography, the study of which in the nineteenth century led to almost all the mathematical information we have on repeated patterns until very recent times.

In the early nineteenth century Hessel found the thirty-two main classes of crystals (i.e., three-dimensional repeated patterns) which are still used today. The names of Bravais, Jordan, Sohncke, Barlow, and Schoenflies figure prominently in the massive effort which culminated in the complete list of all 230 three-dimensional repeated patterns published by Fedorov in 1891. Fortunately, these 230 patterns and the 4,783 four-dimensional patterns recently enumerated by Brown, Bülow, Neubüser, Wondratschek, and Zassenhaus (1978) do not directly concern the student of plane patterns.

One-Color Patterns

The enumeration of the seventeen two-dimensional (one-color) patterns was also published by Fedorov in 1891. Because this paper appeared only in Russian and was of little interest for crystallography, it was not until the 1920s that the classification of one- and two-dimensional patterns became generally known, through the papers of Niggli (1924, 1926) and Pólya (1924).

The second edition (1927) of Speiser's group theory text first called the attention of mathematicians to these results. Speiser adopted the notation used by Niggli, but unfortunately interchanged two of the Niggli symbols. The mathematical literature of the next fifty years was infected by the consequences of this error. It was finally corrected by Schattschneider (1978). Fortunately, the crystallographers continued on their own path, so this error does not appear in their work.

It is to Speiser's student, Edith Müller, that we owe credit for perhaps the first systematic use of these tools in the analysis of material culture. Her 1944 thesis is a detailed study of the patterned art of the Alhambra. Although Müller is often credited with having found all seventeen one-color plane patterns there, she refers explicitly to only eleven; two others have been documented elsewhere. (In the notation explained in Chapter 2, the eleven recorded by Müller are *p1, pmg, cm, pmm, cmm, p4, p4m, p4g, p3, p6,* and *p6m.* Grünbaum, Grünbaum, and Shephard [1986] record *p31m* and *pm* and Jones [1856:P1. 41, 5] records *pg* [ambiguous].) Not until 1987 did the combined efforts of Spanish mathematicians and topologists provide documentation of the presence of all seventeen one-color plane patterns in the Alhambra.

Discussions of the one-color band and plane patterns began to appear more frequently in mathematical texts following Speiser, particularly in Coxeter (1961), Fejes Tóth (1964), Burckhardt (1966), Guggenheimer (1967), Cadwell (1966), and O'Daffer and Clemens (1976). The recent books of Lockwood and Macmillan (1978) and Martin (1982) deal extensively with these topics. Of these references, the last four are perhaps the most accessible to the non-mathematician. The Schattschneider (1978) paper is also recommended.

Two-Color Patterns

The history of the two-color and more highly colored patterns is well described in the treatise of Grünbaum and Shephard (1987), which can be taken as the definitive text for the mathematical theory of patterns in general. The following briefly summarizes the extensive "Notes and References" at the end of their Chapter 8. (They refer to our one-dimensional patterns as "strips," and to our two-dimensional patterns as "periodic patterns.")

The first complete, explicit, and deliberate enumeration of the two-color one- and two-dimensional patterns is found in the papers of the textile physicist H. J. Woods (1935, 1936). The mosaic representations of all forty-six two-color patterns in our Chapter 3 are reproduced from Woods 1936. Other mosaics were used in 1957 by Belov and Belova (excerpted in Shubnikov and Belov 1964), who were presumably unaware of Woods's earlier work (Crowe 1986).

Until very recently the most active study of two-color patterns was conducted by the Soviet school of crystallography, following the lead of Shubnikov (e.g., Shubnikov and Koptsik 1974; Shubnikov and Belov 1964). For reasons related to crystallographic situations (of no importance for the study of patterns as such), they introduced the concept of "gray" patterns to accompany the one-color and two-color (black-white) patterns, and these gray patterns were often pictured along with the others. Since the gray patterns are exactly like the one-color patterns, modern treatments often omit them. However, their inclusion means that in many earlier papers the totals 24 (= 7 one-color

+ 17 two-color) for one-dimensional patterns and 63 (= 17 one-color + 46 two-color) for two-dimensional patterns, which are customary in the most recent literature (including the present handbook), appear as 31 (= 7 one-color + 7 gray + 17 two-color) and 80 (= 17 one-color + 17 gray + 46 two-color).

For the reader who wants to know more about the mathematics of two-color patterns than is in the present handbook, we recommend Woods (1936), Belov and Tarkhova (1956, reprinted in Shubnikov and Belov 1964), Loeb (1971), Lockwood and Macmillan (1978), or Grünbaum and Shephard (1987). A particularly elementary discussion is found in Schattschneider (1986).

The notation we have adopted for the two-color two-dimensional patterns is the "rational symbol" of Belov and Tarkhova. (Some of their misprints are corrected in our Section 3.4.) For the two-color one-dimensional patterns we use the convenient notation of Belov (in Shubnikov and Belov 1964:225). This latter notation is explained in our Section 3.4.

Multicolored Patterns

For patterns with more than two colors, it is only recently that there has been agreement concerning the most reasonable definitions, and there is still no generally accepted nomenclature. The following studies are the most recent statements which may be used to classify multicolored patterns. For detailed bibliographic and historical notes see Schwarzenberger (1984) and Chapter 8 of Grünbaum and Shephard (1987).

Jarratt and Schwarzenberger (1981) determined the number of colorings of one-dimensional patterns with n colors, for all values of n. Wieting (1982) enumerated all possible colorings of two-dimensional patterns by n colors, for values of n up to sixty. He gives detailed drawings for the ninety-six ways of coloring two-dimensional patterns with four colors. Finally, Grünbaum and Shephard (1987) illustrate all twenty-three ways of coloring two-dimensional patterns with three colors.

1.3 Applications of Geometry to Design: Historical Precedents

Interest in the application of the principles of geometric symmetry to fields other than crystallography has been sporadic. "Reinventing the wheel" pervades the literature as a number of individuals have separately discovered that symmetry can be a useful analytical tool. Many authors appear unaware of other similar work and there appears to have been, until the last decade, little follow-up on these isolated pioneering introductions.

Our short historical discussion here can be merely an introduction to the literature in this important field. We make no guarantee to present an exhaustive listing of these efforts. Publication in obscure serials and the isolated, singular nature of many of these studies make omissions almost certain.

Nevertheless, we hope to discuss here the major applications of symmetry to the analysis of decorated objects.

Social and scientific activities around the turn of the century seem to have promoted a focus on design. Because the machines of the industrial revolution could stamp and weave patterns endlessly, there was a great need to codify and order this new wealth of material. At the same time, scholars in the humanistic fields were also categorizing, classifying, and bringing new order to a wealth of artifacts amassed by explorers who had begun to fill museums with objects from their world-wide travels.

It is interesting that during this period, although both crystallographers and designers were describing repeated patterns, neither seemed to take cognizance of the others' work. The crystallographers derived the geometry of crystal structure as a mathematical exercise, but the designers had a practical need to organize the myriad patterns from home and afar in some systematic descriptive fashion. Although the designers saw the rhythm and repetition inherent in the patterns, they never discovered that patterns could be more systematically, precisely, and objectively described by their symmetries.

Men of letters published numerous compendia illustrating patterns from all over the world and from all periods of prehistory and history. An early example is Franz Sales Meyer's *Handbook of Ornament* (1894). Meyer divided "all geometrical ornament" into "ribbon-like forms (bands), bordered figures (panels), and unbordered flat patterns." These generally correspond to the one-dimensional, finite, and two-dimensional categories respectively. Meyer called the system of subsidiary lines (required to form geometrical patterns such as mosaics) "nets," foreshadowing the common use of this term for two-dimensional plane pattern layouts.

Another example, *A Text Book Dealing with Ornamental Designs for Woven Fabrics* (Stephenson and Suddards 1897), showed students how to produce repeated patterns, not by specifying the geometric motions, but by illustrating the basic layouts, such as "drop patterns" (*cmm*), "turnover patterns" (*pg*), "sateens" (various two-dimensional patterns), and "borders" and "stripes" (various one-dimensional patterns). The students were to use these as basic layouts on which they could repeat a variety of motifs. The term *counterchange* was applied to patterns "whose shape is so designed as to leave an exactly similar and equal shape in the ground" (1897:18).

A whole series of encyclopedias of design appeared at this time. Some were in elaborate folio format and illustrated designs from one area or medium, such as Perleberg's *Peruvian Textiles* (n.d.), Clouzot's *Tissus Nègres* (n.d.), Flemming's *An Encyclopaedia of Textiles* (n.d.), Dolmetsch's *Der Ornamentenschatz* (1889), and Racinet's *L'Ornement Polychrome* (1869). Others attempted to cover a world-wide range of designs. Speltz's three-volume *The Coloured Ornament of All Historical Styles* (n.d., 1914, 1915) covers patterns from antiquity to modern times. Hamlin (1916) wrote a systematic history of ornament from the primitive to Gothic periods, and like Meyer divided the patterns into "linear," "all-over," and "radiating"—his names for the three categories of designs we will be examining here: one-dimensional patterns, two-dimensional patterns, and finite designs.

Still other writers attempted to present some discussion on the composition of patterns. Four volumes are of particular note in this regard: Owen Jones's *The Grammar of Ornament* (1856), W. and G. Audsley's *Outlines of Ornament in the Leading Styles* (1882), Lewis Day's *Ornament and Its Application* (1904), and Archibald Christie's *Pattern Design* (1929). Much of their work came very close to describing patterns by their geometric symmetries.

The Audsleys' statement of purpose perhaps best summarizes the activity and interest in design during this period.

> Notwithstanding the numerous and important Works on Ornament which have been published in this and other countries, during the last twenty years, we feel assured that there is still room for the more humble Work which we now lay before the public, differing as it does in aim and treatment from any that have preceded it. In this direction probably Works of such magnitude and elaboration as Owen Jones' *Grammar of Ornament* and Racinet's *L'Ornement Polychrome* will not be again produced in our day. They give superb collections of Decorative and Ornamental Designs, grouped under the respective Nations or Schools which have produced them, and supply the Decorative Artist and Ornamentalist with an almost inexhaustible fount of inspiration. . . . If they fail in anything . . . they do not bring directly and clearly before the eye of the student the true scope of each species of ornamental design, and distinctly impress him with its principles of construction, and point out how these principles have been modified or developed by different artists, and at different epochs of art. (1882: Preface)

The Audsleys classified patterns according to the different layouts: fret, fret diaper, interlaced, powdered, diaper, and conventional foliage.

Christie defined pattern much as we do.

> The term "pattern" necessarily implies a design composed of one or more devices, multiplied and arranged in orderly sequence. A single device, however complicated or complete in itself it may be, is not a pattern, but a unit with which the designer, working according to some definite plan of action, may compose a pattern. (1929:1)

Christie divided all ornament into two main types: isolated units which are "spotted" upon a ground, and continuous units which are "striped" across a ground. (Christie's "ground" is the same as our "background," discussed and defined below.) He gave numerous examples of how various patterns were developed from these types by "processes such as interlacing, branching, interlocking, and counterchanging." He recognized that different designs can be built from the same units simply by arranging them differently in spots and stripes. "The structural method, not the element used, is the sole basis of classification." Christie saw that his pattern classification "follows broadly the lines laid down by the zoologist, who separates into well defined categories all living and extinct creatures" (1929:77, 66, 59).

The work of Andreas Speiser (1927) and his student Edith Müller (1944) (discussed in Section 1.2 above) was perhaps the first attempt by outsiders to describe the symmetries in repeated patterns. By the 1930s both aestheticians and designers had taken note of the geometry inherent in repeated patterns. The mathematician George David Birkhoff, for example, saw that the formal structure of Western music was a mathematical problem that could be defined by the formula $M = O/C$, where M is the aesthetic measure of any object relative to O, its order, and C, its complexity. Later he developed formulas for the aesthetic measure of vases and other objects. He defined *ornament* as "any figure, traced, painted, embossed or otherwise executed on a surface . . . provided there is at least one possible motion which moves the figure, as a whole but not point for point, back to its initial position" (1933:49). Further, he defined and illustrated the four symmetric motions, "fundamental regions," "fundamental portions," as well as finite designs and one-dimensional and two-dimensional patterns, in his famous book *Aesthetic Measure* (1933).

Another early instance of the systematic codification of repeated patterns was by H. J. Woods, from the Textile Physics Laboratory, University of Leeds, who wrote a four-part article for the *Journal of the Textile Institute* (1935–36) describing the geometry behind finite designs and one- and two-dimensional, one- and two-color patterns. He attempted to ease nonmathematicians into understanding the "science" underlying repeated design by pointing out that even in nature patterns are crystalline, "and a crystal is nothing more than a pattern in three dimensions."

The "science" of design is, in fact, only a simplified and specialized part of the branch of physics devoted to the study of crystalline form, "crystallography," just as the latter, to the mathematician, is nothing but an application of the great branch of mathematics, the "Theory of Groups." (1935:197)

Woods claimed to be the first to present this analysis of symmetry to non-mathematical users: "as far as the author is aware there is no work to which the designer unversed in mathematics can go in order to master his fundamentals. The object of these papers is to survey . . . those parts of crystallography which might be of interest to the textile designer" (1935:197). Woods was correct and his papers were landmarks because he made available to the non-scientist a new way of understanding the formation of repeated patterns. Of course, numerous articles and texts by mathematicians and crystallographers had been available for some time but the technicalities of the proofs undoubtedly precluded comprehension of these ideas by a general audience.

Subsequent mention of the applicability of geometry to design then came from other physical scientists. Buerger and Lukesh, in a short article in *Technology Review* (1937), illustrated the two-dimensional patterns with asymmetrical "comma" symbols. These authors classified the patterns both by a crystallographic nomenclature and a symbol system which described the shape of the lattice, the number of rotors (i.e., rotation centers), and the presence and position of the glide and mirror reflection lines.

The classic book *Symmetry*, by the mathematician Hermann Weyl (1952), is a description of symmetry in a variety of contexts. Its scope has recently been updated by Rosen (1975), who points out the myriad presence of symmetry in botany and art as well as in the pure sciences. Another important book, summarizing the impressive work done by the Russian crystallographers, is Shubnikov and Koptsik's *Symmetry in Science and Art* (1974).

A Symmetry Festival, held at Smith College in 1973, was designed to emphasize symmetry's many manifestations. The papers from that conference, *Patterns of Symmetry* (Senechal and Fleck 1977), emphasized that symmetry is not only overtly present in plants and crystal structures but also more subtly in the structure of musical phrases and in literary works.

The most recent compendium of research on the diverse presence and applications of symmetry in the pure sciences and well as in the arts and humanities is to be found in *Symmetry: Unifying Human Understanding*, edited by Istvan Hargittai (1986).

In a very provocative digestion of symmetry, *Gödel, Escher, Bach: An Eternal Golden Braid* (1980), Hofstadter compares Bach's fugues and canons, which transform musical phrases by repetition in different keys and tempos; the periodic drawings of M. C. Escher, whose subtle form shifts from insects to fish to birds suggest potentially infinite transformations; and the mathematical definition of paradoxical loops of logic by Kurt Gödel. Actually, these are just props Hofstadter uses to prod the reader to think about the isomorphisms in human systems of thought and action. That is, he wants the reader to see that isomorphisms lead to symbolic associations of meaning, which in turn are parts of larger formal systems.

Hofstadter uses the decipherment of Linear B script to illustrate how discovery of the system of symbolic association depends on the ability to see isomorphisms. He laments that "it is uncommon, to say the least, for someone to be in the position of 'decoding' a formal system turned up in the excavations of a ruined civilization" (1980:50). But that is precisely what we are about here. We can clearly see that repeated designs are regulated by the formal rules of symmetry. Further, since symmetries restrict the kinds of pattern arrangements possible, they form a sort of grammar. But languages are each characterized by a different grammar; the "grammar" of repeated designs is universal. All patterns are produced by the same rules; that is, pattern structures can change, but the rules for changing them cannot. Meaning in such formal systems is inherent in the structuring of the parts.

An equally intriguing artistic rendering of the principles of symmetry was produced by Scott Kim. *Inversions* (1981), on one level, contains delightful excursions into the world of graphic palindromes. On another level, the implications for understanding art as graphic imagery of our world are almost as infinite as are the tessellations themselves. Kim's wordplay illustrates how different viewers perceive the same scene differently; how viewers perceive only part of what they see; and how perceptions are conditioned by the viewer's specific culture, so that interpretations of partial or obscured images are related to what the viewer already knows and is familiar with in his world (cf. Washburn 1983a).

Perhaps the most fanciful application of the laws of crystallography can be seen in the work of the Dutch artist M. C. Escher, who has arranged people, animals, and insects in two-dimensional one-, two-, and multi-colored symmetrical patterns. Escher began work on these tessellations in the 1920s. By 1942 he had complied a notebook where he illustrated almost all the 2-, 3-, 4-, and 6-color rotational two-dimensional patterns with and without glide reflection. An exhibit of Escher's work was organized on the occasion of the Fifth International Congress of the International Union of Crystallography held in Cambridge, England, in 1960. Subsequently Caroline MacGillavry, a crystallographer, gathered and published a number of these drawings as an aid to teaching the principles of symmetry (1965). The popularity of Escher's work has continually grown and MacGillavry's book was republished under the title *Fantasy and Symmetry* (1976). A complete compendium of Escher's work was recently edited by J. L. Locher; see also Coxeter et al. (1986).

The interest in regular pattern by designers, sparked at the turn of the century by a variety of historical factors, resulted then in the production of a number of surveys of decorative design and continues today in the publication of similar compendia. Arranged culturally, historically, and topically, the early treatises were compiled principally as source books for craftsmen and designers. Current publications, by architects for architects and other designers, include details of the mathematical bases for the repeated patterns.

For example, *The Geometry of Environment* by March and Steadman (1971) illustrates schematically with trapezoidal units the seven one-dimensional and seventeen two-dimensional motion classes. The authors emphasize how Frank Lloyd Wright and Le Corbusier were influenced by the many symmetrical constructions in Owen Jones's *The Grammar of Ornament* (1856). Frank Lloyd Wright was said to "work through the nights training from it to exercise his skill at drafting before applying for a job with Louis Sullivan, the father of modern architecture in Chicago" (March and Steadman 1971:38).

The architect Stevens's 1974 book, *Patterns in Nature,* consists of much photographic raw material awaiting geometric analysis. His subsequent book, *Handbook of Regular Patterns* (1980), extensively illustrates, with patterned art throughout the world, the classes of finite (point), one-dimensional (line), and two-dimensional (plane) pattern classes. His aim is to digest the technical descriptions of crystallographers and chemists so that artists may understand the understructure of their repeated patterns, and indeed gain sufficient knowledge to create new patterns of their own. This book is, in effect, a contemporary version of the pattern encyclopedias produced at the turn of the century, though organized on the very same geometric principles as presented in this volume (except that Stevens treats all patterns as if they were one-color patterns).

Art historians—for example, Gombrich (1979) and Arnheim (1974)—have often used the characteristic of symmetry to assess the formal qualities of a work of art. In fact, the mathematician Niman and the art historian Norman developed a college course to teach the regular and semiregular tessellations and concepts of the arc, circle, polygon, angles, etc. (1978). They used examples from Islamic art to show how certain repeated patterns are represented in a variety of works, including arabesques and calligraphic inscriptions. A chemist and a craft expert have collaborated to show that all seven (one-color) one-dimensional and all seventeen (one-color) two-dimensional patterns have been used in traditional Hungarian needlework (Hargittai and Lengyel 1984, 1985).

Perhaps the first mention of the applicability of the principles of symmetry for anthropological study was by Brainerd, a North American archaeologist (1942). He showed how prehistoric Anasazi pottery from the Monument Valley area, Arizona, and the Mayan site of Chichen Itza in the Yucatan, Mexico, can be described by four one-dimensional symmetries. In fact, Brainerd made a number of observations which continue to be fundamental to the use of symmetry for pattern analysis.

First, he found that all the pottery from the Kayenta, Arizona, area could be classified by one symmetry, twofold rotation, while the Fine Orange Mayan ware had a mixed repertoire of symmetries. Thus, "different types of symmetry predominated in the two groups, and . . . the symmetry of Group B is more diverse than that of Group A" (1942:165). That is, different cultural groups use different symmetries, and homogeneity or heterogeneity in symmetries may be a function of cultural complexity, extent and type of extracultural contexts, or other factors.

Second, Brainerd found that "the occurrence of types of symmetry in primitive conventional design is not mere chance. . . . We do not mean to infer that such symmetry systems were named or recognized by the people using them, but to state that they were followed exactly, even if unconsciously, in the finer pieces of both collections analyzed" (1942:165). That is, within a given culture there will be a preferred symmetry or symmetries used to decorate objects.

Third, Brainerd suggested that use of symmetry as a principle of design arrangement did not arise from copying symmetries in nature. "The predominance of bifold [twofold] rotational symmetry in Southwestern pottery design suggests that this design did not originate in the attempt to copy living things, since this form of symmetry is not found in plants or animals" (1942:165). Implicit in this observation is the idea that these symmetries, and the consistency with which certain motions are used, relate to some other cultural factor. For example, Brainerd suggests that symmetry consistencies may characterize a cultural group. Aberrations from the norm may be "evidence of cultural borrowing."

Fourth, Brainerd showed how the same motif (a fret) could be arranged according to different symmetries and thus be characteristic of different groups. The Kayenta Anasazi arranged the fret in twofold rotational bands; the Yucatecan Maya merely translated the fret in bands.

Each of these simple observations can be fundamental for the study of choices and consistencies in the symmetries of patterned design of any culture. However, although Brainerd published these ideas in *American Antiquity,* the leading archaeological journal in North America, they were not immediately adopted for descriptive pruposes.

In fact, the only other person to have realized the anthropological significance of symmetry analysis was Anna O. Shepard, a geologist at the Carnegie Institution, Washington, D.C., best known as an expert in the petrographic analysis of pottery. Her landmark monograph, *The Symmetry of Abstract Design with Special Reference to Ceramic Decoration* (1948), which explains the method and illustrates its use on design from the Anasazi and Mimbres traditions and the Rio Grande Pueblos of the American Southwest, and the Cocle of Panama, went unheeded for almost thirty years.

Well aware of the prevailing focus on culture history at that time, Shepard pointed out that symmetry analysis would be a good vehicle to describe subtle and varied changes of styles. With this tool the investigator could research a number of questions. "What, if any, characteristics are common to all decorative art, what features are most subject to change, how are new elements assimilated and decorative ideas evolved, and in what ways do artistic standards vary from time to time" (1948:211).

Shepard presents the seven classes of one-dimensional infinite design, describes how to classify patterns with alternating motifs, and discusses at length situations where symmetries may be irregular. Her discussion of pattern design from different cultures highlights how certain symmetries predominate, and how changes within a culture can be pinpointed by symmetry analysis. Although Shepard does not discuss two-dimensional patterns, nor two-color symmetries, her concept of "value," the alternation of light and dark colors on motifs of the same shape, is basically identical to the idea of two-color patterns. The breadth of treatment she gives the finite and one-dimensional classes in both her explanation of the motion classes and her discussion of their presence and variations on numerous examples stand as the cornerstone anthropological study for this exciting new method of analysis.

In her best-known work, *Ceramics for the Archaeologist* (1956), a handbook for the analysis of ceramics, she includes a presentation of the concept of symmetry analysis. But despite the fact that this handbook is a standard reference for technological analyses of ceramics, very few investigators have appreciated her discussion of the usefulness of symmetry for the analysis of design.

There has been a thirty-year hiatus in the use of symmetry analysis between Brainerd's and Shepard's work in the 1940s and the "rediscovery" of their ideas in the 1970s. The recent studies are not numerous. But the success of this more recent research has prompted us to present the method in a more uniform and complete handbook format so that others can avoid a lengthy process of discovery and self-instruction.

1.4 Symmetry Analysis in Anthropological Perspective

In this section we explain why symmetry analysis is an appropriate method for investigating patterning in human behavior, as well as the regularities found in material culture. We first describe symmetry as a property of regular patterns (1.4.1) and then describe the role of symmetry in the process of perception (1.4.2). We then show how symmetry is an underlying feature in style structure (1.4.3) and argue that this property is therefore appropriate for systematic classification (1.4.4). Finally we explore how systematic approaches like symmetry classification are sound methodological bases for understanding aspects of patterning in human behavior as well as material culture (1.4.5).

1.4.1 Symmetry: A Property of Regular Patterns

Although Chapters 2 to 6 describe the concept and procedure of analysis in great detail, it will be necessary to define the properties of symmetry briefly here since the understanding of symmetry as a mathematical entity with specific measurable properties is necessary in order to understand how it can be a useful measure of regularities in culture.

In its most common and popular usage, *symmetry* means bilateral symmetry, that is, mirror reflection of parts in a single (finite) figure. The first definition in *Webster's Third New International Dictionary* reflects this popular usage: "correspondence in size, shape, and relative position of parts that are on opposite sides of a dividing line or median plane or that are distributed about a center or axis." For example, we commonly think of the human body as having bilateral symmetry. Many objects in the natural world (flowers, starfish) have other forms of finite (radial) symmetry. Actually, however, such examples of finite symmetry encompass only a very small subset of the known symmetrical world as defined by geometers and crystallographers. The finite category admits only two symmetry motions about a single point axis: mirror reflection and rotation.

There are other categories of symmetry which also occur in the two-dimensional plane. One-dimensional infinite designs (bands, strips) and two-dimensional infinite patterns (all-over, wallpaper) may admit the above two motions as well as translation and glide reflection. (Still more symmetries may occur in three-dimensional objects, but these will not be considered here.) The symmetries of the plane, then, describe the geometry of repetition of all repeated decorative patterns studied by anthropologists, art historians, craftsmen, or designers. Various combinations of symmetries, herein called *motion classes,* are present in all regularly repeated design. These motion classes have been systematically and objectively classified.

The point of this short excursion is to highlight the fact that some properties of design, such as color and symmetry, can be described by systematically derived units. The use of the series of color hues listed in the Munsell color system to describe painted pottery designs and the use of crystallographic symmetry classifications to describe repeated patterns on material culture are two examples of direct borrowing of a classification system established by another science.

Symmetry, like color, is a property of design. However, unlike color, symmetry in cultural contexts is a non-lexical domain. Where individuals differentiate colors salient to them by naming them (Berlin and Kay 1969) or by comparing them to some other entity (green is "like the color of cooked manioc leaves"), the only names for symmetry classes are the nomenclatures assigned by the crystallographers.

The critical question is, Without the conscious naming which creates categories that anthropologists can study, how can anthropologists know that these crystallographically described arrangements are culturally meaningful and thus relevant for the analytical study of cultural behavior?

There are two ways to ascertain whether symmetry is a culturally meaningful property. One is to study its role in perception and how it is utilized in form recognition. The other is to study its occurrence in cultural contexts—do certain symmetry classes consistently appear in patterns? We shall address both issues in the following sections (1.4.2 and 1.4.3).

1.4.2 Symmetry as a Factor in Perception

Since much of our information about the world comes to us visually, it is important to understand which aspects of the visual process—how information is received, digested, stored, and recalled—are related to cultural factors and which are universal. Information, here, is considered to be anything taken in visually, processed, and used in daily behavior. While the physiology of vision will not be reviewed here, some recent discoveries about cognition are relevant to the study of symmetry as one factor in this process.

Perception is a process by which an individual obtains information from the environment. But since in any given environment there is always more information than an individual can assimilate, a person must learn which stimuli are salient. Thus, perception involves selection. Through socialization, an individual in a particular culture learns to focus on features which will enable him to predict events, reduce uncertainty, and make appropriate responses. The individual stores this information in memory and uses it as baseline data against which to compare new information.

Within a given cultural setting, the same scene may be "seen" differently by different individuals depending upon their particular knowledge and needs. Likewise, persons from different cultures may "see" a given scene differently depending upon their prior knowledge, experience, and immediate context. Thus, a person from a given culture may see that a pattern has symmetry, but may not see the difference between one particular kind of symmetry and another; two "different" colors may not seem to be different to peoples who assign all hues in a certain range to the "same" color category. Individuals recognize redundancy, but not necessarily different variations of the same kind of redundancy. Thus a particular structural relationship may remain potential information; it may never be picked up (perceived) and used (manifested in a cultural institution). In this way, cultural membership and situation influence the information selection process.

The question for the physiologist is, How does the brain process visual input? The question for the experimental psychologist is, What are the fundamental units of perception and how are they organized into features and structures? The question for the anthropologist may be, How are these features and structures used by different cultures?

Research to date by experimental psychologists has not focused on the cultural component of vision. Experimental subjects are commonly the classic "American college sophomore," with no control for ethnic origin. Conversely, anthropologists have not been much interested in the process of vision but only in how a culture relates to the visible environment. The observation from experimental psychologists that not everything in a given environment is "seen," and thus used, is not directly utilized by anthropologists.

Research on the role of symmetry in perception was brought to prominence with Gestalt psychology. For Gestalt psychologists symmetry was one principle that contributed to order and structure in a pattern; that is, symmetry contributed to the "goodness" of the pattern. For the modern information theorist, symmetry is an invariant, a kind of redundancy which the perceptual system uses, among other features, to assess observed information.

Symmetry, of course, is a particularly good feature to use to judge whether an observed object is the "same" or "different" because its various states are truly invariant. Each class of symmetry can be "measured" mathematically, that is, distinguished with replicable precision and accuracy. We shall examine the information carrying capacity of symmetry in this book, from the point of view not of its "goodness" but of its property of invariance.

There are two kinds of features which individuals abstract from environmental stimuli during the perceptual process: 1) universal, invariant relations, such as symmetry or orientation, and 2) distinctive features, such as those peculiar to the aesthetic system of a particular culture. This book is limited to addressing the universal feature of symmetry as it is used to describe shapes.

We wish to use our understanding of the property of symmetry to address several questions. Is symmetry a feature which individuals use to recognize and differentiate categories of objects? Is it involved in the way individuals perceive the environment, make decisions about objects in that environment, and formulate strategies and institutions to cope with it? Does perception of symmetry differ cross-culturally? Do particular world views and cultural institutions predispose individuals in one culture to focus on and use only certain symmetries, while individuals in another culture prefer to use other symmetries?

In order to answer these questions we must consider the findings of other disciplines. Thus, one answer to the question, Why should anthropologists and art historians consider the property of symmetry in the analysis of culturally produced patterns and design? is that by understanding the role of symmetry in the visual recognition process we can better recognize its pervasiveness throughout a number of cultural domains.

Perceptual psychologists have identified a series of features and developed models describing how these features are used, for example, to abstract the shape of an object or to differentiate between a square and a circle. At the other end of the spectrum, anthropologists have developed models and explanations of how information obtained visually is organized within a cultural system. We propose to bridge the two disciplines by developing a model which classifies the cultural applications of symmetry, as observed by anthropologists, according to the basic structural features identified by perceptual psychologists. In sum, if we build upon the knowledges of other disciplines we shall gain greater insight into the many basic properties and features of cultural activity.

In the following pages we summarize the experimental research of psychologists relevant to the processing of visual information. In particular, we discuss how the property of symmetry is a critical feature in the perceptual process. This will partly explain why we have made so great an effort in this book to systematize the property of symmetry for use in pattern analysis. More important, we hope to show how structural consistencies in cultural designs may relate to structural consistencies in other domains of culture.

The Perceptual Process

Perception is a sequence of different stages of information processing: acquisition, storage, retrieval, and utilization. The first stage involves the initial encoding of the stimuli. It is often called pattern recognition (Reed 1973).

Foster (1984:84) has summarized the kinds of features experimental psychologists have discovered are used in the recognition of shape:

1. *Local features* (for example, whether points in a pattern are on straight or curved lines, or whether straight lines form acute or obtuse angles)
2. *Local spatial relationships* (whether points in a pattern are left, right, above, or below the vertical/horizontal reference)
3. *Global features* associated with pattern (for example, symmetry and orientation)
4. *Global spatial relationships* (for example, the position of the pattern in the field)

These features are then used in two different learning processes which enable an individual to perceive the differences and similarities among patterns. The first process is *discrimination learning,* that is, learning the features used to distinguish one pattern from another. For example, to differentiate the letters of the alphabet, an individual uses features of line orientation, line curvature, and symmetry of the parts of the letters. The second process is *generalization learning,* that is, learning the features which are used to group patterns as equivalent. It is this second process which lies at the heart of the processes of classification and categorization. An understanding of these processes will yield insights into how people recognize different examples of a pattern as belonging to a pattern class. From the anthropological perspective this can be restated as how people deal with pattern variability. It is no overstatement that insight into this problem could be of use to many typological and stylistic studies.

Bruner's proposal (1957) that all perceptual experience (e.g., pattern recognition) is the end product of a categorization process is a useful starting point for this discussion. He listed four aspects to the classification process: (1) specifying the critical properties of the structure; (2) specifying how the properties are combined; (3) specifying the weights assigned to each property; and (4) specifying the acceptance limits for each category.

A number of models have been developed to describe the categorization procedure, taking cognizance of these four stipulations: (1) *proximity models,* which show that patterns are compared to a subset of the next closest patterns; (2) *average distance models,* which compute the mean distance between the patterns in question and the pattern categories available; (3) *prototype models,* which are based on a central tendency prototype of the category to which all cases are compared (including the model of "natural" prototypes which may not be the average example); and (4) *cue validity models,* based on the most valid cue (feature) used in the decision-making process.

Debate over which of these models best approximates the categorization process is still ongoing. However, several caveats have emerged from this model-building and testing which are relevant to our understanding of the role of symmetry in perception. First, there is probably an important difference between the features used for form perception and those used in form reproduction. Maccoby (1968) pointed out that form perception is based primarily on whole shapes, while copying is a sequential process in which the divisions of the form into its parts and the spatial relationships of parts is paramount. Second, there is probably a difference between the features used in the perception of the similarity of forms and those used in the classification of forms into categories. In the classification of forms the most relevant features are those used in discriminating among the categories. These may differ from those used in simple similarity decisions.

These two observations lie at the heart of the anthropological search for meaningful *etic* descriptive categories (of the observer), as well as for deeper understanding of the *emic* categories (of the native) which we have been able to discover (see Harris 1968 for a discussion of the *emic/etic* distinction). We do know that pattern recognition begins with the extraction of features from the visual stimuli. It involves features, such as symmetry and orientation, which show relationships between object parts. Features and their relations are combined to form a pattern which is stored in memory and recalled for matching by classification processes in later visual tasks.

How symmetry is specifically involved in these discrimination and generalization tasks is reviewed in the following pages.

Perception of Symmetry

In order to probe the cognitive significance, if any, of symmetry in cultural contexts, it is essential to first review our knowledge about the perceptual process. Understanding which features of a form are salient in the processing of information can help us distinguish between the formation of cultural responses to a particular perceived world, and universal cognitive functions and responses.

In a series of now famous experiments Julesz (1975) demonstrated that the eye distinguishes between sections of dot arrays which are repeated from array sections which are reflected across a mirror plane. He concluded that the visual system encodes reflection symmetry but not direct repetition. These results were duplicated by Bruce and Morgan (1975), using a different set of computer-generated bar patterns. However, while it is gratifying to know that symmetry is an important feature in the shape perception process, at the same time it is curious to note that Julesz did not consider repetition a form of symmetry.

Symmetry is based on superposition. Elements which are regularly superpositioned along an axis are thus regularly repeated. The resulting pattern is said to be symmetrical. This repetition, called translation, is not only a class of symmetry, it is the heart of the concept of pattern.

In fact, for both one- and two-dimensional patterns in the plane, translation—that is, simple repetition of the pattern element along an axis—is a motion inherent in every pattern. For example, the elements in a one-dimensional pattern described as having horizontal mirror reflection also can be said to be translated along that axis.

The failure to distinguish translation from mirror reflection, or from the other symmetries of the plane, is actually symptomatic of a larger problem in many experimental psychological studies—that of assuming that mirror reflection is *the* prototypical symmetry. (Sometimes twofold rotation is considered in this role). That is, symmetry is thought synonymous with mirror symmetry. For example, in many studies the tests for preference of symmetry over asymmetry show forms with mirror reflection symmetry for the "symmetrical" stimuli and translated forms for the "asymmetrical" stimuli.

In fact, there are three pattern categories for plane designs: finite, one-dimensional, and two-dimensional. Designs where only single elements are the stimuli are finite. These have a central point axis around which elements can rotate or through which mirror axes can pass. Other symmetries, such as translation, or glide reflection, are not possible in this category. One-dimensional and two-dimensional patterns have, respectively, seven and seventeen different motion classes, composed of combinations of the four basic motions: translation, rotation, mirror reflection, and glide reflection.

Thus, while important advances have been made in testing human perception of the property of symmetry, not all of the conclusions are useful here, since only a few of the reports even define symmetry, much less test for preference among the different symmetries of patterns in the plane.

Further, there has been no control for cultural differences. This is unfortunate, since focus on certain perceptual features is based on past experience and context. Cross-cultural psychological tests have generally involved non-Western peoples responding to abstract stimuli such as dots or lines in shapes; it is no wonder that non-Western subjects respond more slowly and equivocally to these stimuli than do Western subjects.

With these caveats, the following section reviews the principal literature on symmetry perception.

Most psychological tests have studied the significance of symmetry in the process of shape recognition by (1) testing preferences for symmetry over asymmetry in form and (2) testing ability to reproduce symmetrical and asymmetrical designs.

Symmetry Preferences. Some of the earliest research on the role of symmetry in perception was by Attneave (1954, 1955), who associated symmetry with the concept of information redundancy. His object was to test the Gestalt principle of figural "goodness" by measuring symmetry as a form of redundancy. Gestalt psychologists contended that "good" figures were simple, symmetrical and regular. Attneave suggested that redundant figures (i.e., those with repeated units) actually contain less information. Patterns would be easier to remember and would be judged to be good and pleasing. He was first to show that symmetrical figures were more accurately reproduced than asymmetrical figures.

However, Locher and Nodine (1973) noted that if one begins with the premise that symmetric shapes are preferred (good) because they are redundant (contain less information), the logical hypothesis is that such symmetric shapes should therefore require less time and eye fixations to examine. This is not the case. Results from their tests showed that there is no difference in the number of fixations or the fixation time on the angles and corners of a shape between eye scans, whether viewing half of a symmetrical shape or a whole asymmetrical shape of similar complexity. Other tests have shown that symmetrical shapes are both preferred and preferentially produced and reproduced over asymmetrical shapes, regardless of whether the shapes are simple or complex (Eisenman and Rappaport 1967). In fact, subjects are able to reproduce more accurately figures which have only partial symmetry than figures which have no symmetry (Howe 1980). Indeed, figures which are slightly asymmetrical are "seen" as symmetrical. Freyd and Tversky (1984) found that individuals will distort an image, "seeing" it as symmetrical.

Experimental results on the saliency of vertical orientation give some validity to the experimenters' focus on mirror symmetry, especially vertical bilateral symmetry. Rock (1973) and his associates (Rock and Leaman 1963) have extensively tested how the phenomenal orientation of an object (its orientation in relation to its visible surroundings) or its retinal orientation (its orientation in relation to the eye) affects recognition. Rock concludes:

> For a novel figure, there is little change in appearance when only the orientation of its retinal image is changed. But when the orientation of the figure in the environment is changed, it is generally perceived as different and may not be recognized. (1973:126)

Individuals assign a "top" and "bottom" and "sides" to figures in their environmental contexts. Shifts in position of these objects of 45 or 90 degrees make recognition more difficult than a 180-degree rotation of the object or a top-bottom or left-right mirror reversal. These results confirm the primary importance of bilateral symmetry, especially when the axis of symmetry is oriented vertically, and have led Fox (1975) to suggest that bilateral symmetry is a significant diagnostic feature. In fact he found that recognition of the bilateral symmetry *alone* would result in the correct identification of an object without a total analysis of the object.

There are also experimental results which suggest that symmetry about vertical axes is easier to recognize (i.e., is recognized faster) than horizontal symmetry, and that symmetry about an oblique axis is easier to recognize than symmetry about a horizontal axis (Corballis and Roldan 1975). Palmer and Henenway (1978) retested these observations and found that where the symmetry axes were not shown to the subjects, vertical symmetry was still the easiest to recognize; the next easiest was horizontal symmetry, with diagonal symmetry the most difficult to detect. In all of these tests it appeared that Shepard and Metzler's 1971 findings, that subjects mentally rotated three-dimensional objects in space in order to assess identity of images, were also operative for judging images in the plane. Individuals mentally rotated the images until the symmetry axis was vertical.

Perception of symmetry is related not only to orientation, but also to element proximity and spacing. Corballis and Roldan (1974) investigated the difference between perception of symmetrical figures and repeated figures, using dot figures and "greater than" and "less than" symbols. They found that recognition of symmetrical figures was faster if the units were close together, suggesting that spatial relationship between parts of a figure is important for perception of the figures as discrete units. They also found that perception of symmetrical figures was faster if symbols rather than dots were used. This result reinforces the theory that the perceptual system examines lines and angles for shape perception. Any form which has these cues in particular positions is apparently easier to recognize than one comprised of simple dots. These results also seemed to confirm the perceptual salience of left-right symmetry over left-right repetition where pattern parts in both kinds of stimuli are perceived to belong together as a whole unit.

Very few researchers have examined perceptual differences among the different classes of symmetry. Szilagyi and Baird (1977) found that subjects preferred symmetrical patterns and preferentially produced symmetrical patterns in one-, two-, and three-dimensional space. Hershenson and Ryder (1982), using nonsymmetrical letters which were repeated in different motions (rotation, vertical reflection, horizontal reflection, translation) found that, surprisingly, differences in symmetry type did not affect response time, despite the evidence from earlier studies that vertically bilateral symmetrical figures were easiest to recognize. They have suggested that simple identification of symmetry in a figure is a different perceptual task than identification of the type of symmetry—i.e., the specific kind of structural arrangement of the parts of the symmetrical figure.

Further testing of these principles should (1) use familiar stimuli from the culture of the subject rather than abstract dot patterns, and (2) control for cross-cultural differences in perception of and preference for the whole range of symmetries.

Symmetry Reproduction. The second predominant thrust in cross-cultural studies of symmetry perception are tests of subjects' abilities to reproduce patterns. Although the results are conflicting, the phenomenal orientation and the cultural familiarity of stimuli in perception tests appear to be important limiting factors.

Shapiro (1960) found that African subjects rotated objects more than British subjects, to a position 45 degrees past the perpendicular to the horizontal plane preferred by British subjects. Deregowski studied Zambian subjects' abilities to reproduce symmetrical and asymmetrical patterns but his results have not consistently supported the hypothesis that symmetrical patterns were more easily reproduced than asymmetrical patterns (1972, 1974). Tekane (1963) found that Bantu subjects could complete patterns with bilateral symmetry better than patterns with rotational symmetry.

In 1956 Jahoda first reported that Ghanaian children did not pay attention to orientation, but in a restudy in 1976 he found that as patterns deviated from the horizontal, the children experienced increasing difficulty reproducing them. Serpell retested the effects of orientation with actual objects familiar to the subjects (brooms, arrows, plants) and found that Zambian children were as attentive to the proper orientation of the objects as were American children (1971).

In an effort to further examine these conflicting results, Bentley (1977) tested whether different symmetry classes affected the ease of pattern reproduction and found that both Scottish and Bukusu (W. Kenya) subjects used the redundant property of symmetry to help them recall and reproduce patterns, though the African subjects made more errors reproducing the rotated patterns than patterns with vertical reflections.

A number of researchers have found that increase in age and education improve the accuracy with which subjects reproduce patterns (Bentley 1980; Tekane 1963; Cole, Gay, and Glick 1968). It appears that there are few cross-cultural differences in the long run, although non-Western subjects may be several years behind in acquiring the same perceptual skills (Clement, Sistrunk, and Guenther 1970).

Most interesting for cross-cultural research is Paraskevopoulos's hypothesis (1968) that preference for specific kinds of symmetries is learned. He showed for American elementary school children that "double symmetry" (vertical and horizontal reflection) is preferred at age six, "bilateral symmetry" (vertical reflection) at age seven, and "horizontal symmetry" (horizontal reflection) at age eleven. This suggestion should be tested in different cultural contexts. If symmetry type preference is learned, then this would explain why certain symmetries predominate in the art of a given culture.

Conclusion

Cross-cultural studies suggest that symmetry is a salient feature which all peoples use, to greater or lesser degrees depending on their age and level of education, to assess forms, remember them, compare them with other forms, and reproduce them. That is, with differences in response time and accuracy of reproduction, all peoples use symmetry as a diagnostic feature in the perception of form.

Pick observed that where "there are important similarities in cognitive functioning of diverse groups . . . the similarities help identify aspects of cognition which are universal" (1980:119). Symmetry, then, is a cognitive perceptual universal, basic to the processing of all shape information. A culture's symmetries are part of that culture's cognitive organization map, and the classification of symmetries is a meaningful measure of the way members of a particular culture perceive their world.

1.4.3 Symmetry as a Feature Underlying Style

Symmetry classifications of bodies of data from ethnographic groups have revealed that cultural groups (i.e., interacting peoples who share a common life system) have preferential ways of arranging design elements. That is, rather than randomly using all seven one-dimensional classes and all seventeen two-dimensional classes and numerous of the infinite number of finite classes, a given cultural group will consistently use only several specific symmetries in their design system. The *nonrandomness* of design structure, as measured by symmetry analysis, in any given cultural group is fundamentally significant. Analysis of ethnographic and archaeological data described below demonstrates these nonrandom tendencies.

Crowe, in several studies of African art (1971, 1975, 1980, 1982), has shown that such designs can be described systematically by their symmetries, that repeated designs occur frequently on many types of media, and that a number of different motions characterize the designs. Although all seven one-dimensional and twelve of the seventeen two-dimensional patterns appear on Kuba raffia cloth, carved wooden cups, portrait statues of kings, wall mats for houses, and elaborately decorated masks (1971) and all of the seven band symmetries and twelve of the seventeen two-dimensional symmetries (1975) have been used by Benin artists, in each group certain symmetries predominated.

It is not necessary at this point to fully understand the notations for specific patterns; the aim of the discussion in this section is simply to demonstrate the validity and productiveness of symmetry analysis of material culture data. The basic types of symmetry will be explained in Chapter 2, with the four rigid motions defined in Section 2.2. The symmetry classes and the nomenclature will be explained in Chapter 3.

In a study of decorated stems and bases of clay pipes from the site of Begho K2 in Ghana, Crowe (1982) found that 72 percent of the one-dimensional patterns belonged to a single class (*pmm2*). Only seven of the seventeen two-dimensional classes were recorded and of these seven classes, 55 percent were of one of these classes (*p4m*) and 25 percent were of another class (*pmm*). Checking for temporal changes in use of design symmetries, Crowe noted an early absence but later presence of three of the one-dimensional classes (*p1m1*, *p1a1*, and *pma2*). Conversely, the use of one of the other band classes (*p111*) seemed to decrease. The use of two other classes (*pm11* and *pmm2*) was fairly consistent throughout time. The ability to accurately trace such structural changes affords access to information which the investigator can relate to other shifts in the artifactual record.

In a systematic analysis of Inca quipus, the Aschers (1981) showed how the organized nature of this recording mechanism is but a mirror of similar forces which pervade Inca culture, a characteristic which they call "Inca Insistence." That is, systematic spatial layout of the Empire, careful organization of ancestral lineages within the cities, layouts of house compounds, and even the careful shaping of the mammoth stones in Inca walls—all of these express a cultural coherence of the populace which, in fact, was the very basis for the strength of the Empire.

The careful adherence to a few symmetries in their pottery design was part of this overall "presentation of a coherent self." In the 300 band designs examined, all seven one-dimensional classes were used, but 40 percent were of one class (*pmm2*), 20 percent of another class (*pm11*), and 11 percent of a third class (*pma2*). Of the 120 two-dimensional patterns examined, five of the seventeen classes did not appear; eight other classes were rare; the remaining four classes characterized 70 percent of the designs.

The chemist Zaslow has published a number of statements about the use of pattern mathematics for the study of Hohokam ceramics (1977, 1980, 1981). In collaboration with Dittert (1977b) he has presented a chronicle of changes in symmetries in Hohokam red-on-buff ceramic design at the site of Snaketown during the Pioneer, Colonial, and Sedentary periods and has extended this sequence to include data of unknown provenience from the Soho Phase of the following Classic Period.

The earliest Hohokam designs from the Estrella Phase are finite motifs on bowl interiors. In the following Sweetwater Phase band designs appeared having translation symmetry (*p111*). These were later replaced, in the Snaketown Phase, by designs having rotational symmetry (*p112*). During the following Colonial Period the decorated ceramics exhibit rotational symmetry in both the one-dimensional and the two-dimensional patterns. In the Gila Butte Phase, glide reflections are introduced (*pgg*) and increase throughout the Santa Cruz Phase, but the rotational patterns remain predominant. By the following Sedentary Period, glide reflection patterns occur more frequently than rotational patterns. Early Classic Period Casa Grande red-on-buff vessels continue to show preference for two-dimensional glide patterns, but later this layout is masked almost completely by the introduction of Anasazi designs in one-dimensional glide reflection layout (*p1a1*).

A number of important discoveries about Hohokam prehistory have been made in this study. A design element analysis, noting the continual presence of the scroll throughout Hohokam prehistory, would not have resulted in very specific information about the design system and changes in that system. On the other hand, a classification by symmetry showed how the scroll was rearranged in various layouts through time. Furthermore, symmetry analysis of stratigraphic material showed that these changes were gradual and continuous, supportive of the hypothesis of the presence of a single cultural tradition. Finally, such an analysis enabled archaeologists to postulate an extension of the sequence into the Classic Period, heretofore a problem period because of the lack of documented material.

Van Esterik has analyzed red-on-buff pottery designs from the site of Ban Chiang, Thailand (1981). She describes the Ban Chiang rules for spiral, concentric circle, and sigmoid arrangements finding that two classes (*pmm2* and *pma2*) were the most consistently used for body and pedestal base bands; two other classes (*p111* and *p112*) were used to form the asymmetric spirals on the main body area. She emphasizes that this classification system could be used to compare designs from Ban Chiang to those from other sites in Southeast Asia and to study the process whereby individual variation arises from an established system of acceptable rules for design creation (cf. Van Esterik 1979).

Stewart has analyzed Lincoln black-on-red ware, a body of little-known pottery from the Jornada Mogollon of southern New Mexico (1979, 1983). Major symmetries are two-dimensional rotational (*p2*), finite, and (less frequently) four one-dimensional classes (*p112*, *pma2*, *pmm2*, and *p1a1*). And in a note to an article on Nubian ceramics, Stewart neatly shows how a symmetry analysis could easily demarcate continuities and changes in the structure of Nubian design styles (1980).

Kent (1983) has used symmetry analysis to study temporal changes and continuities in the structure of prehistoric textile designs from the American Southwest. Her studies disclosed a Pan-Southwestern design style in the prehistoric period, marked by the prevalence of rotations in two-dimensional, often truncated layouts. By the mid-fifteenth century there was a return to one-dimensional symmetries, a structural system which continued into the historic period. Kent was able to correlate these structural shifts with other major events in Anasazi prehistory. For example, the A.D. 1100 shift from one-dimensional to two-dimensional patterns correlates with the introduction of the wide loom and of new design ideas from southern Arizona and southwestern New Mexico. The shift back to one-dimensional band designs coincides with the period of massive infusion of different cultural traditions into the Hopi area.

Washburn first applied the principles of symmetry to Pueblo III vessels from the Upper Gila area of west central New Mexico (1977a). Seventy-five percent of the vessels at site 616 were structured by one-dimensional twofold rotation (*p112*); only nineteen percent were structured by two-dimensional layouts and six percent by finite layouts. No differential use of symmetries was found to characterize different areas of this large 500-room, single-component pueblo.

A comparison of these findings with designs from three El Morro sites and the Salmon site along the San Juan River (Washburn 1977b) was made to test whether significant differences in design structure could be observed among these three populations. Although the one-dimensional twofold rotational symmetry (*p112*) was clearly preferred on designs at all sites, it occurred more frequently at the Salmon site (67%) than in the El Morro area (40%) and Upper Gila area (43%).

A more sophisticated extension of the study of cultural interaction was the application of multidimensional scaling techniques to design symmetry from a large number of sites in the Four Corners area of the American Southwest (Washburn and Matson 1985). Scaling was used to show how distance between sites is a factor in pattern similarity. Further, when frequencies of symmetry structures were correlated with sites dated by dendrochronology, a horseshoe-shaped scaling indicated that changes in design structures accurately reflect temporal change. In contrast, a control scaling of type frequencies from the same sites produced a scattering with no clear temporal order.

Since a number of the above studies have shown that design structures within a population group are generally homogeneous and nonrandom, imported materials should be recognizable by their different structural layouts. In a study of black-on-white cylinder jar designs from Chaco Canyon, New Mexico, Washburn found that the locally made Pueblo II one-dimensional rotational (*p112*) design system was replaced in the Pueblo III period by two-dimensional layouts. Formal attributes of these atypical vessels suggested a nonlocal origin and, indeed, likely models for the form and design system can be found in the Mixtec and Toltec cultures of the Valley of Oaxaca (1980).

An excellent body of data to test the sensitivity of structural change to the passage of time in a stable cultural system was available from the site of Knossos, Crete. From a 3,000-year stratigraphic profile, symmetry analysis of incised shards uncovered a dramatic increase in new designs and structures with the beginnings of trade in the Aegean (Washburn 1983b).

An analysis of Early and Late Neolithic wares from mainland Greece (Washburn 1983b) permitted a test of the sensitivity of design structure to geographic factors. Previous studies of the element distributions revealed their presence throughout the occupied area of Greece. However, a symmetry analysis revealed mutually exclusive regions of different arrangements of these common elements (nets, flames, zigzags, and steps) during the Early and Middle Neolithic, but a grouping of symmetry classes, possibly indicating market centers, by the Late Neolithic.

In order to further study these consistencies in symmetry use and to relate these nonrandom distributions to other domains of cultural activity, Washburn turned to a study of well-documented data bases from history and ethnography where the reasons for such consistencies were known or knowable. Washburn reanalyzed informant testimony from northern California basket weavers (O'Neale 1932) and found that one criterion weavers used to judge designs was element arrangement. All design configurations judged as "correct" and tribally appropriate were of two symmetries (*p112* and *pma2*) for the Yurok, Karok, and Hupa, while designs judged as "bad" and "not known" were structured by these as well as a number of miscellaneous other symmetries. In short, (1) designs were consistent in structure within a tribal group and this consistency was clearly definable by summetry analysis, and (2) these structural arrangements were recognized as correct for tribal use by the weavers and users (Washburn 1986a).

Research in progress to make certain that informants use structure as one criterion for judging appropriateness of design involves studies of Laotian weaving categories. Lao women are being shown photographs of a selection of band patterns from cultures all over the world, including those found on Laotian textiles, and are being asked to select those which are Lao. Initial tests suggest that non-Lao patterns with the traditional *pmm2* arrangements are often said to be Lao patterns, while non-Lao patterns generated by other symmetries are almost never said to be Lao.

Design structure is an important feature in a culture's stylistic tradition. Thus, the selection of an attribute or attributes which demonstrate regular nonrandom variation in a structure and which can be studied systematically is crucial to the success of any analysis.

Only a limited number of symmetries are appropriate in any given culture, and adherence to these structures is necessary for approval and use. If, on the other hand, symmetry analysis of the structure of design had shown random use of structural arrangements, then, while the method of symmetry analysis would still have been shown to be a satisfactory classificatory tool, it would not necessarily be better than any other method of classification because it did not isolate and classify an attribute that was sensitive to some aspect of patterned human behavior. But, because symmetry analyses do reveal consistencies in the use of certain design structures, and because informants have indicated that design structure is an important factor in cultural acceptance, we can assume that design structure—and symmetry in particular—is an attribute which merits further systematic investigation.

Since the discovery and explanation of patterned human behavior is the essence of anthropology, it would seem that an analytical technique which can isolate behavior patterns consistently and objectively would be a great asset for the study of certain kinds of cultural activities. Practically every culture in the world is known to decorate at least some portion of its material culture with repeated patterns. It now is possible to systematically describe the structure of these patterns and thus to have a more coherent and precise method of analysis of this activity system. Quite simply, the method is revolutionary in its simplicity of concept, application, and in its ability to uncover significant patterns of cultural behavior.

Two key questions are, Why do people consistently prefer and choose certain ordering systems? and, What kinds of patterned behavior are related to these consistent preferences for structural arrangement?

For many years anthropologists have offered studies which show how consistencies of behavior are symbolic expressions of fundamental cultural values and principles of order. Further, in a given culture, the same principles of order seem to permeate the many subsystems of that culture.

For example, Thompson suggested that Hopi ritual and art is a complex but orderly system which symbolically represents the Hopi concept of the universe (1945:550). Cunningham studied house layout among the Atoni, concluding that

order in building expresses ideas symbolically. . . . Furthermore, order concerns not just discrete ideas or symbols, but a system; and the system expresses both principles of classification and a value for classification per se. (1973:204)

Similar correlations were noted by Roe (1980) for Shipibo residential arrangements and by Arnold for use of environmental space by the residents of Quinua, Peru.

The basic principles of spatial organization in a society are so important to the structure and maintenance of the society that they are reified and reinforced in symbolic space such as ritual, religion, and on textiles and pottery. (Arnold 1983:57)

Similarly, Reichel-Dolmotoff (1971) revealed how the Desana coded and categorized aspects of their environment into symbols which pervaded all art, socioeconomic systems, and value orientations. Adams (1973) found that the dyadictriadic principles which organized Sumba textile design were also found in various social activities: marriage exchange, formal negotiations, frequency of ritual occurrences, structure of ceremonial language, etc.

Mills (1959) sought to understand the relation of art to the psychology and value system of Navajo culture by using the concepts of balance and harmony to study pattern organization in weaving and drypainting. Hatcher (1974) focused on the repetition in Navajo art while Witherspoon (1977) sees symmetry in Navajo design as representing the balance between the static and active forces in Navajo life.

Holm (1965) studied the predominant bilateral symmetry in Northwest Coast art while Critchlow (1976) and El-Said and Parman (1976) noted the correspondence of Islamic tiling symmetries with aspects of Islamic cosmology.

Faris has shown how the Nuba's use of self-decoration to celebrate strong, beautiful bodies also communicates ritual status, age group, patriclan section membership, and physiological condition of the individual through specific combinations of "semantic dimensions" (e.g., color contrast, element spacing, orientation, element size) (1972).

Hanson has found a predominance of bilateral symmetry on Maori painted rafters, textiles, carved wooden boxes and facial tatoos which he suggests mirrors the pervasive duality in Maori culture as seen in their origin myths and social exchanges (1983). In a more recent article Hanson (1985) has suggested that deviations from symmetry (see Donnay and Donnay 1985) are homologous with the hunger for revenge which permeates Maori society and creates constantly unbalanced social relationships. In a short article Knight (1984) has used Maori rafter patterns to illustrate all seven of the one-dimensional, one-color pattern classes. In a later paper (Knight 1984) he discusses the two-dimensional patterns as they appear on cloaks, baskets, and tukutuku weaving.

Recently a number of investigators have attempted to systematize these investigations of cultural order by using the principles of linguistics as a model to decode the structural systematics of various graphic (nonverbal) systems. These investigators contend that the structural arrangement of units of design, like units of language, can be described by a series of rules. The unit parts by themselves are meaningless; meaning only comes with their regular configurations. To nonspeakers of a language, as to nonusers of a design system, the parts and their arrangements are mysterious symbols in a code. Such systems can only be decoded by isolating the regularly repeating units and defining the rules which combine these units.

Some grammar studies, like that of Watt on Nevada cattlebrands (1966) or Korn on Abelam house panel designs (1978), are strictly attempts to test whether the principles of transformational grammar could describe the structure of material culture. However, Munn's use of the method for a grammatical analysis of the structure of Walbiri sand stories (1973) was not an end in itself, but a way to discover how regularities in form relate to activities in cultural context. She was able to define a series of irreducible elements, each with a particular set of meanings, combined in standardized arrangements which produce a form of "discourse through which information is exchanged or experiences and events communicated" (p. 59).

I would stress in particular that a structural analysis of the representational system is essential not only to an interpretation of the dynamics through which the forms are generated, but also to an explanation of the relation between the graphic system and the wider sociocultural order. I am concerned with the structural analysis not simply as an end in itself, but more fundamentally as a means of throwing light on Walbiri society and culture. (p.3)

Likewise, Glassie's transformational grammar of house forms in Middle Virginia (1975) was not only an attempt to abstract a set of rules about house forms which would generate all the house forms in this area, but also to understand how these forms represent cultural ideas about space and privacy.

To date, these design grammars have succeeded in demonstrating that it is possible to reduce the phenomena of a particular design system to a series of component parts that are combined in certain ways and, in some cases, to relate these regularities to activities and meanings. This has been of fundamental importance in the development of the structural approach to material culture. However, none is based upon a set of universal parts analogous to the phonemes and morphemes in language, and thus each is only useful as a descriptor of the peculiar structure of a specific body of data made at a specific time and place. (See, in contrast, Van Esterik 1981 for an example of a successful application of Chomsky's ideas of competence and performance to the analysis of a design system by symmetry analysis.) What is needed is the identification of systematic, universal units of structure which can make possible the development of general statements about relationships between structural regularities in pattern and the other domains of culture.

Such a need has been noted by a number of investigators. Kaeppler found regularities in structure in Tongan music, dance, and bark cloth design and interpreted these as surface manifestations of underlying structures in society. She bemoans the fact that there is no established methodology for understanding the structural principles on which regularities in form are based (1978:262). Likewise, Vastokas discovered correlations between bilateral, tripartite, and quadripartite divisions in Northwest Coast art and concepts of Northwest coast village arrangements and ritual organization (1978). She eschewed linguistic models for her analysis, contending that visual systems are not isomorphic with linguistic systems even though both might be governed by the same rules of order. She advocates a more precise descriptive system than the general divisions she used, and she suggests that "in our striving for descriptive precision, the direct application of mathematics to the study of visual systems would have considerable value" (1978:247).

Thus, of all the approaches which investigators have used to account for patterned behavior, the study of structure appears to be best able to account for regularities in material culture. What began as a study of language as a functional system, showing how individual elements are systematically arranged to achieve intelligible communication, has been adopted by other anthropologists to study other kinds of regular activities (see the extensive discussions in Gardner 1981; Roby 1973; Hawkes 1977). It has as its premises that there is structure underlying all human behavior, that this structure can be discovered by orderly analysis, that this structure has meaning, and that there are as many kinds of structure as there are kinds of behavior. It stresses that the cultural world is made up of relationships among things and that it is the anthropologist's task to decode, that is, to discover the structure expressed in these relationships. It stresses further that these relationships are meaningful—that they communicate values, ideas, and rules to live by. Since communication can be nonverbal as well as verbal, this approach has been extended to the study of other aspects of culture which are also thought to communicate information.

If meaning is produced by the articulation of parts, the problem for analysts of nonverbal culture is, What are the parts which hold meaning? And what kinds of articulations hold what kinds of information? The first need is to define universal parts—analogous to the phonemes and morphemes of language. In this light geometric symmetries can be considered universal parts, since they are present in all regularly repeated patterns.

The second step is to qualify this universal by stipulating that different kinds of order can exist in the same design system. Symmetry is one kind of order, but probably not the only ordering system which is contributing to the total structure of a given design system. Thus, a system may be characterized by symmetric structure, rhythmic structure, repetitive structure, etc. Each is a different kind of order which encodes different kinds of information.

Earlier we reviewed studies which indicate that structural aspects of patterned design are used by members of a culture to recognize what is "correct" and what is culturally inappropriate. What is now needed is knowledge of what kinds of order determine some of these responses. We propose here that symmetry is one such kind of order. It is probable that there are other orders but they have not been systematized and we do not discuss them here.

Descriptions of symmetry in the arrangement of parts are superior to data-specific grammars because the units, symmetry motions, are universally present in all repeated designs from all cultural groups. In this book we treat only the symmetry of plane patterns—those which are on a flat two-dimensional plane or those which can be conceptually flattened to such a plane (e.g., designs on a rounded ceramic surface). In this class of phenomena there are three categories: finite, one-dimensional, and two-dimensional. In each of these categories there are a given number of motion classes each consisting of certain combinations of the four basic geometric motions (rotation, mirror reflection, glide reflection, and translation). One might say that these mathematical principles constitute the rules which govern their composition and juxtaposition, as in a language grammar. Thus, classificatory replication among investigators is assured and systematic comparison among data sets is possible.

Symmetry classification is also superior to typological classifications because the classification of designs by their symmetries, like the classification of objects by their color, focuses on only one attribute. By isolating one attribute and studying the persistence and/or change in that attribute we can more systematically determine the actual behavior(s) which relate to these patterns. In contrast, a type encompasses a number of attributes and is thus a bundle of different kinds of cultural information. The combination of all these different behaviors in one analytical unit makes it extremely difficult to use this unit to study any one of the activities encompassed in the type. Further, because the typological process involves subjective judgments, it does not produce replicable results among investigators for a given body of data. This problem renders comparative studies noncomparable and thus of limited value (cf. Washburn 1984).

It should be pointed out here that symmetry classifications do not address developmental issues or issues of cultural complexity. They describe the way a pattern is organized, not whether one pattern is more or less complex than another. Geometers do not consider one kind of symmetry more or less complex or higher on a hierarchical scale than another symmetry. Symmetries are different; they are not more or less complex.

Such confusion about what symmetry means is seen in the work of J. L. Fischer, where he correlated "designs repetitive of a number of rather simple elements" with "egalitarian societies," and "designs integrating a number of unlike elements" with "hierarchical societies." Since Fischer considered that symmetrical designs were a "special case of repetition," he correlated these with egalitarian societies. Conversely, he claimed that "asymmetrical designs should characterize the hierarchical societies" (1961:81).

These correlations are both simplistic and ethnocentric. In the first place, many examples can be cited where they do not exist. For example, the incredibly sophisticated colored patterns with two-dimensional symmetries on pre-Columbian Peruvian textiles were produced by the many empires along the coast of Peru—societies hardly to be classified as egalitarian. In fact, most designs produced by most societies are symmetrical, whether the societies are egalitarian or hierarchical. While one might expect, given the systematic nature of culture, to find "formal themes" (Armstrong 1971:33), that is, modes of organization, in the many facets of culture—music, dance, narrative, design—and even that some of these structures mirror organizational modes in house form or village layout, this is not the same as proposing that all symmetrical designs are produced by egalitarian societies while asymmetrical designs are produced by complex, hierarchical societies.

In the second place, Fischer has assumed that symmetry is synonymous with bilateral mirror reflection. We have shown (1.4.2) how this mistake has also been made by experimental psychologists who have tested white, middle-class, American college sophomores for preferences among symmetrical patterns: the "symmetrical patterns" were geometrical shapes arranged in bilateral symmetry, and the "asymmetrical patterns" were composed of repeated shapes (actually patterns with translation symmetry). This Western preference for bilateral mirror reflection has obscured the fact that other cultures may prefer other kinds of symmetry and may perceive only these as "symmetrical."

With our presentation in this book of a more complete definition of symmetry classes in the plane it is clear that such simplistic correlations cannot be sustained. We have shown in the examples cited that different societies do choose and use different symmetries preferentially to structure their patterns. No longer can we sustain such simplistic either/or correlations of "symmetry" (bilateral) vs. "asymmetry" (repetition).

The analysis of design structure by the symmetries which generate the pattern is a replicable, objective way of describing pattern arrangement. Since pattern arrangement appears to reflect culturally meaningful patterns of behavior, then a systematic way of describing and studying this arrangement should be the first order of business for the archaeologist or any other investigator studying design. This analytical tool not only isolates an attribute which has been shown to be culturally significant, but also measures it systematically.

1.4.4 Systematic Classifications: The First Step in Theory Building

In this section we explain why the use of systematic classificatory units and procedures must be first, foremost, and fundamental to research. We take as our model the pure sciences, for from them we can learn the importance of defining the problem and isolating and classifying systematically the units to be used in analyzing the problem. One of the clearest discussions of this problem-solving arena specifically written for social scientists can be found in the first section of Dunnell's *Systematics in Prehistory* (1971).

Dunnell observes that the pure sciences are the Western "folk theories" of the phenomenological world (1971:13). For example, biologists developed a system, the Linnaean taxonomy, to organize and describe the changes in the various kinds of life forms. Likewise, crystallographers developed the series of symmetry classes to systematically describe the different crystal structures in minerals. Both of these classificatory schemes are "folk taxonomies" in the sense that they were developed by a particular group of people (Western scientists) in order to facilitate exploration of specific problems—the evolution of life and the properties of matter.

There is nothing inherently final or exclusive about these classifications. They were developed and persist because they work. That is, they make possible systematic study of data, replication of results among researchers, and formation of plausible hypotheses and explanations. Other classifications could have been developed and still are possible.

Our task as social scientists is to create a science of systematics for our particular data base, "categorizing historical events in such a manner as to create ahistorical units upon which predictions and explanations can be based" (Dunnell 1971:20). A perusal of archaeological investigations reveals, however, that many classificatory units (typologies, horizon styles) are, in fact, historically based temporal or spatial markers rather than ahistorical analytical units. When the reconstruction of the culture history of a site was the object of archaeological analysis, such classificatory units were admirably suited to this problem. But with the changing focus to other problems, such as the definition of ethnic groups or the interactions of such groups, archaeologists must develop units and methods of analysis which will measure material culture related to these activities.

For example, both F. Plog (1977:19) and Muller (1977:28) have questioned studies of ceramic design elements which assume that variability in this attribute correlates with individual variation. Evidence which particularly places this correlation in doubt comes from Hardin's studies of San José painters (1977:135) which indicates that whole families of painters use the same design elements.

In short, classifications need to fit the problems being investigated. Questions of chronology need analytical units that reflect changes and continuities in historical events. Questions of group composition, interaction, and communication need analytical units that reflect those particular behavior patterns.

Chronological schemes, per se, are "folk taxonomies." They are the Western investigator's way of classifying regularities in the successive events of prehistory and history. They are kinds of classifications which have withstood the test of time. Chronological schemes are, however, no more or less "folk taxonomies" than the Linnaean taxonomies or crystallographic symmetry classes, and in this sense they must serve the problems for which they were created.

We might well reflect further on why chronology has been such a successful classificatory tool for the social sciences and humanities. Perhaps the most important factor is that chronology is based on the principles of stratigraphy and superposition which indicate specific relationships between a series of units.

> . . . the system from which the relationship between categories is derived must be explicit. One must not be in the position of having to assume the nature of the relationship between a given set of categories—but rather one must know. If the relationships must be assumed, they will in part be a function of the in-

dividuals employing them, thus not replicable and ultimately lacking in ability to organize phenomena in a fashion amenable to prediction or control. (Dunnell 1971:25)

Thus, while the interpretation of a given chronological unit based on a separate geologic stratum may allow some controversy regarding what kind of activity it encompasses, there is no question regarding the extent of the unit or the succession of the units. Types, in contrast, although designed to be equally systematic, are not successful invariant analytical units. The investigator who names a type may have an explicit list of attributes which characterize that type, but subsequent users often find classification difficult when these attributes are present in conjunction with others not included in the original description or when some of the attributes in the original list are absent.

Such difficulties in the application of the unit of analysis are not due to investigator carelessness, but to the nature of the unit itself. One can define the necessary and sufficient conditions for membership in a type, yet each attribute in a type changes according to different conditions through time and space, and these conditions do not usually conveniently change simultaneously. There will almost never be a type which remains invariant in all its attributes wherever it is found. Thus, while we can, in theory, define type, in practice such a unit of analysis regularly fails to be replicable and thus does not yield systematic analyses.

The current interest in understanding culture in terms of the categories of the maker and user requires investigators to replace the descriptive categories that were the "artifacts" of the analyst with new classifications which directly relate to the behavioral regularities being investigated. In this book we offer an analytical technique which isolates behavioral regularities that, our investigations now suggest, relate to group identity, conscious or unconscious, and group interaction. These activities are not the only ones which can be analyzed by a symmetry classification; nor, conversely, can symmetry classification address all types of behavioral regularities. More classifications are needed, each treating a property of order by a different attribute (cf. Brew 1946).

1.4.5 Concepts and Theories: The Next Steps to Understanding Culture

We have seen that systematic science depends on classification of explicitly defined, replicable units. These units allow us to systematically observe phenomena and describe their regularities. In the following sections we will discuss further why such precise classificatory tools are fundamentally necessary for hypothesis formation and theory testing.

Biologists use the concept of evolution to explain the successive changes in life forms over time. Physicists use the concept of gravity to explain the movement of mass. Likewise, anthropologists and art historians have attempted to use the concept of style to explain consistencies or differences in the appearance of objects. Style can be a valid concept at the descriptive level of analysis. In the past many investigators based their stylistic descriptions on formal or functional differences (cf. Kroeber 1957:26; Schapiro 1962:278). Currently, many anthropologists are focusing on structural differences, borrowing the principles of linguistics, as we have described, in an attempt to define style more systematically (cf. Muller 1979). Many have sought to interpret particular features of style as information codes or ethnic identity markers.

For example, Wobst (1977:323) relates artifact style to the process of information exchange in his proposal that only simple, invariant, recurrent messages will be transmitted stylistically; his supporting data are drawn from studies of dress in Yugoslavia. Salvador (1978) has shown how Kuna women use molas to express their ethnic identity. Hodder (1977, 1982) has studied styles of clothing as they symbolize and reflect tribal identities, boundaries, and interactions in the Baringo area of Kenya.

In a study of metallurgical style, Lechtman (1977) demonstrates how a stylistic message was transmitted throughout Inca culture by means of a specific technology. She describes a technique which gave the appearance of gold to a body that was actually an alloy of 80 percent copper and only 20 percent gold. This deceptive technique reflected the Inca idea that superficial appearance is a reliable indicator of content; the "goldness" of objects associated with the Inca emperor represented and reinforced his identification as a divine descendant of the (golden) sun.

The Problem with the Concept of Style

However, the concept of style is not very useful for general theoretical development unless it and its relationships are rigorously defined. Even very elegant and specific statistical analyses of style are only able to describe a particular style in more detail, rather than clarifying what aspect of style makes it communicate or symbolize. For example, Roaf (1978) analyzed twenty-one attributes of twenty-four Persian archers carved in relief at Persepolis to see if they would reveal the style of individual sculptors. Cluster analysis differentiated the work of three sculptors and these results were corroborated by sculptor's marks. What Roaf presents is an example of the way statistics can be used in the service of more exact description of a body of data. His statistical procedures produced more precise knowledge about the Persepolis style, but they did not contribute to our understanding of the general concept of style.

This is because Roaf, like most investigators, treats specific attributes—such as size of projectile point, shape of the shoe of the archer, distance between the hatching lines—as stylistic. If these attributes are found to occur consistently and if they are found to coincide with tribal boundaries, language differences, etc., then they are stated to be identity markers or interaction indicators. While this relationship between a specific attribute and a specific type of behavior may hold for a particular cultural group, it may not hold for any other culture. Thus, such a specific approach to style cannot lead to the definition of general relationships and thus not to the development of theories about these relationships.

The problem is that instead of being universal properties of a class of phenomena, the attributes used are too data-specific. For example, while size and shape are formal properties of objects just as symmetry is a formal property, the different kinds of sizes and shapes are quite artifact specific. It is not possible to make statements about general relationships with data-specific units of analysis. Thus, no general theory of style or of any other concept may be derived from such units. To say that a certain design motif is the tribal symbol of a given population group is a specific statement about a specific stylistic pattern for a specific group of people. But it can say nothing about the general relationships of decorative motifs (a class of phenomena) to population groups. Consequently, it is not surprising that such attributes can function as identity codes for one group and age group markers for another. As such they can only be used as the unit of analysis for a descriptive study of a specific body of data. They can be of no help in formulating more general statements about units of stylistic meaning or mechanisms of stylistic transmission.

In contrast, in this book we are looking at a basic property which is present throughout a class of phenomena. The different kinds of symmetry are not artifact specific, but are based on a universal system of motion classes that may appear on any type of artifact with a repeated design. We can observe whether they occur consistently or not in a number of bodies of data and in this way observe trends which enable us to make general statements about the relationships of certain structures with certain types of behavior. Should we wish to use the concept of style, we could say that the consistent use of a certain symmetry is a stylistic behavior.

Style is not a theoretical concept like evolution or gravity. That is, it does not summarize a specific kind of relationship within a general class of phenomena. Quite the opposite: style summarizes the general similarity within a specific body of things. Styles, like types, are merely descriptive classifiers. Both describe attributes which co-occur consistently enough to be recognizable. They concern similarities in a specific body of phenomena (designs from one place), rather than generalizations about a class of phenomena (design). They do not describe a specific kind of relationship and the implications of the relationship. It is this very lack of explicitness about relationships that renders the concept of style, as currently used, an ineffective explanatory concept.

Systematic classificatory schemes, rather than general concepts (like style), can better support the process of hypothesis building and theory testing. First, theories are ideas about general classes of phenomena. Second, theories involve principles which relate classes of phenomena. Only if the classes and the relationships between the classes are explicitly defined is theory—that is, postulation of systemic relationships among the classes—possible. "Progress towards general theory (sufficient explanation) must be built on the examination of relationships, not things" (Faris 1972:121n).

Unfortunately many anthropological "theories" about design systems do not encompass these two components: precisely defined classes of phenomena and precisely defined relationships between these phenomena. Most common are the studies which postulate a relationship between social and political units and consistencies in style. Some propose that stylistic homogeneity is correlated with isolated and closed societies, while stylistic diversity is characteristic of open societies (cf. Englebrecht 1974). Others propose that stylistic homeogeneity is correlated with intensity of interaction with other cultures (Redman 1977); that is, widely dispersed homogeneous styles indicate intense interaction while different styles juxtaposed indicate little or no interaction.

A number of archaeologists have challenged some of these proposals and offered examples where they are not true (cf. S. Plog 1980). All of these case studies add to our knowledge about human behavior under a variety of conditions and situations, and any of these postulates may, in fact, be true in a specific situation. However, the mission of those who use the concept of style must be to first establish the criteria which define it.

The lack of a definition and understanding of the basic, universal properties of style presents a dilemma to those who examine how data-specific attributes express social affiliation and group relations (cf. Wobst 1977, S. Plog 1980, Hodder 1982, Wiessner 1983). As Wiessner admits, there is no "coherent theory of stylistic behavior in the archaeological literature" (1983:273). Sackett's critique of Wiessner's study of Kalahari San projectile point styles (1985) is actually a discussion of whether styles are consciously manipulated, purposely active messages, or passive, unconscious, tradition-bound learned behaviors. Such a controversy may arise when the units of "style" are poorly defined and thus the relationships between the parts and the behaviors which produced them have not been specified. One must first know about the stylistic attribute itself—its general and universal properties and how they vary—before postulating its social referents. We need to understand more about the behavior which produced a particular consistency of form, and by this we do not mean ethnic identity or interaction behavior, but the way people discriminate and categorize and, specifically, what features and properties are used as the basis for these categories.

1.5 Conclusion

We have seen that the only research on material culture to date which has attempted to discover general structural relationships is that which has borrowed the idea of language grammars. But, when applied to design, the grammars can only extract some invariant principles of form applicable to particular data sets. The units are data-specific and technologically limited. There are no theories to date which treat the entire phenomenon of design. In order to build theories about design we need classifications which define specific units and specific relationships among the units in a whole class of phenomena.

All of the above arguments of systematic classifications notwithstanding, users must be satisfied that abstract properties characteristic of a wide class of phenomena from the natural world can be successfully and meaningfully used to classify material culture. Gumerman and Phillips have justly criticized the archaeologists' practice of rather freely borrowing models from a number of different disciplines.

> Archaeologists cannot simply adopt models because they are useful ways to organize particular sets of data; a more adequate justification for the process of selection is needed, one that examines the basic validity of these models in their new application. (1978:187)

The use of symmetry analysis, however, meets the two criteria for validity in that: (1) there is the *same* measurable order in the phenomena which the classification systematizes and reveals; and (2) it solves or accounts for the data.

We now can ask whether the model of a culture as a structured, orderly whole and the method of symmetry classification can entertain questions of ethnic identity and interaction. Earlier research has shown that not every attribute of design is sensitive to those issues. Friedrich's now classic Tarascan study (1970) has shown that design elements are very easily dispersed among groups, but layout configurations seem to be more specific indicators of shared work groups. Washburn's restudy of comments made by O'Neale's informants (1986a) suggests that northern California basket weavers recognize a small subset of element configurations as tribally correct and appropriate. These and many other studies cited above have shown that the structural approach seems to best allow explicit statements of behavior patterns which stem from cultural preferences and choices.

Clearly symmetry classification of motif arrangement—which is a systematic measure of what is commonly referred to as design structure, arrangement, or layout—results in replicable description. It reveals that design elements are arranged in consistent nonrandom structures by artisans within a cultural group. It is a powerful tool to organize and objectively present these cultural preferences. It does not explain these preferences, but it does organize the data in such a way that hypotheses may be formulated and tested and, ultimately, theories developed. Without explicitly defined classes of phenomena, the formation of general theories about design relevant to all cultures cannot be achieved.

Design is a multifaceted phenomenon which can be subject to a number of different categorizations. We present here one kind of classification scheme which focuses on the attribute of design structure, an attribute which prior investigations have shown to be sensitive to problems of group identity, exchange, and interaction—problems which are foremost in the minds of anthropologists, archaeologists, and other humanistic theoreticians of behavior today.

If the aim of history, art history, archaeology, and anthropology is to describe and study the products of human behavior which consistently reoccur and thus form nonrandom patterns, and if we treat these patterns as manifestations of ideas held in common by makers and users of the artifacts, then we must, first of all, give our attention to classificatory aspects of those phenomena which relate to those nonrandom ideas and patterns of behavior. We offer here one way of more rigorously defining the units of analysis for a whole class of phenomena—repeated design—in a way which enables us to address important problems relating to group formation, maintenance, and interaction. The problem of why people do things similarly is pervasive, profound, and not trivial. It deserves our best systematic efforts.

Ceremonial digging board, Ica Valley,
Peru (Lowie Museum of Anthropology,
University of California, Berkeley,
no. 4-4663)

2 *Mathematical Principles and Terminology*

> Nowhere will any great knowledge of mathematics be required, as illustrations rather than proofs will be given of most of the statements.—H. J. Woods (1935)

2.1 Introduction

As DISCUSSED in Chapter 1, a number of investigators have proposed the description of repeated patterns by the four basic geometric motions which generate any such pattern. Since the publication of these initial papers prospective users have been enthusiastic about the method, but have had difficulty carrying out the analysis since the requisite geometric concepts are not part of traditional anthropological or art training.

In response to this we have developed a clearly defined procedure for symmetry analysis, which uses the flow charts presented in Chapters 4 and 5. We believe these flow charts will expedite adoption of the methods of symmetry analysis. The flow charts lead the user to a complete description of a pattern through a series of questions, each easily answerable with a basic understanding of a few principles of geometry. The purpose of the present chapter is to give some explanation of these geometric principles. Chapter 3 is devoted to the refinements necessary when color alternation is considered along with the geometric symmetries.

We will first describe briefly the kinds of figures with which we are concerned: *figures in the plane.* These are figures on surfaces which can, conceptually at least, be flattened out into a plane. Many decorated objects, e.g., textiles, tiles, decorated walls, and the flat sides of containers, are themselves planar; their decorations are already figures in the plane.

We will briefly discuss some cases where the decorated object is nearly cylindrical or spherical. The cylinder is the easiest case (aside from the plane itself), for its decoration can be unrolled without distortion onto a plane. Indeed for some objects, such as carved rolling pins for making patterned shortbread, or cylindrical seals, this is their actual intended use. Figure 2.1 shows the band pattern obtained by unrolling a cylindrical stamp from Mexico. Many other examples of patterns on cylinders which are easily converted to actual patterns in a plane by this unrolling process are shown in Figures 5.106, 5.109, 5.123, 5.127, 5.129, 5.157, 5.184, 5.186, and 5.197.

A cone which is nearly cylindrical can be treated in the same way. (An example is the basket hat of Figure 5.126.) In the case of a sphere the pattern units may be sufficiently small in relation to the size of the sphere that it can be considered a plane pattern (just as a city map is drawn on a plane sheet of paper, even though the city is actually sitting on the spherical earth). The jar in Figure 5.227 and the cap on the wood statue in Figure 5.291 are examples of this type.

Patterns on cones and spheres are very often bands around the object. These bands can also be unrolled into the plane with only moderate distortion. Examples of such bands can be seen in Figures 4.32, 4.35, 4.45, 4.61, 4.76, and 4.122.

2.1 Cylinder unrolled to show band design. Stamp, pre-Columbian, Mexico. From Enciso 1953, 29.

2.2 Engraved gourd, Luba, Zaire (Musée Royal de l'Afrique Centrale, Tervuren, Belgium, no. RG37067)

Finally, on spherical bowls there are often circular designs, centered at the top, front, or bottom of the bowl. An example of this general type, but square instead of circular, is shown on the Baluba calabash in Figure 2.2. These will generally be treated as "finite designs," though with some distortion some could be unrolled to become bands. More detailed criteria, together with examples, for distinguishing such finite designs from circular band designs, are found in Chapter 6.

We will assume that the figures to be studied are actually located in a plane. (Indeed all illustrations in this or any other book are necessarily plane representations of figures which may originally appear on more complicated surfaces.) We will then analyze these plane figures by simple tools of plane geometry, the *rigid motions*. By a *rigid motion* we mean a *distance-preserving transformation* of the plane onto itself. Schematically this means that the points P, Q, . . . of the plane are assigned new positions P', Q', . . . in such a way that the distance PQ between any two points P and Q is always the same as the distance P'Q' between the transformed points. Rigid motions are often also called *motions, symmetries, isometries,* or *distance-preserving transformations.* The next section is devoted to a description of the rigid motions of the plane.

2.2 Symmetries of the Plane: The Four Motions

We will take as our starting point the fact (proved in Appendix 1) that every rigid motion of the plane, no matter how complicated, is one of four basic rigid motions:

1. reflection (in a line in the plane)
2. translation
3. rotation (about a point in the plane)
4. glide reflection

The only tool needed for the analysis of patterns as described in this book is the ability to recognize each of these four motions and note its occurrence (or non-occurrence) in a given pattern. A brief description of these motions is given in Section 2.2.1, below.

As a preliminary to a more formal discussion of the four basic rigid motions, imagine some plane figure F, for example the triangle of Figure 2.3a, drawn on a piece of paper. Then lay a piece of transparent paper over the triangle and draw an exact copy of it, F*. Now, for the particular triangle shown, there is no way to move the transparent paper and then replace it so that F and F* exactly match up, *except* by putting it back down in exactly the same place it was. This is another way of saying that this triangle has *no symmetries,* or is *asymmetrical.*

2.3a Asymmetrical triangle

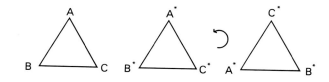

2.3b   Equilateral triangle showing rotation symmetry

However, if the triangle is an equilateral triangle ABC, as in Figure 2.3b, then when we trace the copy A*B*C* there are several ways to replace it so that it coincides with ABC. We can, for example, rotate the transparent sheet by 120° (one-third of a complete turn) so that A* lies on B, B* on C, and C* on A. This shows that the equilateral triangle has *rotational* symmetry, or *admits rotation* by 120°. A synonymous expression is that the triangle is *invariant under rotation* by 120°.

In the case of the equilateral triangle, the triangle can also be turned over on itself, so that A* still lies on A but B* lies on C and C* lies on B. This shows that the triangle also *admits reflection* in line L, which is the perpendicular bisector of side BC (Figure 2.3c). In the case of the equilateral triangle there are two other such lines of reflection symmetry, the perpendicular bisectors of sides AB and AC. Here again we say that the triangle is *invariant under reflection* in any one of these three perpendicular bisectors.

In some infinite figures, for example the figure consisting of the infinite row of equally spaced triangles in Figure 2.3d, when the traced copy is made of the whole infinite figure, it would be possible to match the copy with the original (without cutting the paper) by shifting T_1^* onto T_1, T_2^* onto T_2, etc. This shows that the original row of triangles has *translation symmetry*, because the motion which shifts the whole figure one triangle to the left is called *translation*. Of course, we could also shift each triangle two or more triangles to the left. Again we say that the infinite row of triangles is *invariant* under any such translation.

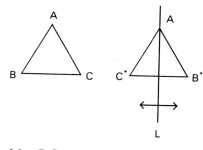

2.3c   Reflection line L on equilateral triangle

2.3d   Pattern with translation symmetry

Notice the transparent paper experiment shows that no finite figure admits a translation, since no translation can move a finite figure so that it will coincide with itself. In this book, the word *pattern* will be used to refer only to (potentially) infinite figures.

A plane figure is said to be *symmetrical* if it admits one or more of the four plane isometries. For example, in this general sense, the infinite band of triangles in Figure 2.3d is symmetrical because there is a translation, a shift, which moves each triangle onto the next triangle. This is a more general concept than the popular understanding of symmetry to mean only *bilateral symmetry* (cf. Brainerd 1942). That is, in popular usage, a plane figure is considered symmetrical only if it admits a reflection. We will say more about this in the following section. First, we turn to a more detailed description of each of the four rigid motions of the plane.

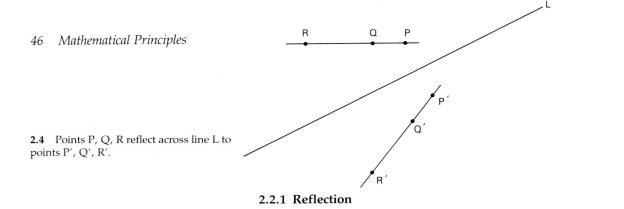

2.4 Points P, Q, R reflect across line L to points P′, Q′, R′.

2.2.1 Reflection

A *reflection* in line L or across line L (also called *line reflection* or *mirror reflection* for emphasis) moves each point P to the point P′ obtained by drawing a perpendicular to L and extending it the same distance on the other side of L. (If P is *on* the mirror line then P′ = P, i.e., P is a *fixed point*.) A good way to visualize this is to draw points P, Q, . . . and line L on a piece of paper (the plane). Then fold the paper along L and mark where the points P, Q, . . . lie on the other side of L. These new points, P′, Q′, . . ., are the *mirror images,* in L, of P, Q, . . ., as shown in Figure 2.4. Thus, any figure which can be "folded in half" so that one half coincides exactly with the other *admits a reflection,* and the line of the fold is the mirror line for that reflection.

The isometry which takes each point of the plane into its mirror image in line L is called *reflection in line L.* The line L is called the *mirror* or *axis of reflection.* Remember that points on the mirror line do not move at all: they are the fixed points of this isometry. The triangles of Figure 2.5a are related by reflection in line L. The upper and lower halves of the San Ildefonso Pueblo pattern in Figure 2.5b are related in the same way, by reflection in a horizontal line through the middle of the band. In our illustrations we use a solid line to indicate an axis of *mirror reflection.* (A dashed line is an axis of *glide reflection,* to be discussed in Section 2.2.4, below.)

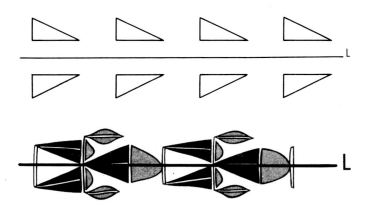

2.5a Mirror reflection across central horizontal line

2.5b Ceramic design, San Ildefonso Pueblo. From Chapman 1970, pl. 96m.

In band (or strip) patterns any axis of reflection must necessarily lie along the axis of the band, as in Figures 2.5a and 2.5b, or perpendicular to that axis, as in Figures 2.5c and 2.5d. Note that for bands there can be at most one "horizontal" line of reflection, but there may be many "vertical" lines of reflection. Indeed, in an infinite band which admits translations, as in all those of Figure 2.5, there will necessarily be infinitely many vertical lines of reflection (if there are any at all). Only two reflection lines are marked in Figures 2.5c and 2.5d; the translations move each vertical reflection line to another reflection line.

2.5c   Mirror reflection across vertical lines

2.5d   Ceramic design, San Ildefonso Pueblo. From Chapman 1970, pl. 109o.

In two-dimensional patterns, the presence of two intersecting mirror lines implies the presence of a rotation (by an angle which is twice the angle of intersection of the two lines) about their point of intersection. (This is discussed in more detail in Appendix 1.) For example, in Figure 2.6a, a Chinese window lattice, there are mirror lines at right angles (90°); hence there is a half-turn (180°) about their point of intersection. In the Japanese pattern of Figure 2.6b mirror lines meet at 60° angles; hence there is a rotation by 120° about their point of intersection.

In Appendix 1 it is shown that the reflections are the building blocks out of which all rigid motions are constructed, in the sense that every rigid motion (of the plane) is the result of applying either one, two, or three reflections. The products of *two* reflections are translations and rotations, discussed in Sections 2.2.2 and 2.2.3, below.

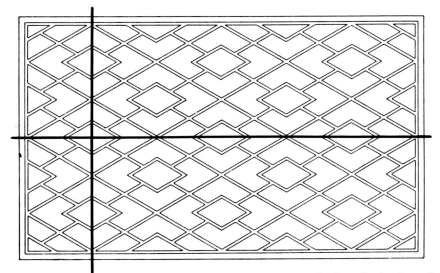

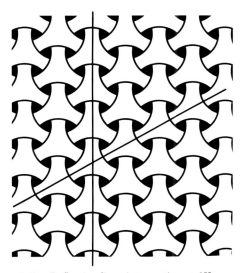

2.6a   Perpendicular reflection lines. Tomb carving, Han dynasty, Kiating, Szechwan. From Dye 1974, Z3a.

2.6b   Reflection lines intersecting at 60°. Japanese design. From Wade 1982, no. 452.

A plane figure which admits a reflection is often said to have *bilateral symmetry*. Indeed in many expositions (as discussed in Section 1.4.2 of this book) this is the only kind of symmetry which is recognized. However, we use the word symmetry in its more general sense. A plane figure is said to be *symmetrical* if it admits any one (or more) of the four rigid motions. For example, a Greek cross is symmetrical because it admits reflections. But a swastika is also symmetrical, because it admits a rotation of 90° (or 180° or 270°) about its center. A swastika has *no* (mirror) symmetry, and hence has *less* symmetry (i.e., admits fewer rigid motions), but still retains the same rotational symmetry as the Greek cross.

2.2.2 Translation

A *translation* of the plane is just a *displacement* or *shift* by a certain distance *d* along a certain line L (or any line parallel to it). Thus a *vector* $\vec{v}$ (which has length *d* and direction parallel to L) completely defines a translation. More specifically, if the tail of the vector is placed at each of the points P, Q, . . . and the head of each vector is labelled P', Q', . . ., then the rigid motion of the plane which takes P, Q, . . . to P', Q', . . . is a translation by vector $\vec{v}$ (or equivalently, by distance *d* in direction L). Figure 2.7a illustrates a pattern of triangles which (when interpreted as an infinite band) admits translation, but no other isometries. The minimal translation, taking triangle A to triangle B, and triangle B to triangle C, etc., is shown as vector $\vec{v}$ in Figure 2.7a. In Figure 2.7b a minimal translation vector is $\vec{w}$.

2.7a   Translation by vector $\overrightarrow{v}$

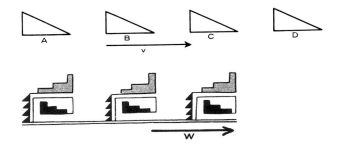

2.7b   Ceramic design, San Ildefonso Pueblo. From Chapman 1970, pl. 108m.

Of course, a pattern which admits a translation by some vector $\vec{v}$ also admits a translation by $2\vec{v}$, $3\vec{v}$, and so on, as well as translation in the reverse direction, that is by $-\vec{v}$, $-2\vec{v}$, $-3\vec{v}$, and so on. Referring to Figure 2.7a again, this means that if some translation (by $\vec{v}$) moves each triangle one step to the right, then when this translation applied twice, to yield a new translation by $2\vec{v}$, each triangle moves two steps to the right. Likewise, the translation by, say, $-3\vec{v}$, moves each triangle three steps to the left.

Note that under a translation there are *no* fixed points. Every point moves, by exactly the same distance, *d*.

2.2.3 Rotation

A *rotation* has exactly one fixed point, the *center of the rotation*. A rotation is completely specified when we know its center, the angle of rotation, and its *sense*, clockwise or counterclockwise. Counterclockwise is generally taken to be the positive sense. It is apparent that rotations are the only symmetries (other than reflection) admitted by finite (i.e., bounded) figures. Figure 2.8a shows a simple finite design (two hooks, A and B) whose only symmetry is a *twofold* (i.e., 180°) rotation. Figure 2.8b shows a twofold finite ceramic design from Cochiti

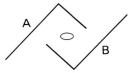

2.8a   Twofold (180°) rotation, finite design

2.8b   Ceramic design, Cochiti Pueblo. From Sides 1961, pl. 33b.

2.8c   Leaf-shaped element, cotton print block, India. From Christie 1929, fig. 94.

Pueblo. Figure 2.8c does not have rotational symmetry; it has no center point of rotation.

It is equally apparent that the only rotations a band pattern can admit are half-turns (180° rotations). As is the case with vertical reflections, if a band pattern (which admits translations) admits one such rotation it admits infinitely many, since each translation moves any rotation center to a new rotation center. Figure 2.9a shows the hooks of Figure 2.8a repeated by translation to make a band pattern. Exactly the same symmetries are shown, using triangles, in Figure 2.9b. The pattern admits twofold rotations about points like P and Q. Note that a rotation about P or Q by any angle other than 180° (or some multiple of 180°) would leave the strip at an angle from its original position; hence the strip of hooks or triangles could not possibly match its original position. This is the reason band patterns can only admit twofold rotations and no others. Figure 2.9c shows a San Ildefonso Pueblo pattern whose symmetries are exactly the same as the two preceding examples.

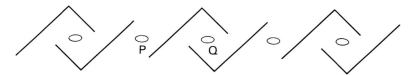

2.9a   Twofold rotation, one-dimensional design

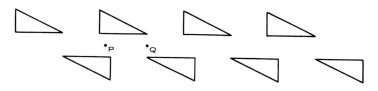

2.9b   Twofold rotation around points P and Q

It is a remarkable fact (the "crystallographic restriction") that the only possible rotations admissible by two-dimensional repeated patterns in the plane are half-, third-, quarter-, and sixth-turns (180°, 120°, 90°, and 60° rotations respectively). A simple proof of this is given by Stevens (1980:380–81). Figure 2.10a illustrates "hooks" arranged so that the whole (infinite) figure admits 180° ("twofold") rotations. Such hooks could be arranged in a different two-dimensional repeated pattern to admit 120° (threefold) rotations, 90° (fourfold) rotations, and 60° (sixfold) rotations, but *not*, for example, to admit fivefold or eightfold rotations in an infinite repeated pattern. Figure 2.10b shows a two-dimensional twofold rotational pattern incised on Mississippian tradition ceramics. We have drawn translation vectors on Figures 2.10a and 2.10b to show how they move by translation.

2.9c   Ceramic design, San Ildefonso Pueblo. From Chapman 1970, pl. 101c.

2.10a Twofold rotation, two-dimensional pattern

2.10b Incised ceramic design, Mississippian tradition, American Southeast. From Naylor 1975, 29.

2.2.4 Glide Reflection

A *glide reflection* can be simply described as a translation ("glide") followed by a reflection in a line parallel to the direction of translation. The reflection could be performed first, followed by the glide, with the same result. In practice, these are the hardest motions to recognize and identify with certainty.

A prototype example is the characteristic human footpath created by the alternating left-right-left-right movements of the two feet when walking, as in Figure 2.11a. This is broken down into glide followed by reflection in Figures 2.11b, 2.11c, and 2.11d. The original position is shown in Figure 2.11b. After a glide, by vector $\vec{v}$, the intermediate position is shown by the dashed triangles in Figure 2.11c. (Note that each solid triangle A, B, C, etc. has moved to the right by $\vec{v}$ to become a dashed triangle A′, B′, C′, etc.) Then finally the glide reflection is completed by reflection in the dashed line L. The result of the whole glide reflection is shown in Figure 2.11d where A has moved to A″ (= B), B to B″ (= C), and so on, so that the original pattern coincides with itself. Figure 2.11e illustrates a San Ildefonso Pueblo ceramic design whose sole symmetries (other than translation) are glide reflections. We use dashed lines, as in Figure 2.11, for the axes (i.e., reflection lines) of glide reflections.

Any rigid motion admitted by a figure is a *symmetry of the figure*. The classification of patterns in this book is a classification according to the symmetries which the figure admits, and the process of classification is called *symmetry analysis*.

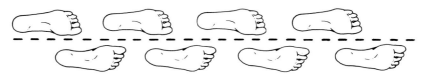

2.11a   Human footprints related by glide reflection. From Martin 1982, fig. 8.3. Redrawn by A. Pertschuk.

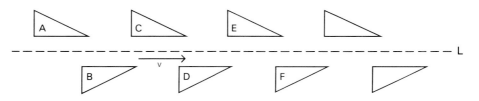

2.11b   Original position in a glide reflection

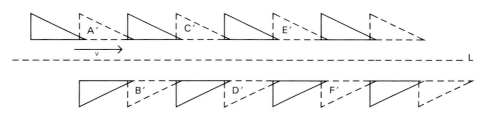

2.11c   Intermediate position in a glide reflection

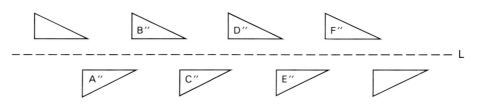

2.11d   Completed glide reflection

2.11e   Ceramic design, San Ildefonso Pueblo. From Chapman 1970, pl. 100g.

2.3 Designs, Repeated Patterns, and Dimension

We are now in a position to define more exactly what is meant by *design, pattern,* and *dimension.* We have been using, and will continue to use, the term *figure* to apply to any drawing, painting, set of points, etc. in the plane. That is, the word figure is not intended to have any specialized meaning. This book, however, is concerned with figures which have some kind of symmetry. We apply the term *design* to these special figures. Thus a design is a specific kind of figure, one which admits at least one (non-trivial) isometry. A circle is an example of a design, since it has both rotation and reflection symmetry.

We reserve the term *pattern* (or *repeated pattern,* for emphasis) for those designs which have translation symmetry. No bounded figure, such as a circle or rosette, is a pattern even though it may have reflection or rotation symmetry. A pattern must conceptually extend to infinity; otherwise it cannot have translation symmetry. A pattern may have no other symmetry at all, as in Figure 2.3d, but because of its translation symmetry, it will necessarily extend infinitely far, as in band patterns or wallpaper patterns. Thus, in this hierarchy, a pattern is a special kind of design, and a design is a special kind of figure.

We can use earlier illustrations of this chapter to elucidate this hierarchy: Figure 2.8c is a "figure," but not a design or pattern because it has no symmetry at all. Figure 2.8b shows a "design" (which is of course also a figure) which is not a pattern because it does not have translation symmetry. Figure 2.9c is a "pattern" (as well as a figure and a design) because it has translation symmetry to the left and to the right, imagined as extending infinitely far in both directions. Two-dimensional patterns which are thought of as extending infinitely far in all directions, such as those in Figure 2.6, are also "patterns."

Many of the examples in this chapter illustrate colors and complex motion classes which will be treated in more detail in Chapters 3, 4, and 5. The reader may wish to refer back to these finer points and exceptions after reading those chapters.

If a design does not admit any translations then it is called a *finite design* (see, for example, Figure 2.8b). Notice that some "finite" designs, such as a sun with rays extending to infinity in all directions, may be infinite. We still call them finite designs if they do not have any translation symmetry.

If a design admits translations in only one direction (and its "opposite direction") the design is called a *band, strip, frieze,* or *one-dimensional pattern* (see, for example, Figure 2.9).

If a plane figure admits translations in two or more directions it is a *two-dimensional pattern* (see, for example, Figure 2.10). (In Grünbaum and Shephard 1987 and in some technical mathematical literature these are also called *periodic patterns.*)

We emphasize here that, given the four motions, only seven one-color classes are possible for one-dimensional bands and only seventeen one-color classes are possible for two-dimensional patterns. Proofs for the existence of only seven

2.12a   Finite motif on a shard, Mesa Verde black-on-white. Photo by D. Washburn.

2.12b   Finite motif on a shard, McElmo black-on-white. Photo by D. Washburn.

2.12c   One-dimensional design on a shard, Santa Fe black-on-white. Photo by D. Washburn.

2.12d   Two-dimensional pattern on a shard, American Southwest. Photo by D. Washburn.

classes of band patterns are found in Appendix 2. Proofs for the existence of only seventeen classes of two-dimensional patterns can be found in Martin 1982 (Chapter 11) and Schwarzenberger 1980 (Chapter 1).

Notice that one- and two-dimensional patterns are necessarily infinite, for the fact that they admit a translation by distance *d* implies that they admit translations by distances *2d, 3d*, and so on. That is, they admit an infinite number of translations, and hence cannot be finite in extent.

Of course, what we call a one- or two-dimensional design on a textile or jar, is not, literally, infinite. Such patterns are terminated by the edge of the cloth or by completely encircling the vessel. In most cases it is quite clear in what sense such patterns are infinite: there are enough repetitions of some basic figure to make it apparent how the pattern could be extended to fill a whole infinite strip or the whole plane. Ordinary brickwork on the wall of a building is a good example of a pattern we can all agree is "infinite, two-dimensional."

However, there are cases that are not so clear, and we need to establish some general "minimal repetition" rule to decide whether a figure is really a *repeated* pattern. We first note that in every repeated pattern there is some basic unit ("fundamental region" or "motif") whose repetition, by certain isometries, generates the whole pattern. Our general rule is that a one-dimensional pattern must have at least the original basic unit and one copy of it by translation. Rotation or reflection are not enough. (The problem of deciding whether a circular band, where the "translation" is really a rotation, is finite or one-dimensional is treated in Chapter 6.) A two-dimensional pattern must have at least the original basic unit, one copy by translation, and a copy of these two by translation in a second direction. That is, there must be at least two rows, each one at least two units long. These rules are particularly useful for the classification of fragmentary material, such as the designs on artifacts recovered by archaeologists.

For example, if the investigator knows that the decorated material of the particular period is banded, then he could reasonably assume that a shard from this design system with two units in translation was part of a longer one-dimensional band.

Figure 2.12 shows four ceramic shards from the American Southwest, selected to illustrate aspects of this rule. Shards a and b each have only one unit, or set of units, related by twofold (180°) rotation, and hence are classified as finite designs even though they appear to be located in a band design field. If the second triangle, in each case, had been obtained from the first by a translation (instead of rotation) we would call them one-dimensional.

In contrast, shard c does contain a repetition, *by translation,* of the triangle and thus qualifies as a one-dimensional pattern. Shard d shows a fragment of a two-dimensional checkerboard pattern. In this case, even though the investigator does not know the shape of the larger figure which contains the checkerboard,

2.13   One-dimensional design, ceramic design, San Ildefonso Pueblo. From Chapman 1970, pl. 4m.

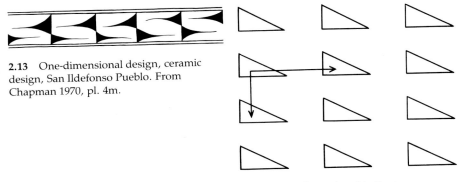

2.14a   Two-dimensional pattern

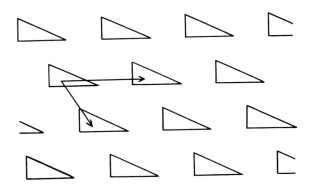

2.14b   Two-dimensional pattern

2.15   Two-dimensional pattern, ceramic design, San Ildefonso Pueblo. From Chapman 1970, pl. 4l.

this pattern within it can be classified as two-dimensional because there are more than two copies, by translation, of the basic unit (a black and white square together) in each of the two directions. Some more examples follow.

In one-dimensional patterns, the units extend infinitely in both directions along a single line axis. The San Ildefonso Pueblo ceramic design in Figure 2.13 is a clear example of a one-dimensional pattern.

In two-dimensional patterns, the units extend infinitely in many directions. Figures 2.14a and 2.14b are schematic drawings of two such two-dimensional layouts. Note, as in Figure 2.14b (and Figures 5.67, 5.68, 5.123) that the translation directions, some of which are indicated by arrows, do not have to be at right angles to each other. Two-dimensional patterns are commonly found on wallpaper, tile, textiles, and other media where broad areas are covered by motif repetitions. Figure 2.15 shows an actual San Ildefonso ceramic design which is a two-dimensional pattern. Note that it is very similar to the example in Figure 2.13, only differing in the presence of translations in several directions.

2.16 Truncated two-dimensional pattern. Chief's blanket, Third Phase, Navajo (California Academy of Sciences, San Francisco, no. 370-699; photo by C. Thomas).

2.17 Two-dimensional pattern on a lime container from Madang District, New Guinea. From Hanneman 1969.

2.18 Two-dimensional pattern. Detail, sleeping hammock, Cashinahua, Peru (Haffenreffer Museum, Brown University, no. 69-10278).

We have specified that a two-dimensional pattern must have at least two rows in each of two directions. A nearly minimal example of this rule is seen on a Navajo chief's blanket (Figure 2.16) where only one repeated unit is visibly complete. However, the truncation of the pattern units along the edges strongly implies that there are three rows horizontally and three rows vertically. The minimal two-row rule is easily satisfied on a lime container from the Madang District in northeastern New Guinea, shown in Figure 2.17. There are three horizontal rows of the basic unit as well as four vertical rows. Finally we show a truncated two-dimensional pattern on a Cashinuahua hammock (Figure 2.18). Only two horizontal rows of this pattern are present. Discussion of other special examples of problems of dimension is found in Section 7.1.

2.4 Recapitulation

From the above discussion it should be clear that symmetry classification is not concerned with the shape of the unit, but with the motions which move the pattern along an axis or around a point. These motions can be thought of as *generating* the design. The symmetry motions describe the specific configuration of parts for each design. Symmetry does not describe the parts, but how they are combined and arranged to make a pattern. It is concerned with only one aspect of design—its structure. In these ways, classification by symmetry is fundamentally different in *procedure* from typology or other taxonomic efforts.

Furthermore, because the same unit may be moved by different motions to produce different patterns, the results of symmetry classification differ markedly from the results of studies which tabulate occurrences of design elements or of types. For example, for illustrative purposes we have modified a San Il-

2.19a *pma2* Ceramic design, San Ildefonso Pueblo. Modified from Chapman 1970, pl. 3l.

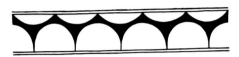

2.19b *pm11* Ceramic design, San Ildefonso Pueblo. From Chapman 1970, pl. 3m.

2.20 *p112* Ceramic design, San Ildefonso Pueblo. From Chapman 1970, pl. 98p.

2.21 *p112* Ceramic design, San Ildefonso Pueblo. From Chapman 1970, pl. 138k.

defonso ceramic design (Figure 2.19a) to show what we will learn to call a *pma2* structure for the continuous arc units in the center of the band line. This line of arcs has vertical reflections and twofold rotation symmetries. However, if the arcs are squashed against the upper band line, as in Figure 2.19b, then the symmetry changes to *pm11*, having only vertical reflections. Recent research has shown that these structural differences may have profound cultural implications (cf. Washburn 1983, Van Esterik 1981, Ascher and Ascher 1981).

We emphasize that, for maximal information, a pattern should be classified two ways: first, to describe the symmetry of the basic underlying structure; and second, to describe the symmetry of the complete design with all the added embellishments. Some patterns will have the same symmetry of structure and final design; others will have different symmetries of structure and final design. When these are different, the elaborations either maintain or reduce the symmetry. We examine here a number of situations to clarify this point.

For example, a San Ildefonso Pueblo ceramic pattern (Figure 2.20) shows a *p112* pattern that does not change symmetry from structure to fully elaborated design. The parallel line elaborations on two sides of the right triangles do not alter the *p112* symmetry. Similarly, on the San Ildefonso design in Figure 2.21 the band has been subdivided into parallelograms and triangles with flowers have been added. The symmetry of a band of parallelograms is *p112* and the symmetry of the arrangement of triangles and flowers is still *p112*, so no symmetry reduction has occurred from design field to complete design.

However, some patterns have a design field that has a different symmetry from that of the complete design. For example, in the San Ildefonso design in Figure 2.22, the center zigzag pattern structures the space between the two banding lines with *pma2* symmetry. Addition of pendants on the banding lines, if all were all black, would not alter the *pma2* symmetry. However, because small white ovals are inserted in only the upper row, the symmetry of the entire design has been reduced to *pm11*.

Likewise, in the San Ildefonso pattern in Figure 2.23, we see a pattern that has been first demarcated by rectangular panel design fields with *pmm2* symmetry. The mirror symmetries have subsequently been cancelled by the addition in each panel of motifs having only rotational symmetry, to give a *p112* design.

2.22 *pm11* Ceramic design, San Ildefonso Pueblo. From Chapman 1970, pl. 100i.

2.23 *p112* Ceramic design, San Ildefonso Pueblo. From Chapman 1970, pl. 132i.

2.5 Notation for One-Color Designs and Patterns

In this section we discuss the notation for the finite designs; for the seven one-color, one-dimensional patterns; and for the seventeen one-color, two-dimensional patterns. (The notation for the corresponding two-color versions of these patterns will be discussed in Section 3.4.)

2.5.1 Notation for Finite Designs

We recall that finite designs are those which admit no translations (and hence no glide reflections). Thus a finite design can have only reflection and/or rotation symmetry. Such designs were already known by Leonardo da Vinci (cf. Section 1.2) to fall into the two infinite classes cn and dn, where n is some integer.

The designs of type cn (c for "cyclic") are those which have n-fold rotational symmetry, but no mirror symmetry. Figure 2.24 shows some examples. Note that $c1$ is the name for a finite figure which has no symmetry at all—neither reflection nor rotation.

The designs of type dn (d for "dihedral") have reflection symmetry as well as n-fold rotational symmetry. Figure 2.25 shows some examples. Note that $d1$ is the name for designs which have bilateral, but no other, symmetry. More generally, dn has exactly n distinct mirror reflection lines.

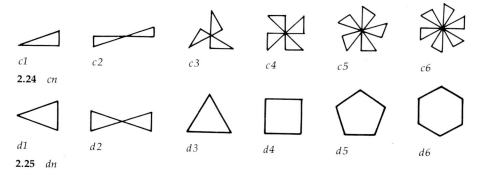

c1   *c2*   *c3*   *c4*   *c5*   *c6*

2.24 *cn*

d1   *d2*   *d3*   *d4*   *d5*   *d6*

2.25 *dn*

2.5.2 Notation for One-Color, One-Dimensional Patterns

For the seven one-dimensional, one-color patterns we use the generally accepted four-symbol notation, of the form $pxyz$. Each begins with p. The second, third, and fourth symbols respectively describe vertical reflections, horizontal reflections or glide reflections, and half-turns, as follows:

If there is a vertical reflection x is m (for "mirror"); otherwise x is *1*.
If there is a horizontal reflection, y is m; if there is a glide reflection but no horizontal reflection, y is a; otherwise y is *1*.
If there is a half-turn, z is *2*; otherwise z is *1*.

There is also an abbreviated, two-symbol notation which is sometimes used for the seven one-dimensional patterns. This abbreviation is obtained from the four-symbol notation by deleting the first and fourth symbols and replacing *a* by *g*. (There is one exception: the symbol *p112* becomes *12*.)

Alternatively, we can describe the two-symbol notation as follows:

The first symbol is *m* if there is a vertical reflection; otherwise it is *1*.

The second symbol is *m* if there is a horizontal reflection; otherwise it is *g* if there is a glide reflection (but no horizontal reflection), *2* if there is a half-turn (but no reflection or glide reflection), and *1* otherwise.

This two-symbol notation was proposed by Senechal (1975). Its extension by Coxeter to describe two-color strip patterns is described in Section 3.4.2.

The seven one-color bands and their names, in both the full and abbreviated versions, are shown in Figure 2.26.

2.5.3 Notation for One-Color, Two-Dimensional Patterns

For the seventeen one-color, two-dimensional patterns our notation is the short form of that adopted in the *International Tables for X-Ray Crystallography*, Vol. 1 (Henry and Lonsdale 1952). Consequently, our explanation of the notation is preceded by a short discussion of certain special features of patterns on which the notation is based. This explanation is not needed for the identification of patterns using our flow charts, but is included here to give some understanding of the origin of the symbols. Our discussion closely follows Schattschneider 1978, which may be consulted for more details. The reader who is only interested in the practical question of identifying patterns may skip the rest of this section. Section 4.1 gives a self-contained description of the use of the flow charts to identify the seventeen one-color, two-dimensional patterns.

Associated with every two-dimensional pattern is a *lattice* of points. The points of this lattice are obtained by taking any point of the pattern and all of the points obtainable from it by applying translations of the pattern. A parallelogram whose vertices are lattice points, but which contains no other lattice points inside it or on its edges, has the property that the translations of the pattern completely cover the plane with non-overlapping (except at the edges) copies of this parallelogram. Such a parallelogram is called a *primitive cell* for the pattern. Sometimes, but by no means always, the pattern is built up in a simple way on such a primitive cell, and in such cases, the primitive cell can readily be seen. However, it is often the case that the primitive cell cannot easily be seen and for this reason in this book we have based our analysis of the patterns themselves on the motions of the pattern rather than on a primitive cell.

Table 2.1

Crystallographic Notation for One-Color, Two-Dimensional Patterns

Short Form	Full International Symbol	Lattice
p1	*p1*	parallelogram
p2	*p211*	parallelogram
pm	*p1m1*	rectangular
pg	*p1g1*	rectangular
cm	*c1m1*	rhombic
pmm	*p2mm*	rectangular
pmg	*p2mg*	rectangular
pgg	*p2gg*	rectangular
cmm	*c2mm*	rhombic
p4	*p4*	square
p4m	*p4mm*	square
p4g	*p4gm*	square
p3	*p3*	hexagonal
p3m1	*p3m1*	hexagonal
p31m	*p31m*	hexagonal
p6	*p6*	hexagonal
p6m	*p6mm*	hexagonal

2.26   The seven one-color, one-dimensional patterns

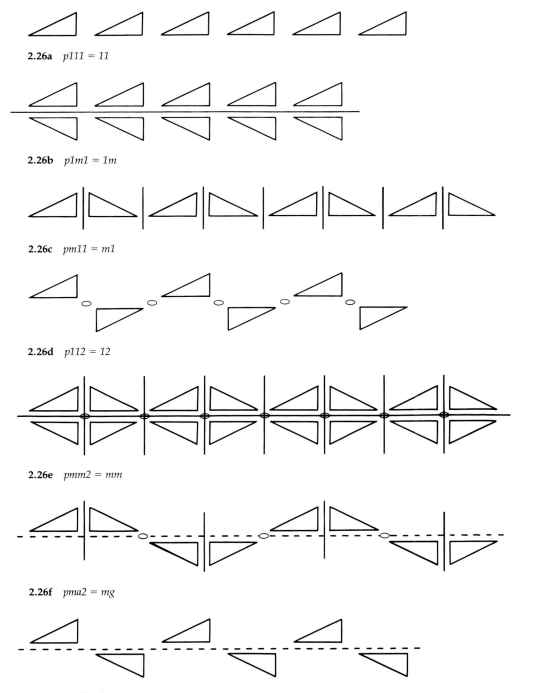

2.26a   *p111 = 11*

2.26b   *p1m1 = 1m*

2.26c   *pm11 = m1*

2.26d   *p112 = 12*

2.26e   *pmm2 = mm*

2.26f   *pma2 = mg*

2.26g   *p1a1 = 1g*

2.27   The five primitive cells for two-dimensional patterns

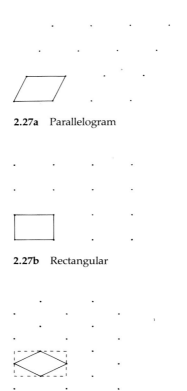

2.27a   Parallelogram

2.27b   Rectangular

2.27c   Rhombic

2.27d   Square

2.27e   Hexagonal

For purposes of notation, a certain primitive cell is conventionally chosen for each pattern. It has the rotations of highest order at its vertices and its left side is called the *x-axis*. There are five types of these primitive cells which lend their names to the corresponding lattices: parallelogram, rectangular, rhombic, square, hexagonal (the cell in a hexagonal lattice is a rhombus consisting of two equilateral triangles). The five lattices, each with its conventionally chosen primitive cell, are shown in Figure 2.27.

The full crystallographic notation consists of four symbols which identify the conventionally chosen cell, the highest order of rotation, and the symmetry axes in two directions. In the two cases where the lattice is rhombic, a *centered cell*, shown by dashed lines in Figure 2.27c, is chosen which is twice the size of the primitive cell. Hence the first symbol of the notation for these two cases only is *c* instead of *p*.

The full international four-symbol notation is then read as follows:

1. Letter *p* or *c* denotes primitive or centered cell.
2. Integer *n* denotes the highest order of rotation.
3. The third symbol denotes a symmetry axis perpendicular to the x-axis: *m* (mirror) indicates a reflection axis, *g* indicates glide reflection but not reflection, and *1* indicates no symmetry.
4. The fourth symbol denotes a symmetry axis at angle α to the x-axis, where α = 180° if *n* (the second symbol) is *1* or *2*, α = 45° if *n* = *4*, and α = 60° if *n* = *3* or *6*. Then the symbols *m*, *g*, and *1* are interpreted as in (3). The absence of a symbol in the third or fourth position means the pattern admits no reflections or glide reflections.

We ordinarily use the internationally accepted short forms of this four-symbol notation. The two forms are listed in Table 2.1.

Examples of each of the seventeen one-color, two-dimensional patterns are shown in Figure 2.28. The use of flow charts for identification of these patterns and their two-color versions is described in detail in Chapter 5.

2.28   The seventeen one-color, two-dimensional patterns

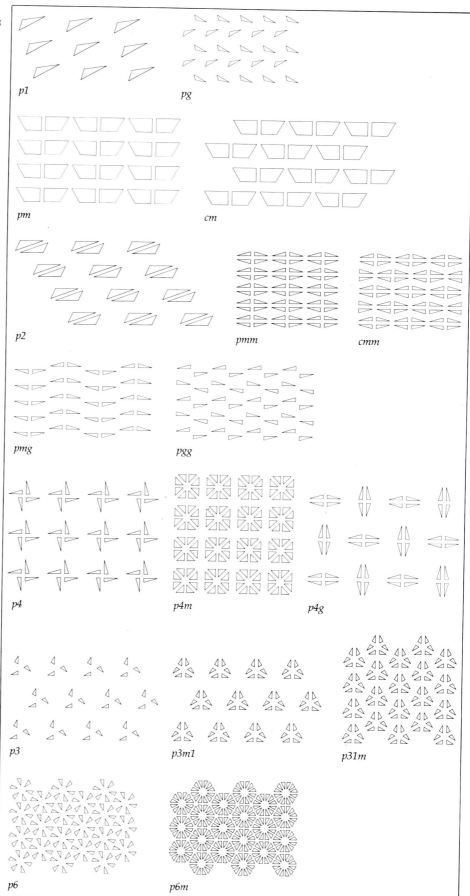

Raffia cloth, Kasai region, Zaire (University
Museum, University of Pennsylvania, no.
AF 1416)

3 *Color Symmetry*

The symmetry operations which we have so far discussed have been purely geometrical, that is, movements of various kinds which were such that each movement of the figure resulted in an equivalent position exactly superposible on the initial one. By this we mean that if the figure is drawn in black and white, black falls on black and white falls on white. It may happen, however, that a figure is such that it can be moved to a new position in which black and white are exactly interchanged.—H. J. Woods (1935)

3.1 Introduction

THERE OFTEN APPEAR designs in which some basic pattern has been "colored" in some way. However, not every such pattern will be defined as a "colored pattern" for the purposes of symmetry analysis. One purpose of the present chapter is to make this distinction explicit.

When only two colors are present, we will often refer to the colors as "black" and "white," even though they may be red and green, or some other color combination. Because this two-color case is by far the most common, we discuss it in detail in this chapter.

There is some technical disagreement about the meaning of "colored pattern" for cases of more than two colors, but we will not deal with these technicalities. For three colors we recommend the classification and terminology for the twenty-three three-colored patterns given by Grünbaum and Shephard (1977, 1987) as definitive. Three-color patterns, where the three colors occupy three equivalent parts of the pattern, are comparatively rare. We have only found illustrated examples of twelve of the twenty-three types in the literature, including five among the drawings of M. C. Escher. (Reproduced in Mac-Gillavry 1976. These are Plates 36, 38, 39, 40, and 41 which represent types $pg[3]_1$, $p3[3]_1$, $p6[3]_1$, $p31m[3]_2$, and $p6[3]_2$ respectively in the Grünbaum and Shephard notation. In their straightforward notation, for example, $pg[3]_1$ is the first of the versions of pg which are three-colored; $p31m[3]_2$ is the second of the versions of $p31m$ which are three-colored, and so on.)

For the four-colored patterns the ninety-six illustrations of Wieting (1982) are definitive. This number agrees with the calculations of Grünbaum and Shephard (1987) as well as those of Jarratt and Schwarzenberger (1980). However, such four-color and more highly colored patterns appear to be extremely rare in real life contexts.

This handbook focuses on the seventeen colored classes of the seven one-dimensional patterns and the forty-six colored classes of the seventeen two-dimensional patterns.

3.2 General Principles for Two-Color Patterns

This section gives some general definitions, which are illustrated with specific examples in Section 3.3.

The patterns we call two-color fall into two broad categories. The first con-

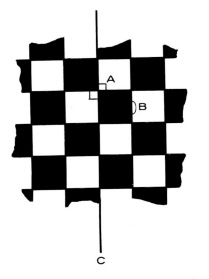

3.1   Color reversals around centers A and B and across line C

sists of those in which the entire plane (or an entire strip, or an entire finite region) is indeed completely covered with exactly two colors. A design or pattern of this type is called a *two-color pattern* (or *two-color design* for finite designs) if there is some rigid motion of the plane which interchanges the colors everywhere. An infinite checkerboard is a typical two-color, two-dimensional example. In the literature of art (e.g., Christie 1929, Gombrich 1979, Woods 1935) these patterns are often called *counterchange* patterns.

The checkerboard in Figure 3.1 is a two-color pattern because there is a quarter turn about any corner point A where four squares meet which interchanges the black squares with the white squares. There is also a half-turn about the midpoint (B) of an edge of any small square which interchanges black and white squares. Likewise, a reflection in any line such as C containing an edge of one of the squares interchanges the two colors.

Rigid motions which interchange the colors everywhere, like those just described for the checkerboard, are said to be *consistent with color*; rigid motions which move each color onto the same color are also *consistent with color*. (The equally descriptive phrase, *compatible with color*, is used in Grünbaum and Shephard 1987).

The motions consistent with color are thus of two types: those which *reverse* (or *interchange*) colors and those which *preserve* colors. This is the terminology used in our flow charts in questions like, "Is there a rotation which reverses colors?" In the case of the checkerboard we have just seen that the answer is "yes." For the checkerboard the question, "Is there a rotation which preserves colors?" also has the answer "yes," since a quarter-turn (or half-turn) about the center of any square takes black squares to black squares and white squares to white squares. More examples, to illustrate the meaning of the concept "consistent with color," are given in Section 3.5.

This first category of two-color pattern (where the whole plane is colored with the two colors) is also called a *mosaic* or *tiling*. Woods (1936) was the first to illustrate all the forty-six types of two-color mosaics. Belov and Belova (1964) have similar illustrations of these "dichromatic" mosaics.

The second broad category of two-color pattern is more common and somewhat harder to discuss because of the possible presence of other colors as background. These patterns are obtained when two colors are used to cover *part* of the plane, or *part* of a strip, or *part* of some finite region, which is the design proper, while some remaining part is either not colored or is colored with one or more different colors. We will call this remaining part *background*. On occasion one of the two colors of the pattern proper will also appear in the background. An example of this is seen in Figure 3.6b, where the narrow band of white separating the white and black floral patterns has no black counterpart and hence must be considered background. Further discussion of the meaning of "background" appears below.

3.2 Two-color (gray, black) pattern on white background. Painted house decoration, fifteenth century, Cairo. From Christie 1929, fig. 344.

However, the crucial property that makes such patterns true two-color patterns is the same as that for the mosaic patterns just discussed. As for the checkerboard, a true two-color pattern (as opposed to a pattern on which two colors appear) is one in which the part of the pattern which is colored one of the colors is exactly like the part of the pattern which is colored the other color: that is, *some rigid motion of the plane interchanges the two colors.*

In the remainder of this book we do not distinguish between the two categories of two-color patterns. The flow chart analysis of a given two-color pattern does not depend in any way on whether the two colors cover the whole plane or not. When necessary we will point out explicitly that what might be thought of as part of a pattern is to be considered background *because no rigid motion moves this background onto the pattern proper.*

The concept of *background* becomes important only when two or more colors are involved in a pattern. In a one-color pattern such as Figure 2.17 (on page 55, above), it makes no difference whether we call this a black pattern on a white background or a white pattern on a black background. The symmetries of the black pattern must move black to black; hence necessarily white moves to white. That is, the symmetries of this or any other one-color pattern are the same whether it is considered a black pattern on white background or a white pattern on black background. This is true even in extreme cases, where the background dominates the pattern (for example, a field of black with a few evenly spaced tiny white motifs on it) or where the background is almost entirely absent (for example, the thin black lines separating tightly packed white squares). If we find that what we called "background" can be moved by a symmetry of the whole figure to coincide with what we called "pattern," then what we have is not in fact a one-color pattern, but a two-color pattern of the first category described above.

In two-color patterns of the second category, where the two colors do not cover the entire plane, the areas of background may have the same shape as the motifs in the pattern. A typical example is Figure 3.2, where there are identical small shapes in black, gray, and white. However, in the pattern as a whole there is twice as much white as black or gray. Consequently, there is no rigid motion which moves all the white to coincide with all the black; likewise, the white cannot move to gray. There is, however, a rigid motion which exactly interchanges black and gray (for example, a half-turn about a point of contact between a black shape and a gray one). This rigid motion also moves white to white. Hence this is a two-color pattern, the colors being black and gray. White must necessarily be treated as background in such cases.

For a more intricate example, see the San Lorenzo tiling in Figure 5.173 (on page 202, below). Here only the hatched diamonds and the dotted diamonds are interchangeable. Consequently this is a two-color pattern, the two "colors" being hatched and dotted; the black and white, taken together, form the background.

3.3 Examples of Two-Color Patterns

In this section we give specific examples to illustrate the ideas of Section 3.2. Figure 3.3 shows part of a pattern whose two colors fill the whole plane. However, there is no rigid motion which takes gray to white throughout. For example, if we reflect gray row D to white row C, then white row E goes to white row B. That is, the colors do not systematically interchange. Nor will translations or rotations fare any better. For example, the translation which takes gray row D to white row C will take white row F to white row E. Again, the colors are interchanged in some places only, not everywhere. Thus, this is only a one-color pattern.

In Figure 3.4 there is a design with three colors. However, this is only a two-color pattern. There are rigid motions which interchange white and gray everywhere: for example, a *reflection* in line L, or a *translation* by a vector $\vec{v}$. But any such motion always takes black to black. There is no rigid motion which takes black to white everywhere, or black to gray everywhere. All the rigid motions which are consistent with this coloring take black to black. Hence black is the background and we have a two-color (gray, white) pattern.

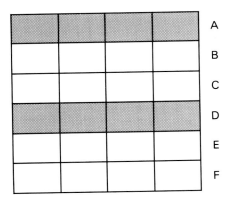

3.3 This is not a two-color pattern. No symmetry moves gray to white.

3.4 Two-color (gray, white) pattern on black background. Women's cloth, Ibo, Akweto, Nigeria. From Kent 1972, 25. Redrawn by D. Crowe.

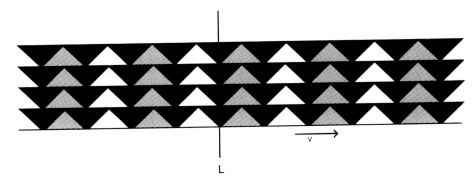

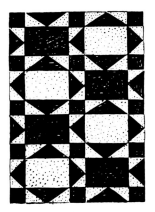

3.5 This is not a two-color pattern. No symmetry moves black to white. Roman marble pavement, Trieste. From Christie 1929, fig. 297.

Figure 3.5 illustrates a more complicated Roman mosaic which looks very much like a two-color pattern. However, careful examination shows that no rigid motion interchanges black and white because there is no white counterpart of the black triangles. This is a one-color pattern.

Figure 3.6 illustrates genuine two-color patterns, though at first glance this might not be apparent. Figure 3.6a is a two-dimensional pattern with a diagonal translation as well as a glide reflection which interchanges black and white. Figure 3.6b shows a two-color, one-dimensional border on a Persian rug. It has a half-turn as well as a glide reflection which interchanges black and white, except for the small interval of white separating the two floral patterns. This small band of white is the background. A finite two-color design is the familiar Yin-Yang symbol of Figure 3.6c, in which a half-turn about the center of the circle exactly interchanges the black and white portions. Again, the white border is background.

3.6 Two-color designs

3.6a   A glide reflection interchanges white and black. Floral design. From Christie 1929, fig. 341.

3.6b   A half-turn interchanges white and black. Rug border, sixteenth century Persia. From Christie 1929, fig. 185.

3.6c   A half-turn interchanges white and black. Yin-Yang symbol, China. From Christie 1929, fig. 93.

3.4 Notation for Two-Color Patterns

The reader may want to review Section 2.5 concerning the notation for the one-color designs and patterns, as the notation we describe below for two colors (especially the finite designs and one-dimensional patterns) is an extension of the notation described there for the corresponding one-color cases.

3.4.1 Notation for Two-Color Finite Designs

We recall that finite designs are either of type cn (for some integer n) if no reflections are present and the smallest rotation is by $360°/n$, or of type dn if exactly n reflections are present. (Cf. Section 2.5.1.)

There is only one way of coloring a cn design with two colors, consistent with all its isometries, and that is to alternate the colors around the design. Even this is only possible when n is an even number. Such a two-color coloring of cn (where n is even) is denoted by cn'. Schematic examples are shown in Figure 3.7.

3.7 cn'

$c2'$ $c4'$ $c6'$

In the case of finite designs, dn, which admit reflections, there are two subcases. If n is an odd number there is only one way of coloring dn with two colors consistent with all reflections. It is denoted $d'n$. All reflections reverse the colors; all rotations preserve the colors.

In case n is even there are two different colorings of dn with two colors. The first is like the odd case: all reflections reverse the colors; all rotations preserve the colors. It is called $d'n$, exactly as for odd n. In the second coloring of dn, where n is even, half of the reflections reverse colors and half preserve colors; rotations by one nth of a full turn reverse colors. We denote this design by dn'. Examples are shown in Figure 3.8.

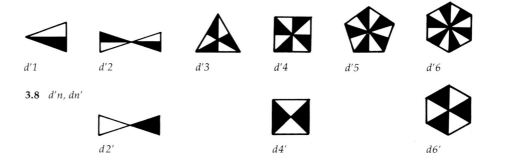

$d'1$ $d'2$ $d'3$ $d'4$ $d'5$ $d'6$

3.8 $d'n, dn'$

$d2'$ $d4'$ $d6'$

3.4.2 Notation for Two-Color, One-Dimensional Patterns

The notation for the seventeen two-color, one-dimensional patterns is also a quite straightforward modification of the corresponding notation *pxyz* for the seven one-color bands (cf. Section 2.5.2). This is the internationally accepted notation of Belov in Belov and Shubnikov (1964:225). Generally, a prime (') is attached to one of the four symbols if the corresponding operation reverses colors. (For this purpose *p* is understood as representing translation.) More exactly, the notation is determined in the following way:

The first symbol is *p* if no translation reverses the two colors; it is *p'* if some translation does reverse the colors.

The second symbol, *x*, is *1* if there is no vertical reflection consistent with color; *m* if there is a vertical reflection which preserves color; *m'* otherwise (i.e., if all vertical reflections reverse the colors).

The third symbol, *y*, is *1* if there is no horizontal reflection or glide reflection; *m* if there is a horizontal reflection which preserves color; *m'* if there is a horizontal reflection which reverses colors (except in the two cases beginning with *p'*, in which two cases *y* is *a*); *a'* if there is no horizontal reflection, but the shortest glide reflection reverses colors; and is *a* otherwise.

The fourth symbol, *z*, is *1* if there is no half-turn consistent with color; *2* if there are half-turns which preserve color; *2'* otherwise (i.e., if all half-turns reverse colors).

Although the description just given of the two-color, one-dimensional notation is a complete prescription for writing the name of any two-color strip pattern, another completely authoritative way of determining the notation is given by the flow chart in Chapter 4. There the flow chart is accompanied by a detailed step-by-step analysis of each of the twenty-four one- and two-color strip patterns.

For occasional use, the advantage of the flow chart is that it does not require memorization of the rules we have just stated for determining the last three symbols of the notation.

Coxeter (1985) has recently observed that each two-color pattern involves *two* one-color pattern types. First, the underlying pattern *type,* T; this underlying pattern type is obtained by considering all the symmetries of the pattern which are consistent with the coloring, both those which preserve color throughout, and those which interchange the two colors everywhere. Second, a *subtype,* T*, which is the symmetry type of the pattern formed by *one* of the colors alone. In the case of one-dimensional patterns the type/subtype pair T/T* gives a complete description of the two-color pattern. Two examples follow.

Consider the band in Figure 3.9a, which is *p'111* in the Belov notation. Since the only symmetries of the pattern which are consistent with the coloring are translations, the underlying pattern type is *p111*. The pattern formed by the black part alone also has type *p111* symmetry. Hence, the two-color pattern is described by writing *p111/p111*. This can be abbreviated by using the two-symbol abbreviation *11* for *p111* (described in Section 2.5) so that it becomes *11/11*. Likewise, for the band in Figure 3.9b the underlying pattern type is *p112* since the only symmetries consistent with the coloring are half-turns. The black portion by itself has type *p111*. Hence the two-color pattern is *p112/p111*, which abbreviates to *12/11*.

Figure 3.9 shows all the two-color bands as given by Woods (1935). Each is labelled by both the Belov notation and the (abbreviated) type/subtype notation.

3.4.3 Notation for Two-Color, Two-Dimensional Patterns

Although there is no universally accepted international notation for the forty-six two-color, two-dimensional patterns, the notation of Belov and Tarkhova (1964) is widely used. (However, there are a number of misprints in that article. Their Table 11 inadvertently omits the primes in p'_cgg, p'_c4, and p'_c4mm. Furthermore, in Belov and Belova 1964 the names of *pm'*, *cm'*, *pm'g*, *pmg'*, *pgg'*, and *cmm'* have been given as *p1m'*, *c1m'*, *pgm'*, *pg'm*, *pg'g*, and *cm'm*. When in doubt we have taken the names in Figure 141 of Belov and Tarkhova 1964 as the standard.) We have adopted it because of its general acceptance and recognition. Incidentally, we read symbols such as p'_cgg as "*p c prime, g, g.*"

Grünbaum and Shephard (1987) as well as Loeb (1971) have correlated this notation with their own notations and Lockwood and Macmillan (1978) have adopted it with several minor changes. Although the notation of Woods (1935, 1936) with its modification by Washburn (1977a) has other advantages, it seemed to us to have less international recognition.

The reader may recall (Section 2.5) that the one-color notation is based on a primitive (or centered) cell of one of the five lattices which underlie all two-dimensional patterns. The two-color notation is also based on this underlying lattice, but in a more complicated way; we only give some hints as to the rationale for these symbols.

As a general rule (not without several exceptions!) a prime (') attached to a symbol indicates a color change when the corresponding operation is performed. If a translation makes the color change, the *p* of the symbol is changed to p'_b when the translation is along an edge of the primitive cell, or to p'_c when the translation is along a diagonal of the primitive cell. (However, when *p* is changed to p'_b or p'_c in this way, no other symbol has a prime attached.) When all the mirror reflections in one direction reverse the colors then the corresponding *m* becomes *m'*; when all the glide reflections in one direction reverse the colors then the corresponding *g* becomes *g'*.

We give just one series of examples to illustrate the above principles. A *pmg*

3.9 The seventeen two-color, one-dimensional designs. From Woods 1935, T207–8.

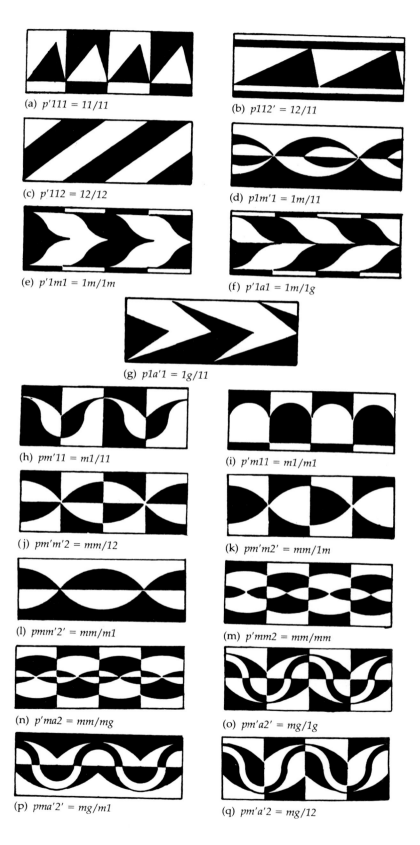

(a) $p'111 = 11/11$

(b) $p112' = 12/11$

(c) $p'112 = 12/12$

(d) $p1m'1 = 1m/11$

(e) $p'1m1 = 1m/1m$

(f) $p'1a1 = 1m/1g$

(g) $p1a'1 = 1g/11$

(h) $pm'11 = m1/11$

(i) $p'm11 = m1/m1$

(j) $pm'm'2 = mm/12$

(k) $pm'm2' = mm/1m$

(l) $pmm'2' = mm/m1$

(m) $p'mm2 = mm/mm$

(n) $p'ma2 = mm/mg$

(o) $pm'a2' = mg/1g$

(p) $pma'2' = mg/m1$

(q) $pm'a'2 = mg/12$

pattern is shown in Figure 3.10a, together with the five distinct ways of coloring it with two colors consistent with all its motions (Figs. 3.10b,c,d,e,f). Two typical mirror lines (solid) and two glide lines (dashed) are shown.

In Figure 3.10b the pattern has been colored in such a way that all the mirror reflections reverse colors. No translation reverses colors and no glide reflection reverses colors. So the notation is obtained by putting a prime (') on the m, but not on the p or the g; it is $pm'g$.

Likewise, in Figure 3.10c all glide reflections reverse colors, but no translations and no mirror reflections reverse colors. Its notation is thus pmg'.

In Figure 3.10d a translation (along the edge of a primitive cell) reverses colors (so that p becomes p'_b), but no mirror reflection reverses colors and not all of the glide reflections reverse the colors. The notation is thus p'_bmg. There are no primes on the m or g.

In Figure 3.10e no translation reverses colors, but all mirror reflections and all glide reflections reverse colors. The notation is $pm'g'$.

Finally in 3.10f these nomenclature principles fail. (Perhaps because all combinations have been used up!) The name of this pattern is p'_bgg. The symbols do not even record the underlying pmg structure.

This is perhaps enough to indicate that a complete statement of the crystallographic rules which determine the notation is too complicated to be practically useful. For exactly this reason we have developed the flow charts in Chapter 5. They can be thought of as a complete set of rules for determining the notation for any given pattern in terms entirely of the rigid motions of the pattern, without reference to the underlying primitive cells or lattices.

3.4.4 Type/Subtype Notation

Coxeter (1986) has developed an alternative "type/subtype" notation which avoids the extensive two-color flow chart of Figure 5.2. We briefly repeat that description. Suppose the underlying one-color pattern has type T (as determined by applying the one-color flow chart in Figure 5.1 to all the symmetries which are consistent with the coloring). Suppose also that the pattern formed by one of the two colors alone has type T* (also as determined by the one-color flow chart). Then the notation T/T* describes the two-color pattern completely, *except* in the two cases of p'_b1m (or pm/pm) and p'_bm (or pm/pm). In order to distinguish between these two we write $pm/pm(m')$ for the first one, where the prime indicates that some (mirror) reflections interchange the two colors. For the second we write $pm/pm(m)$, where the last (unprimed) m indicates that no (mirror) reflections interchange the two colors.

Figure 3.11 shows the forty-six two-color, two-dimensional patterns as given by Woods (1936), together with both the crystallographic notation and the type/subtype notation just described.

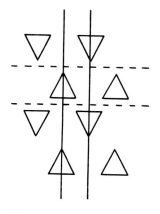

3.10a *pmg*

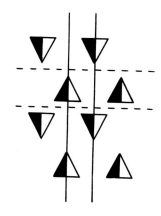

3.10b *pm'g*

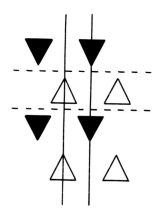

3.10c *pmg'*

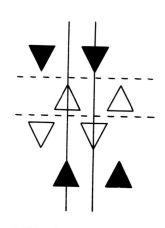

3.10d *p'_bmg*

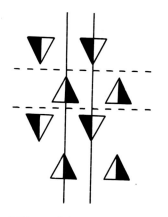

3.10e *pm'g'*

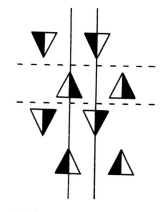

3.10f *p'_bgg*

74   *Color Symmetry*

3.11 The forty-six two-color, two-dimensional patterns. From Woods 1936, T312–16.

1. $p'_b1 = p1/p1$

2. $p2' = p2/p1$

3. $p'_b2 = p2/p2$

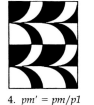
4. $pm' = pm/p1$

5. p'_b1m
 $= pm/pm(m')$

6. $p'_bg = pm/pg$

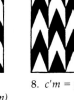
7. p'_bm
 $= pm/pm(m)$

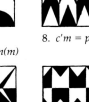
8. $c'm = pm/cm$

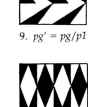
9. $pg' = pg/p1$

10. p'_b1g
 $= pg/pg$

11. pmm'
 $= pmm/pm$

12. $pm'm'$
 $= pmm/p2$

13. p'_bgm
 $= pmm/pmg$

14. p'_bmm
 $= pmm/pmm$

15. $c'mm$
 $= pmm/cmm$

16. pmg'
 $= pmg/pm$

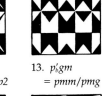
17. $pm'g$
 $= pmg/pg$

18. $pm'g'$
 $= pmg/p2$

19. p'_bgg
 $= pmg/pgg$

20. p'_bmg
 $= pmg/pmg$

21. pgg'
 $= pgg/pg$

22. $pg'g'$
 $= pgg/p2$

23. p'_cm
 $= cm/pm$

24. p'_cg
 $= cm/pg$

25. cm'
 $= cm/p1$

26. p'_cgg
 $= cmm/pgg$

27. p'_cmm
 $= cmm/pmm$

28. p'_cmg
 $= cmm/pmg$

29. cmm'
 $= cmm/cm$

30. $cm'm'$
 $= cmm/p2$

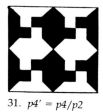

31. *p4′ = p4/p2*

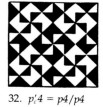

32. *p′_c4 = p4/p4*

33. *p4′m′m*
         = p4m/cmm

34. *p4′mm′*
         = p4m/pmm

35. *p4m′m′*
         = p4m/p4

36. *p′_c4mm*
         = p4m/p4m

37. *p′_c4gm*
         = p4m/p4g

38. *p4′gm′*
         = p4g/pgg

39. *p4′g′m*
         = p4g/cmm

40. *p4g′m′*
         = p4g/p4

41. *p31m′*
         = p31m/p3

42. *p3m′*
         = p3m1/p3

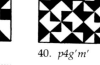

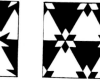

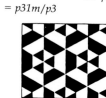

43. *p6′ = p6/p3*

44. *p6′mm′*
         = p6m/p3m1

45. *p6′m′m*
         = p6m/p31m

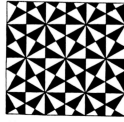

46. *p6m′m′ = p6m/p6*

3.5 Coloring Consistent with Motion

Because the concept "consistent with color" is so essential in classifying two-color patterns, we will discuss some examples in detail.

It sometimes happens that a pattern is colored in such a way as to reduce the symmetries of the original pattern; that is, some of the symmetries of the original pattern are not consistent with the coloring. For example, a zigzag line is a band of type *pma2*, but colors may be filled in so that some of the original *pma2* symmetries are no longer consistent with the coloring. This particular situation is analyzed in the next three examples.

The first example is a simple design, Figure 3.12a, which appears in the San Ildefonso Pueblo ceramic design repertoire. The design has *pma2* symmetry for the one-color structural layout. With the coloring shown, the *pma2* symmetry is reduced to *p'112* for the following reasons.

With reference to the schematic version in Figure 3.12b, the pattern (ignoring colors) has a vertical mirror axis X through triangle C. (Recall that such axes are the reason for the *m* in the symbol *pma2*.) But the coloring is not consistent with reflection in axis X. For example, two sides of triangle C, which are interchanged by this reflection, have the same color; on the other hand, triangles B and D, which are also interchanged by this reflection, have opposite colors. Any other mirror line we choose, for example Z, gives some such inconsistency.

By way of contrast, the uncolored pattern also has a 180° rotation around point Y. (Such rotations are the reason for the *2* in the symbol *pma2*.) The coloring is, however, completely consistent with this rotation. That is, white triangle C is superimposed on white triangle D, black triangle A is superimposed on black triangle F, and so on. Similarly, for any other choice of twofold center, the colors are either consistently preserved (for centers like Y) or consistently reversed (for centers like W). Thus, we can say that the motion of twofold rotation is consistent with color. Keying out the design on the flow chart gives us the symmetry type *p'112*. This agrees with the "type/subtype" notation since the only symmetries consistent with the coloring are half-turns and the only symmetries of the black triangles alone are also half-turns. Thus the type is *12/12*, which is just another name for *p'112*.

The second example (Figure 3.13) is an invented design where a different coloring of the same underlying *pma2* structure reduces its symmetry in a different way. In this case reflection in a vertical mirror axis such as X preserves all colors, and reflection in any axis such as Z reverses all colors consistently. Hence the coloring is consistent with all vertical reflections.

However, in this case a 180° turn about point Y is not consistent with color, since the two-color triangle D is superimposed on the single color triangle C; the single-color triangle E is superimposed on the two-color triangle B; and so on. Whatever center we choose, for example W, or V, some such inconsistency is found. Keying this design through the flow chart we arrive at class *p'm11* of *pm11*, not the underlying *pma2*.

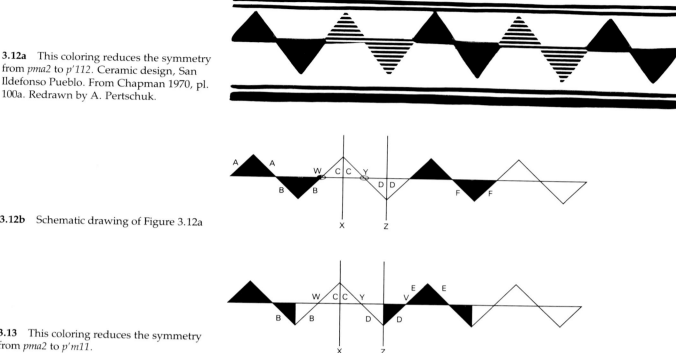

3.12a This coloring reduces the symmetry from *pma2* to *p'112*. Ceramic design, San Ildefonso Pueblo. From Chapman 1970, pl. 100a. Redrawn by A. Pertschuk.

3.12b Schematic drawing of Figure 3.12a

3.13 This coloring reduces the symmetry from *pma2* to *p'm11*.

3.14 Ceramic design, San Ildefonso Pueblo. From Chapman 1970, pl. 132g. Redrawn by the University of Wisconsin Cartographic Lab.

3.15a *pmg*

3.15b *p'_bgg*

3.15c *p'_b2*

A final example for band patterns is on the San Ildefonso ceramic design in Figure 3.14. This pattern has rectangular design fields with *pmm2* symmetry but the series of right triangles reduces the symmetry to *p111*; coloring them alternating colors yields class *p'111*. The reader should note that it is not the coloring which reduces the pattern to *p111*, but the arrangement of the right triangles with one narrow slit on the side which does not allow 180° rotations of the colored units into the white units.

We turn now to two two-dimensional examples which illustrate this same phenomenon. Figure 3.15a shows a *pmg* structure. One line, M, of mirror reflection symmetry has been drawn. Figure 3.15b shows a common two-color version. This coloring is completely consistent with all the motions of the underlying *pmg* pattern. It is class *p'_bgg*. (An African basket with this pattern is shown in Figure 5.157, on page 196, below.)

A schematic drawing of a basket from East Africa (not illustrated) uses three colors of which the white is background to make the two-color (black, gray) pattern drawn in Figure 3.15c. In this version much of the symmetry of the original *pmg* is no longer consistent with the coloring. For example, none of the original reflections is consistent with this coloring. Reflection in one of the original mirrors M moves black to the white background and gray to the white background. It might seem at first that the mirror reflection axis M has become a glide reflection axis, since some black parallelograms directly along M move to black parallelograms on the other side of M. Likewise, gray moves to gray and white to white. However, if we look at parallelograms one step further away from M we see that the same glide reflection which appeared to preserve colors now takes black parallelogram A to gray B, a color reversal. In fact, no glide reflection is consistent with color. Indeed, the only motions consistent with color are half-turns about points like C (which reverse both colors and preserve the white background) or D (which preserve all colors). It is class *p'_b2*.

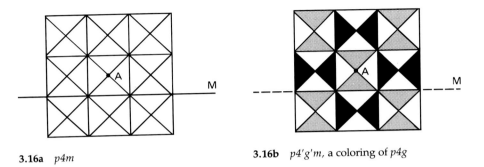

3.16a   *p4m*

3.16b   *p4'g'm*, a coloring of *p4g*

Our final example appears in Figure 3.16, where colors have been added to the *p4m* pattern in 3.16a to obtain 3.16b. If all the colored triangles in 3.16b were the same color, it would be of type *p'c4gm*, in which the coloring is consistent with all the motions of the original *p4m* (cf. the Roman mosaic from Timgad in Figure 5.244, on page 228, below).

However, the exact coloring of Figure 3.16b (where the two colors are black and gray, against a white background) is not consistent with all the motions of *p4m*. In particular, reflection in line M (which is a mirror line in the original *p4m* pattern) moves all the black and gray triangles onto the white background. There is, however, a glide reflection in line M which preserves all colors, and hence is consistent with the coloring. Furthermore, although *p4m* allows a quarter-turn about point A, in Figure 3.16b a quarter-turn about A takes black and gray onto the white background. However, a half-turn about A preserves all colors. The flow chart yields *p4'g'm* (a coloring of *p4g*) for this pattern.

Finally, one of the most frequently occurring problems is the irregular coloring of a design so that not all areas are colored consistently to give proper color alternation upon superposition. For example, on the Maori rafter in Figure 3.17 we see that not all the areas of the same shape are colored consistently either gray or black. If there are only a few such cases in a long band of design, they can be overlooked, but if, as in the case of most Maori designs, such color inconsistencies are persistent, then the design coloring can only be considered asymmetrical.

3.17   The irregular coloring makes this figure asymmetrical. Rafter pattern, Maori. From Hamilton 1896, no. 15.

Jar by Mary Juan, Maricopa, Arizona
(California Academy of Sciences, San
Francisco, no. 370-544)

4 One-Dimensional Patterns

4.1 Introduction to the Flow Charts

TWO KINDS of flow charts are presented for both one- and two-dimensional patterns. Table 4.1 gives the flow chart for one-color, one-dimensional patterns and Table 4.2 gives the flow chart for one- and two-color, one-dimensional patterns. Likewise, Table 5.1 gives the flow chart for one-color, two-dimensional patterns and Table 5.2 gives the flow chart for one- and two-color, two-dimensional patterns. The shorter one-color flow charts in Tables 4.1 and 5.1 can be used for patterns which are clearly one-color, but in ambiguous cases and obviously two-color cases the user will have to use the longer flow charts in Tables 4.2 and 5.2. The following points apply to both one- and two-color, one- and two-dimensional patterns.

First, both kinds of flow charts query the user about the presence and coloring of specific rigid motions. The order in which these queries arise is strictly arbitrary. The fact that the flow chart for two-color, one-dimensional patterns begins with a query concerning half-turns, i.e., twofold rotation, or that the flow chart for the two-dimensional patterns begins with a query about the size of the smallest rotation *does not* mean that there is a hierarchical order of importance among the motions of rotation, translation, mirror reflection, or glide reflection. Flow charts could be devised which begin with queries about other motions; indeed, the one-color, one-dimensional flow chart begins with a query about reflections.

Second, it is important to remember that in some cases not all symmetries present in a pattern are mentioned in the flow chart.

Third, we use three important phrases: *preserves colors, reverses colors,* and *consistent with color*. Because it is essential to understand the meaning of these terms we recapitulate some of the discussion from Chapter 3 here.

Preserves colors means that the same coloring is maintained; i.e., all white units superimpose on white units and all black units superimpose on black units. No color changes (i.e., reversals) occur.

Reverses colors means that color changes have occurred everywhere; i.e., all white units superimpose on black units and all black units superimpose on white units.

The phrase *consistent with color* asks the user to determine whether only color reversals or only color preservations are present from one point of rotation or line of reflection in the pattern. To do this the user rotates or reflects the entire pattern about this point or across this line. It is important to recognize that, in a given design, different points of rotation or reflection may or may not produce symmetries consistent with color, or consistent in the same way.

Recall, for example, that in Figure 3.12b rotation of the pattern about W means that all black triangles will fall on white triangles, and all white triangles will fall on black triangles. In short, in a half-turn about center W all colors are reversed. The motion of twofold rotation about W is said to be consistent with color.

Additionally, rotation of the pattern about center Y places white triangles on white triangles and black triangles on black triangles. Thus, about center Y all colors are preserved. This motion of twofold rotation is also said to be consistent with color, although rotation about Y preserves all colors, in contrast to rotations about W (which reverse all colors).

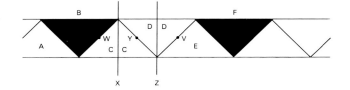

4.1   Flow chart example of motions not consistent with color

Figure 4.1 shows another coloring of the same underlying structure, *pma2*. This is an extreme version of the reduction of symmetry by addition of color since none of the motions of the original *pma2* pattern reverse colors consistently. For example, rotation about point W would place white triangle C on black triangle B (a color reversal), but white triangle D on white triangle A (a color preservation). This rotation, as well as any other, is inconsistent with color. Similarly, vertical reflections in lines like X are inconsistent with color. Ultimately, there are only two motions consistent with color: reflections in lines like Z (but not in lines like X), and translations such as those which take triangle B to triangle F and triangle A to triangle E. These motions all preserve colors, none of them reverse colors. Consequently, when this apparently "colored" pattern is keyed out on the flow chart, we find the one-color class *pm11*.

Fourth, there are basically two types of questions in the flow charts. One asks whether or not there exist in the pattern *any* cases of the particular motion in question. This may be one of several which the pattern possesses.

The other type of question asks about the color-preserving or color-reversing effects of a particular symmetry motion. This query does not ask whether a particular motion is present. Rather, the question concerns a motion already identified in a previous question.

4.2 Flow Charts for the One-Dimensional Patterns

In the following discussion, the process of design classification is illustrated by examining a series of bands on historic pottery from San Ildefonso Pueblo, New Mexico (Chapman 1970). This is a particularly convenient source of one-dimensional patterns, as all but three of the twenty-four classes of one- and two-color bands are represented in this sample. In the following pages we will "key out" one example of each of the one- and two-color classes of one-dimensional patterns. The reader will need to follow this section with flow chart (Table 4.2) in hand.

83   4.2 Flow Charts

Table 4.1   Flow chart for the seven one-color, one-dimensional patterns

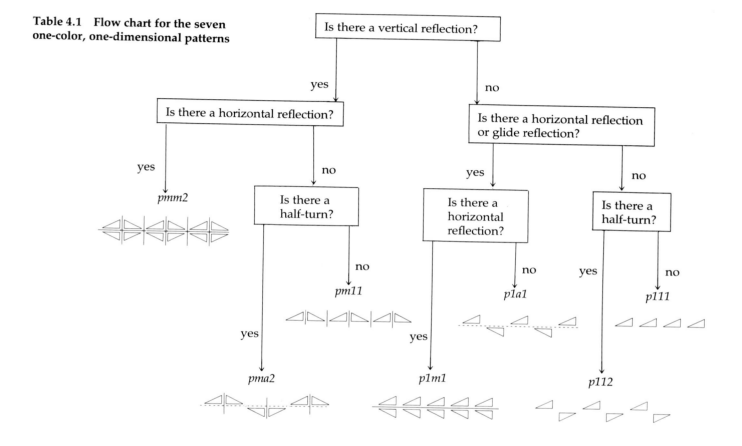

**Table 4.2   Flow chart for the twenty-four
one-color and two-color, one-dimensional patterns**

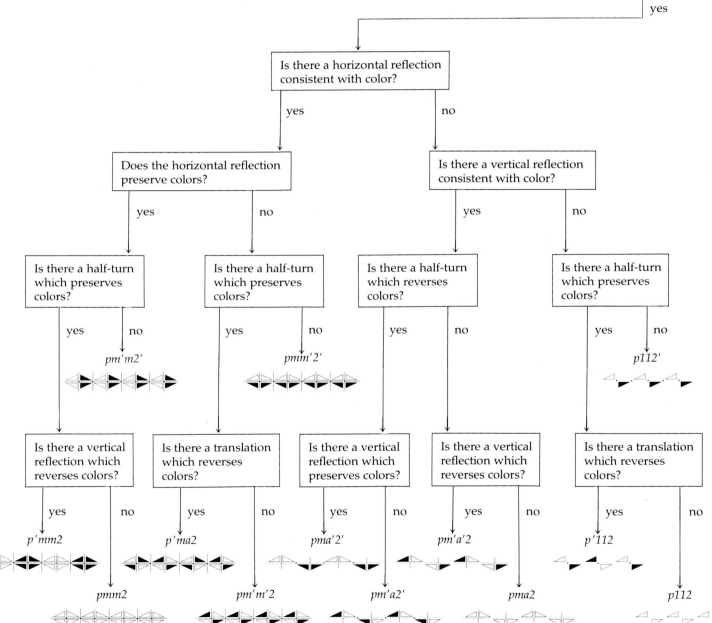

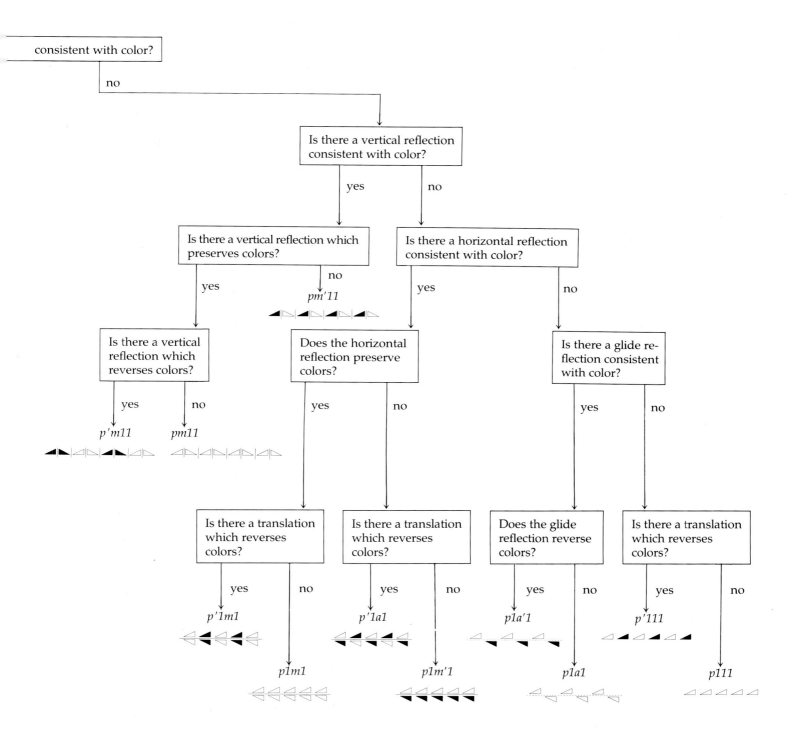

This flow chart falls into two sections, after the initial question is answered. Let us begin with the "yes" side of the chart and examine the pattern in Figure 4.2a. A schematic drawing of the same pattern, with centers of rotation and lines of reflection indicated, appears in Figure 4.2b.

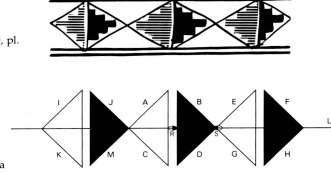

4.2a *pm'm2'* Ceramic design, San Ildefonso Pueblo. From Chapman 1970, pl. 132r. Redrawn by A. Pertschuk.

4.2b Schematic drawing of Figure 4.2a

A "yes" answer to the question, "Is there a half-turn consistent with color?" means that either (1) there is some half-turn (i.e., twofold rotation) which preserves all colors, or (2) there is some half-turn which reverses all colors.

In the case of the pattern in Figure 4.2b, a half-turn about center R puts the white A and C sections onto the black D and B sections and puts the white E and G sections onto the black M and J sections, and so on, always interchanging black and white throughout the whole pattern. Thus, the answer to the first question is "yes"; there is a half-turn consistent with color because this 180° turn about R reverses the colors. A half-turn about center S, a different center, also reverses the colors throughout the pattern. In fact, for the pattern in Figure 4.2a, there are color reversals about all twofold centers. The small ovals at these centers in Figure 4.2b are colored black-white to indicate this reversal.

The next question, "Is there a horizontal reflection consistent with color?" asks the same type of question as the first, but this time we must determine whether color reversal or color preservation occurs consistently across the horizontal reflection line. In Figure 4.2b, the horizontal mirror reflection line has been marked with a solid line L. In this pattern the answer to the second query will again be "yes" since, for example, the white sections I, A, and E will reflect onto the white sections K, C, and G respectively. Likewise, the black sections J, B, and F will reflect onto the black sections M, D, and H respectively. Thus the horizontal reflection preserves colors and the answer is "yes," horizontal reflection is consistent with color.

The next question, "Does the horizontal reflection preserve colors?" has, in fact, already been answered in the preceding paragraph. The answer is "yes." The next question, "Is there a half-turn which preserves colors?" has also already been answered: all half-turns reverse the colors. (There are really only two kinds of half-turns in this pattern: those about points like R, by which the colors are reversed, and those about points like S, by which the colors are also reversed.) Thus, the colors are not preserved and the answer is "no."

For this particular pattern, we have reached the end of the flow chart. No more questions are required to determine the symmetry class of the pattern. The notation for Figure 4.2 is *pm'm2'*.

Suppose, however, we examine a pattern where the answer to the last question, "Is there a half-turn which preserves colors?" is "yes." The pattern in Figure 4.3 is one such case. Note that in this design the two colors are black and gray; white is the background.

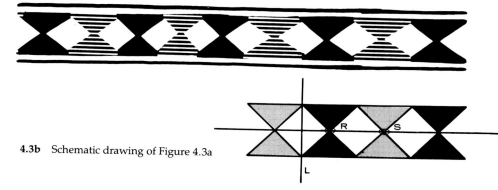

4.3a *p'mm2* Ceramic design, San Ildefonso Pueblo. From Chapman 1970, pl. 132n. Redrawn by A. Pertschuk.

4.3b   Schematic drawing of Figure 4.3a

Going back to the beginning of the flow chart we see that all the half-turns around centers R and S (Figure 4.3b) are consistent with color because they all preserve colors. Half-turns about the centers of the white diamonds reverse the colors black and gray. Hence they are also consistent with color. The horizontal reflection along the axis of the band preserves colors, and thus is consistent with color, giving a "yes" answer to the second and third questions. We have already seen that some half-turns preserve color, so the answer to the fourth question is "yes." The answer to the final question, "Is there a vertical reflection which reverses colors?" is "yes," because examination of the colors across the reflection axes which pass between the hour glass figures, such as the mirror line L, shows that color reversal occurs. Thus, the classification of the pattern in Figure 4.3 is *p'mm2*.

Finally, we examine a pattern, Figure 4.4, which is consistent with color in its half-turns and horizontal reflections, because there is no color change anywhere in the pattern. The answer to the next two questions is also "yes" since the horizontal reflection and all half-turns preserve colors. The answer to the last question must be "no" as there are no vertical reflection axes which reverse colors. The classification for the pattern in Figure 4.4 is *pmm2*, one of the seven classes of one-color, one-dimensional patterns.

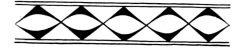

4.4   *pmm2* Ceramic design, San Ildefonso Pueblo. From Chapman 1970, pl. 3f.

Let us examine another pattern, Figure 4.5a, which requires different answers to the last of the series of questions on the left side of the flow chart. The horizontal reflection line (L) and points of rotation in the pattern are indicated in Figure 4.5b.

4.5a *p'ma2* Ceramic design, San Ildefonso Pueblo. From Chapman 1970, pl. 95o. Redrawn by A. Pertschuk.

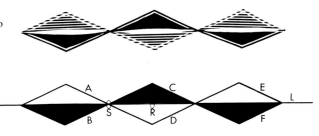

4.5b   Schematic drawing of Figure 4.5a

For this pattern, the answer to the question, "Is there a half-turn consistent with color?" is "yes" because rotation about point R places the white A, D, and E sections in the black F, C, and B sections. Notice that a half-turn about point S is also consistent with color because it places all the colors in the upper half in the same colors in the lower half of the design; e.g., white A moves onto white D and black B moves onto black C. That is, colors reverse everywhere for center R but are preserved everywhere for center S. The answer to the next question is also "yes" because a reflection across the horizontal center line will cause a color reversal in all parts of the pattern. Thus, the horizontal reflection is consistent with color.

However, in the next query, "Does the horizontal reflection preserve colors?" our course down the flow chart changes. We have just determined that, although the horizontal reflection is consistent with color, the consistency in this case is in the reversal of the colors in all parts of the pattern. Thus, the answer to the query whether the horizontal reflection preserves colors is "no."

Proceeding to the next question, "Is there a half-turn which preserves colors?" the answer is "yes" because, as we saw in answering the first question, a rotation about point S will take white A to white D, black B to black C, and so on. Given this "yes" answer, we proceed to the final question, "Is there a translation which reverses colors?" A translation of the pattern which moves the top white section A to the top black section C, and moves the bottom black section B into the bottom white section D and so on reverses all colors. Thus, the answer is "yes" and the pattern is classified as *p'ma2*.

For this next series of questions we examine a pattern that is not from San Ildefonso. In an earlier report (Crowe and Washburn 1985) we found that only three of the seventeen one- and two-color, one-dimensional patterns did not occur at San Ildefonso (at least, in Chapman's extensive sample of 1970). Class *pm'm'2* was one of these missing two-color classes and so we substitute here a Maori rafter design, Figure 4.6.

4.6 *pm'm'2* Painted wood rafter, Maori. From Bossert 1955, pl. 29, no. 23. Redrawn by A. Pertschuk.

4.7 *pmm'2'* Ceramic design, San Ildefonso Pueblo. From Chapman 1970, pl. 124i. Redrawn by A. Pertschuk.

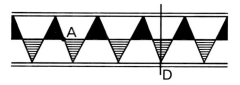

4.8 *pma'2'* Ceramic design, San Ildefonso Pueblo. From Chapman 1970, pl. 131j. Redrawn by the University of Wisconsin Cartographic Lab.

We find that this pattern has half-turns consistent with color. In all cases the colors are preserved. The horizontal reflection is consistent with color because all colors are reversed across the horizontal mirror axis. So we have to answer "no" to the question, "Does the horizontal reflection preserve colors?" But to the next question we can answer "yes," because we found previously that all the half-turns preserve colors.

The final question distinguishes this pattern from *p'ma2* patterns because a translation preserves, not reverses the colors, with the gray sections moving to the corresponding gray sections and the black to black. Thus, the classification for this Maori rafter pattern is *pm'm'2*.

Suppose, however, that we examine a San Ildefonso pattern, Figure 4.7, where there are half-turns consistent with color (colors are reversed around center A) and the horizontal reflection is consistent with color (colors are reversed across the horizontal mirror axis), thus making the answer to the third question "no," the horizontal reflection does not preserve colors. The answer to the next question, "Is there a half-turn which preserves colors?" must be "no" since 180° rotations around all centers such as A or B reverse the colors. The classification for this pattern is *pmm'2'*.

Let us now identify a pattern with no horizontal reflection at all. We stay on the left side of the chart to analyze Figure 4.8, but this time, after the initial "yes," the answer to the question "Is there a horizontal reflection consistent with color" is "no." To the question "Is there a vertical reflection consistent with color?" we answer "yes" because reflection across mirror axis D, for example, will superimpose gray on gray and black on black. Thus, vertical reflection across axis D preserves colors.

We have already answered the next question, "Is there a half-turn which reverses colors?" because we saw in the first question that a half-turn about center A would reverse black triangles and gray triangles. Furthermore, we have also already answered the final question, "Is there a vertical reflection which preserves colors?" because we found that reflection across vertical mirror line D preserves colors. Thus the "yes" answer gives us a classification of *pma'2'*.

Let us remain in this left-hand section of the flow chart and examine several more patterns. It should become clear that this section is dealing with *pma2* patterns because we always answer "no" to the question whether there is a horizontal reflection consistent with color and "yes" to the question whether there is a vertical reflection consistent with color. Since there are no horizontal

L

4.9 *pm'a2'* Painted wood rafter, Maori. From Bossert 1955, pl. 29, no. 4. Redrawn by A. Pertschuk.

reflections, the remaining questions deal with half-turns and vertical reflection, the two motions (together with glide reflection) characterizing class *pma2*.

Again we examine a Maori rafter design, Figure 4.9. In this pattern we first answer "yes" to the question whether there is a half-turn consistent with color, because we see that half-turns around all centers, for example the one marked by a small oval in the center of the figure, reverse colors and thus are consistent with the coloring. Since there is no horizontal reflection, we move to the question "Is there a vertical reflection consistent with color?" The answer is "yes" because inspection of any vertical mirror line such as line L shows that the colors reverse and thus are consistent. We can answer "yes" to the next question also, because we have already found that half-turns reverse the colors. But to the final question we answer "no" because, as we have found, there are no vertical reflection axes which preserve colors. Thus, the classification of the pattern is *pm'a2'*.

Let us now move on to a new set of questions and examine the pattern in Figure 4.10. This San Ildefonso Pueblo design has a half-turn consistent with color since all half-turns around the centers of the leaves preserve color. The answer to the next question, "Is there a horizontal reflection consistent with color?" is an easy "no" since there are no horizontal reflection axes in this pattern. There are, however, vertical reflection axes.

To answer the next question, "Is there a vertical reflection consistent with color?" we see that reflection across any vertical mirror axis, such as line M, reverses colors everywhere, and thus is consistent with color, and the answer to the question is "yes."

Moving to the next question, "Is there a half-turn which reverses colors?" the answer is "no" since we have already determined that all half-turns preserve colors. The final question, "Is there a vertical reflection which reverses colors?" must be answered with a "yes" as we have already determined this in the third question which asked whether the vertical reflections were consistent with color. The classification of the pattern in Figure 4.10 is thus *pm'a'2*.

Finally we come to the underlying one-color pattern of all these two-color classes of *pma2*. We use a simple zigzag pattern from San Ildefonso in Figure 4.11 because it has the structural layout of so many *pma2* designs.

Since it is a one-color pattern, all its rotations and vertical reflections are consistent with color. That is, there are no half-turns or vertical reflections which reverse color. There is no horizontal reflection line. The above responses lead

M

4.10 *pm'a'2* Ceramic design, San Ildefonso Pueblo. From Chapman 1970, pl. 131e. Redrawn by A. Pertschuk.

4.11 *pma2* Ceramic design, San Ildefonso Pueblo. From Chapman 1970, pl. 3c.

to a "no" answer to the final question about color reversal across a vertical mirror line, and a classification of *pma2*.

Thus far we have completed most of the left side of the flow chart by illustrating class *pmm2* and its five color classes and class *pma2* and its three color classes. We now move toward the center of the chart to classify patterns whose only motions (aside from translation) are half-turns.

Our first pattern, Figure 4.12, has such half-turns which are consistent with color because rotation around centers either in the middle of the white diagonals or the middle of the white verticals will reverse all colors. Rotation about these points moves the black triangles into the gray triangles, and vice versa.

The answer to the question concerning horizontal reflection is "no" simply because there are no horizontal reflections in this pattern. Likewise, the answer to the question concerning vertical reflections is also "no" since there are no vertical reflection axes in the pattern.

We return to queries about half-turns in the next question, "Is there a half-turn which preserves colors?" Since we have already determined in the first question that all the half-turns reverse the colors, the answer to this question must be "no." We are thus at the end of the sequence in the flow chart, at the pattern classification *p112'*.

If we examine another pattern, Figure 4.13, we can see that a rotation about the center of a black or gray flag preserves colors everywhere in the pattern, but a rotation about a corner between flags reverses all colors. Thus, for any given rotation, the coloring is consistent—either it is always preserved or it is always changed.

Since there are no horizontal or vertical reflections, the answer to the next two questions is "no." Since we have already seen that a rotation about a flag center preserves colors, the answer to the following question is "yes." Likewise, the answer to the question whether a simple translation would reverse the colors is "yes" since movement of the gray flag into the succeeding black one reverses the colors. This "yes" answer gives us a classification of *p'112*.

We turn now to keying out a one-color twofold rotational pattern. Since Figure 4.14 is one-color, we can easily see that the half-turns around points A or B always preserve colors, and thus are consistent with color. We see that there are no horizontal or vertical reflection lines and also that there is no translation which reverses the colors, since movement of the separate motifs maintains the black color. Thus we classify our pattern as *p112*.

We turn now to the right-hand side of the flow chart, where the answer to the first question, "Is there a half-turn consistent with color?" is "no." We will first consider patterns which have neither half-turns nor horizontal reflections, *pm11*. The "no" answer to the first question indicates (1) that there are no half-turns in the pattern or (2) that there are half-turns in the pattern which are not consistent with color (i.e., half-turns around a given center reverse some colors and preserve others).

4.12   *p112'* Ceramic design, San Ildefonso Pueblo. From Chapman 1970, pl. 132f. Redrawn by the University of Wisconsin Cartographic Lab.

4.13   *p'112* Ceramic design, San Ildefonso Pueblo. From Chapman 1970, pl. 96i. Redrawn by the University of Wisconsin Cartographic Lab.

4.14   *p112* Ceramic design, San Ildefonso Pueblo. From Chapman 1970, pl. 4i.

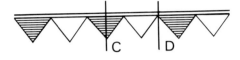

4.15 *p'm11* Ceramic design, San Ildefonso Pueblo. From Chapman 1970, pl. 109c. Redrawn by the University of Wisconsin Cartographic Lab.

4.16 *pm'11* Ceramic design, San Ildefonso Pueblo. From Chapman 1970, pl. 109g. Redrawn by A. Pertschuk.

4.17 *pm11* Ceramic design, San Ildefonso Pueblo. From Chapman 1970, pl. 3b.

4.18 *p1m1* Ceramic design, San Ildefonso Pueblo. From Chapman 1970, pl. 4d.

For the patterns based on *pm11*, as in Figure 4.15, the answer is "no" because there are no half-turns. The answer to the second question, "Is there a vertical reflection consistent with color?" is "yes." In the case of a vertical reflection across a mirror axis such as C, since gray triangles reflect into gray triangles and white into white, the colors are preserved. For vertical reflection across a mirror axis such as D, the colors are reversed between the triangles. Although there is a difference between the two different axes, for *any one axis,* the reflection is consistent with the coloring and thus the answer is "yes."

For the next question, "Is there a vertical reflection which preserves colors?" the answer is "yes" again because, from the preceding question, vertical reflection across axis C preserves all colors. To the final question, "Is there a vertical reflection which reverses colors?" we answer "yes" again since we saw that a vertical reflection across axis D reflected the white triangles into the gray triangles. This pattern is class *p'm11*.

Another coloring of a *pm11* pattern is shown in Figure 4.16. In this case, since there are no half-turns in the pattern, we are again on the right-hand side of the flow chart. To the question, "Is there a vertical reflection consistent with color?" we reply that color reversals always occur across *both* mirror axes C and D, and thus the answer is "yes." However, since all mirror reflections reverse the colors, the answer to the next question, "Is there a vertical reflection which preserves colors?" must be "no." At this point we find that the classification for this pattern is *pm'11*.

Finally we can key out the one-color class *pm11* by examining the pattern in Figure 4.17. There are no half-turns and since all units in the design are the same color, the vertical reflections all preserve color and are thus consistent with color. The absence of any color reversals requires a "no" answer for the fourth question, which leads to the classification *pm11*.

Let us now examine patterns without half-turns or vertical reflection but with horizontal reflection. The answers to the first and second questions will be "no." A "yes" answer to the third question, "Is there a horizontal reflection consistent with color?" leads us to examine patterns admitting horizontal reflection. For the pattern in Figure 4.18 the answer to the fourth question is "yes" because horizontal reflection preserves colors. And since there are no translations which reverse colors, the classification is *p1m1*.

There are three colorings of class *p1m1*.

In the pattern in Figure 4.19, after our "no" answer to the first two questions, we see that the colors are all preserved across the horizontal reflection line because all the upper sections are the same color as the lower sections. Hence for the next question, "Does the horizontal reflection preserve colors?" we answer "yes." Finally, we answer "yes" to the last question, "Is there a translation which reverses colors?" since the shortest translation shifts the gray units to the black units, and vice versa, throughout the design. The notation for this pattern is *p'1m1*.

4.19 *p'1m1* Ceramic design, San Ildefonso Pueblo. From Chapman 1970, pl. 97j. Redrawn by A. Pertschuk.

4.20 *p'1a1* Ceramic design, San Ildefonso Pueblo. From Chapman 1970, pl. 140i. Redrawn by A. Pertschuk.

Suppose, however, that we examine a pattern with horizontal reflection that is consistent with color in the sense that all colors are reversed, not preserved. In Figure 4.20 the black units reflect into the gray units and vice versa. This means that the answer to the fourth question is "no," and we have but to see that a shortest translation reverses the colors, both above and below the horizontal axis; black units translate into gray units and vice versa. Thus the classification is *p'1a1*.

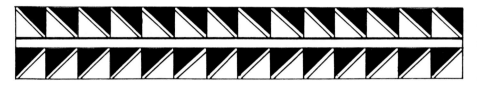

4.21 *p1m'1* Detail, "Birthday for *African Arts* and the United States Bicentennial," by Tita Zungu, South Africa. *African Arts* 10, no. 2 (1977), back cover. Redrawn by A. Pertschuk.

Finally we come to the third case of a color symmetry class not found in Chapman's illustrations of San Ildefonso ceramic repertoire, that of class *p1m'1*. Figure 4.21 is a rendering of a section of a contemporary drawing by a South African artist for the United States Bicentennial. In this example, the horizontal reflection reverses the colors of the units, so the answer to the fourth question is "no." But translation does not reverse the colors, so the answer to the last question is "no," giving the classification *p1m'1*.

For patterns which have no half-turns, vertical reflection, or horizontal reflection, we can go to the fourth question, "Is there a glide reflection consistent with color?" For example, in Figure 4.22 the glide reflection axis passes horizontally through the middle of the band. Because the answer to this question is "yes," and because the pattern in question has no color reversals, the classification is *p1a1*.

4.22 *p1a1* Ceramic design, San Ildefonso Pueblo. From Chapman 1970, pl. 100g.

If, however, we examine the pattern in Figure 4.23 we see that by a glide reflection there are color reversals consistently superimposing the lower black sections upon the upper gray sections and vice versa. Thus, the answer to the final question, "Does the glide reflection reverse colors?" is "yes," since we have just determined that all motions along the glide axis reverse the colors. The notation for the pattern is *p1a'1*.

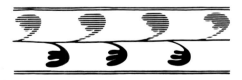

4.23 *p1a'1* Ceramic design, San Ildefonso Pueblo. From Chapman 1970, pl. 99l. Redrawn by A. Pertschuk.

We move now to the far right-hand side of the flow chart to key out the simplest designs, those whose only motions are translations. "No" answers all down the flow chart will key out the one-color pattern, class *p111*, as in Figure 4.24.

If the answer to the question "Is there a translation which reverses colors?" is "yes" because the units alternate color, the notation will be *p'111* (Figure 4.25).

4.24 *p111* Ceramic design, San Ildefonso Pueblo. From Chapman 1970, pl. 108d.

4.25 *p'111* Ceramic design, San Ildefonso Pueblo. From Chapman 1970, pl. 113e. Redrawn by A. Pertschuk.

4.3 Examples of One-Color and Two-Color, One-Dimensional Patterns

In this section we describe actual examples of the one- and two-color classes of one-dimensional patterns. We begin with translation symmetry, although this was not the first symmetry discussed in Section 4.2. Moving from left to right in the flow chart enabled us to show how alternative answers to questions changed the symmetries. However, for the purpose of studying examples of each symmetry class, we feel that it will be easier if we begin with and build on knowledge of the symmetry present in all the other classes—translation.

4.26 Schematic *p111*

p111

This is the most fundamental of all the one-dimensional pattern classes since it admits only the motion of translation—the movement of parts a given distance in a single direction. None of the other motions of mirror or glide reflection or rotation is present.

(Although translation is present in all the other one-dimensional pattern classes, we ordinarily describe these other classes by the other motions which clearly distinguish them. Thus, for example, we may refer to class *p112* as the "twofold rotation class," or to *p1a1* as the "glide reflection class," without explicit mention of the translations which are present, by definition, in all repeated patterns.)

A typical *p111* pattern consists of a number of individual asymmetrical motifs, or units, repeated in one direction. The motif itself, as a finite figure, will not have vertical or horizontal reflections, or half-turns, for if it did then each of these symmetries would also be a symmetry of the entire repeated pattern. The asymmetry of the motif is seen quite clearly in the examples in Figures 4.26–4.32. In Figures 4.33 and 4.34 the asymmetry is more subtle and only apparent on closer scrutiny.

A schematic drawing of a *p111* pattern is shown in Figure 4.26. Each right triangle represents an asymmetrical unit which is moved a given distance into the next right triangle.

A number of good examples of class *p111* are found on San Ildefonso Pueblo ceramics. Figure 4.27 illustrates the minimum number of units (two) necessary for a pattern to be considered one-dimensional. If only one unit is present, then it would be considered finite, but if at least two units are present, arranged along a line axis, then the pattern can be considered one-dimensional.

Actual examples of this class are legion. Animals, plants, or human figures are frequently represented in side view. For example, the decoration on a San Ildefonso ceramic vessel (Figure 4.28) has birds in translation and a carved wood border from Norway (Figure 4.29) has leaves in translation.

A purely geometric example of a simple *p111* pattern is found on a Tlingit basket (Figure 4.30) where each diagonally arranged line of three at-

4.27 Ceramic design, San Ildefonso Pueblo. From Chapman 1970, pl. 108e.

4.28 Ceramic design, San Ildefonso Pueblo. From Chapman 1970, pl. 109a.

4.29 Carved wood border, Norway. From Arneberg 1951, pl. 61, no. 2.

tached triangles moves along the horizontal axis. No other symmetry motion is present along *this* axis, although the rectangular units above and below this row of diagonal triangles are moving by a different symmetry, *pmm2*.

It should be noted that many motifs of *p111* patterns are composed of smaller components which may have other symmetries. For example, although the gray isosceles triangles on the San Ildefonso design in Figure 4.31 have mirror symmetry as separate

4.31 Ceramic design, San Ildefonso Pueblo. From Chapman 1970, pl. 108f. Redrawn by the University of Wisconsin Cartographic Lab.

design elements, their arrangement with the other design elements gives a basic unit which does not permit any other symmetry.

It should also be noted that although this pattern has two colors, it is not a two-color pattern because the two colors are not symmetrically placed within the motif, nor do the colors alternate between motifs; hence no motion interchanges the colors. Careful consideration of each pattern is required. Many complex patterns have only translation symmetry because motif elaborations and added colors have violated the initial layout symmetries. Several examples follow.

A Pueblo III period McElmo black-on-white bowl from the Four Corners area of the American Southwest (Figure 4.32) has a band pattern which is

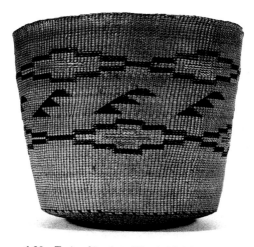

4.30 Twined basket, Tlingit (California Academy of Sciences, San Francisco, no. 145-37). Photo by C. Thomas.

4.32 McElmo black-on-white bowl, Anasazi tradition (Colorado State Historical Society, Denver, no. 0125). Photo by D. Crowe.

basically demarcated by a zigzag so that all the upper and lower triangles formed by the zigzag are the same shape. However, the zigzag layout is elaborated so that the upper triangles have a hooked unit and the lower triangles have slanted lines parallel to one side of the triangle. Each of these elaborated triangles moves by translation. The whole pattern is reduced from the *pma2* symmetry of the zigzag structure to the *p111* symmetry of the final fully elaborated pattern.

4.33   Carved wood border, Gudbrandsdal, Norway. From Arneberg 1951, pl. 25, no. 4.

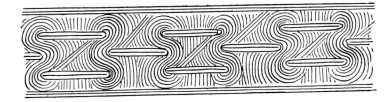

4.34   Incised ceramic design, Mississippian tradition, American Southeast. From Naylor 1975, 29.

Another border pattern from Norway (Figure 4.33) appears to have a horizontal reflection axis (*p1m1*) through the hearts but closer inspection reveals that this is canceled by the intertwining of the rope-like braid which surrounds the hearts. Because some braids go over others, perfect horizontal reflection cannot occur and the only symmetries of the pattern are translations. (In our analysis of this pattern we are ignoring the left end

with its reversed heart and braid. If we were to take this into account here, there would no longer be any translations, and the whole figure would be finite, with no symmetries at all.)

A more difficult pattern to classify is incised on Mississippian tradition ceramics from the southeastern United States (Figure 4.34). In this pattern individual units with a diagonal line between the two horizontal lines move by half-turns. However, because the intervening area between these units has a diagonal above but not below the central horizontal line, half-turns of the entire design cannot occur. Again, only translation can move the final pattern.

Finally, what appears to be a very symmetrical pattern on a bronze vessel from the Late Shang dynasty, China (Figure 4.35) can only be moved by translation. The vertical hooked units appear at first to contain left and right hooks which are related by glide reflection (along a vertical axis). But closer examination reveals that the hooks are attached to the lower border of the strip, but not to the upper border in the same way. Hence, it is indeed only a one-dimensional pattern and the only symmetries are the translations which move one vertical set of hooks horizontally into the next set of hooks.

4.35   Bronze P'ou, Late Shang, China (Avery Brundage Collection, Asian Art Museum of San Francisco, no. B60 B47)

4.36   Schematic *p'111*

p'111

The only two-color version of class *p111* is *p'111*, where the successive units alternate colors (Figures 4.36). This involves a translation which moves the unit parts into succeeding parts having the same shape but different color.

A very simple San Ildefonso pottery pattern (Figure 4.37) and a Hopi basket with deer (?) in alternating black and brown (Figure 4.38) illustrate this color class.

Of course, the pattern on the Hopi basket is placed betwen two bands of isosceles triangles, each belonging to class *p'm11*. This is a good example (similar to Figure 4.30) of three bands which, although they appear together on the basket, are considered separately for classification purposes. (There are cases, however, in which the artist composes a pattern consisting of two bands which are intended to be considered as a single band. An example is Figure 4.106, below, in the section describing class *p'mm2*.)

In another example, small birds alternate colors on the border of a

Chancay-style Peruvian textile (Figure 4.39). Yet another Peruvian example of this color class is found on the upper and lower pattern bands of a vessel from the Nazca Valley (Figure 4.88, below). This case is slightly more complicated because there appear to be three colors in the band—black, gray, and white. However, close inspection reveals that the design alternation sequence is actually black-gray-white-gray-black-gray-white-gray and so forth. Thus, gray appears twice as often as either white or black and so cannot exchange with either of them and must be considered a background color. The colors which do alternate are black and white and they alternate in perfect *p'111* symmetry. This is a very frequently occurring color situation which appears, at first glance, to have a higher color symmetry (i.e., more colors alternating regularly) than it really has.

4.37   Ceramic design, San Ildefonso Pueblo. From Chapman 1970, pl. 111o. Redrawn by A. Pertschuk.

4.38   Coiled basket, Hopi (California Academy of Sciences, San Francisco, no. 370-872). Photo by C. Thomas.

4.39   Fragment, mantle border, Peru, Central Coast, Chancay, Late Intermediate (A.D. 900–1476). Courtesy of the Ross Collection, Museum of Fine Arts, Boston (no. 10.263).

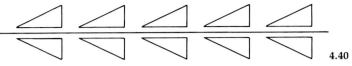

4.40 Schematic *p1m1*

p1m1

The characteristic motion of class *p1m1* is horizontal mirror reflection across a central axis. In the schematic drawing of Figure 4.40 this reflection axis is shown as a solid line.

Figure 4.41 shows several designs from San Ildefonso ceramics, the first three of which have *p1m1* symmetry. The succession of patterns in Figure 4.41 is an important demonstration of how different arrangements of the same motif alter the pattern structure and hence its symmetry class.

Figure 4.41a shows a very simple *p1m1* pattern. The basic design field is undivided, and the units are simply placed regularly within that field. Figure 4.41b, however, differs markedly. Now it appears that the design field has been subdivided into rectangular panels, by themselves of class *pmm2*, which are then elaborated into class *p1m1* by coloring two of the four corners black. Figure 4.41c is the same except that the horizontal line through the center of the panels reminds the reader of the presence of the horizontal reflection axis. In Figure 4.41d two rows of what appeared in b and c are aligned, creating a two-dimensional pattern, class *pm*, a two-dimensional version of *p1m1* with multiple axes of horizontal reflection symmetry. If, however, two rows of panels alternate direction, as in Figure 4.41e, the pattern no longer has translations in a second direction and is a one dimensional *p112* pattern.

Complex patterns sometimes require careful scrutiny. In Figure 4.42a we see a complex San Ildefonso pattern and close examination reveals that all parts reflect with perfect *p1m1*

4.41a Ceramic design, San Ildefonso Pueblo. From Chapman 1970, pl. 4n.

4.41b Ceramic design, San Ildefonso Pueblo. From Chapman 1970, pl. 4o.

4.41c Ceramic design, San Ildefonso Pueblo. From Chapman 1970, pl. 4p.

4.41d Ceramic design, San Ildefonso Pueblo. From Chapman 1970, pl. 4q.

4.41e Ceramic design, San Ildefonso Pueblo. From Chapman 1970, pl. 4r.

4.42a Ceramic design, San Ildefonso Pueblo. From Chapman 1970, pl. 96n.

4.42b Ceramic design, San Ildefonso Pueblo. From Chapman 1970, pl. 97m.

4.43 Painted wood rafter, Maori. From Hamilton 1896, no. 28.

symmetry. However, Figure 4.42b shows another San Ildefonso pattern which differs in the elaboration of some upper elements so that it can only have *p111* symmetry.

Other examples of *p1m1* patterns are found on a Maori rafter (Figure 4.43) and the upper carved band on a wooden vessel from Zaire (Figure 4.44).

4.44 Wood container, Zaire (California Academy of Sciences, San Francisco, no. 389-1439). Photo by C. Thomas.

On a storage jar from Zia Pueblo (Figure 4.45) the upper and lower bands have *p1m1* symmetry. In these bands the pattern was first structured by dividing the space between the upper and lower banding lines into rectangular panels. The symmetry of this simple panel layout is *pmm2,* because each panel can be subdivided by horizontal and vertical mirror reflection lines. However, when motifs were placed in each panel, the vertical symmetry of the panels was canceled since the motifs themselves have only horizontal mirror reflection.

The central band of design on this Zia jar, although narrower than the upper and lower bands, is generated by horizontal mirror reflection, but because there are the required minimum two rows of triangles, it should be classified as a two-dimensional pattern, class *pm*. (Cf. Figure 4.41d, above.)

Finally, it should be noted that the curvature of the vessel wall on the Zia jar causes distortion in the shape of the panels and the patterns in the panels. Technically, this distortion cancels the *pmm2* symmetry of the square panel, because in the upper band the lower part of the panel is broadened in the flare of the jar shoulder, and in the lower band the lower part of the panel is narrowed as the jar diminishes in size toward the base. However, if we considered all these particular form restrictions they would mask the underlying importance of the geometric motions used to arrange the design parts. For this reason, we shall proceed as if all patterns are intended to be seen in a flat plane.

4.45 Ceramic jar, Zia Pueblo (California Academy of Sciences, San Francisco, no. 370-106). Photo by C. Thomas.

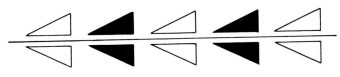

4.46   Schematic *p'1m1*

4.47   Ceramic design, San Ildefonso Pueblo. From Chapman 1970, pl. 129q. Redrawn by A. Pertschuk.

4.48   Section, man's blanket, Chichicastenango, Guatemala (Lowie Museum of Anthropology, University of California, Berkeley, no. 3-121)

p'1m1

In this coloring of *p1m1*, reflections across the horizontal mirror axis preserve colors but some translations (the shortest ones) reverse the colors (Figure 4.46).

A San Ildefonso pattern (Figure 4.47) illustrates this color reversal (if the tips of the units are ignored), as does the center band pattern on a Guatemalan textile (Figure 4.48). Note in Figure 4.48 that the colors are reversed only on the arrows. A series of triangles on a schematic drawing of a beaded Sioux moccasin (Figure 4.49) also has *p'1m1* color reversals. Although to the wearer the pattern appears to be oriented vertically, the symmetry classification is determined by the movement of the units along the long axis.

4.49   Detail, beaded moccasin, Sioux. (California Academy of Sciences, San Francisco, no. 539-13a). Redrawn by A. Pertschuk.

4.50   Schematic *p1m'1*

p1m'1

A second coloring of *p1m1* is *p1m'1* (Figure 4.50), where the color reversals occur across the horizontal mirror axis and not along the axis of translation as in the *p'1m1*.

An example of this color class is on the center band of a Navajo blanket (Figure 4.51). The background red color serves as the center horizontal axis for the band. Additionally, the top

and bottom bands are of class *p1m'1*, but unfortunately their color reversals are not clear on this photograph.

A more complex example is on a basket from East Africa (Figure 4.52), where the two horizontal banded design fields have been subdivided into rectangular panels. Thus, both the pattern, which mimics Figure 4.50, and the "background," that is, the remaining space between the banding lines, alternate color according to *p1m'1*.

4.52   Basket, East Africa (Musée Royal de l'Afrique Centrale, Tervuren, Belgium, no. 80383)

4.51   Blanket, Navajo. Courtesy of the Museum of New Mexico (no. 44487/12). Photo by A. Taylor.

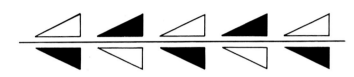

4.53   Schematic *p'1a1*

p'1a1

A third coloring of *p1m1* is illustrated in Figure 4.53. Here the colors reverse both across the horizontal mirror axis and by translations.

Simple examples are a San Ildefonso ceramic design (Figure 4.54) and the lower left and upper right sections of a tapa strip from Fiji (Figure 4.55). A *p'1a1* band is also present on a beaded Plains Indian sleeve (shown schematically in Figure 4.56). Note that

in this last case we consider the body and head of the bird background; it is the alternation of the wing colors that makes the color class *p'1a1*. Note also that this is another example where the particular orientation of the horizontal axis is up and down, not left and right. Whatever the position of the axis, it is the position of the units relative to the axis that determines the symmetry classification.

4.54   Ceramic design, San Ildefonso Pueblo. From Chapman 1970, pl. 140i. Redrawn by A. Pertschuk.

4.55   Section, tapa, Fiji (Pitt Rivers Museum, University of Oxford, no. V118)

4.56   Detail, beaded sleeve, Plains (Rochester Museum and Science Center, no. AE9250). Redrawn by A. Pertschuk.

4.57   Schematic *pm11*

pm11

In contrast to class *p1m1,* where the mirror reflection occurs across the central horizontal axis of the band, in class *pm11* the mirror reflections occur across (vertical) axes perpendicular to this central axis of the band. Note that the position of the *m* in the nomenclature indicates whether the reflection occurs across horizontal or vertical mirror lines. That is, the *m* in the second position (*pm11*) indicates vertical reflection, while the *m* in the third position (*p1m1*) indicates horizontal reflection. Figure 4.57 shows a schematic pattern where the mirror reflection occurs across all the vertical lines between the triangles.

Four San Ildefonso ceramic patterns with *pm11* symmetry of their underlying structure are illustrated in Figure 4.58 to show the effect of various modifications. Figure 4.58a is a simple series of pendant triangles with *pm11* symmetry. Figure 4.58b is similar, with the triangles reversed 180°. Additionally, in this design, since both the upper and lower banding lines are demarcated, the white background as well as the black design has *pm11* symmetry. Thus, users should not be concerned whether they are classifying the positive or negative aspects of the pattern, since they will have the same symmetry.

A slightly tricky pattern is found in Figure 4.58c, where the pendant triangles alternate in color as well as motif elaboration. However, even though they alternate in color, it is not a two-color design because the motifs are somewhat different in the alternating triangles. Thus, the black triangles cannot superimpose in shape on the white triangles, but only on other black triangles. Hence, vertical lines between two triangles are no longer reflection axes, but vertical lines through the apexes of the triangles are still reflection lines of the elaborated pattern. The elaborated pattern remains class *pm11*.

In contrast, the San Ildefonso pattern in Figure 4.58d has no color alternation and the motif elaboration reduces the *pm11* symmetry of the pendant isosceles triangles to *p111* symmetry for the final pattern.

Other *pm11* examples are found on an Iroquois beaded moccasin where elements with *pm11* symmetry are

4.58a   Ceramic design, San Ildefonso Pueblo. From Chapman 1970, pl. 109h.

4.58b   Ceramic design, San Ildefonso Pueblo. From Chapman 1970, pl. 3j.

4.58c   Ceramic design, San Ildefonso Pueblo. From Chapman 1970, pl. 109m. Redrawn by the University of Wisconsin Cartographic Lab.

4.58d   Ceramic design, San Ildefonso Pueblo. From Chapman 1970, pl. 109n.

4.59 Beaded moccasin, Iroquois (Rochester Museum and Science Center, no. 70.89.52). Photo by D. Washburn.

sewn around the decorated flap as well as on the top (Figure 4.59), and on enameled bricks from the palace of Darius I at Susa (Figure 4.60).

On a Santo Domingo Pueblo vessel (Figure 4.61) motifs with *pm11* symmetry appear on the upper band around the neck. Interestingly, the same motifs, arranged differently, produce the band around the jar body, which has *pma2* symmetry. This is a classic example of the advantage of structure analysis over design element analysis for many types of investigations. Structure analysis distinguishes between different *arrangements* of the same elements, which element analysis cannot detect.

It should be noted that the uneven rendering of the design on the Santo Domingo jar yields elements that are not exactly identical in size and shape. This kind of variation may be important for studies of individual artisans, but is not relevant for classification of the basic motions which structure the design and thus should not affect the symmetry classification.

A more complex *pm11* pattern is found on a man's shoulder or waist cloth from Sumba (Figure 4.62). Here stags, cockatoos, and cocks face each other in *pm11* symmetry. Recall that if the animals were simply lined up, all facing one direction, as on the Hopi basket (Figure 4.38), they would have only *p111* symmetry. But in the head-to-head arrangement, each linear row has *pm11* symmetry, with vertical reflections both between their heads and between their tails.

4.61 Black-on-cream jar, Santo Domingo Pueblo (California Academy of Sciences, San Francisco, no. 370-116). Photo by C. Thomas.

4.60 Enameled brick pattern, Palace of Darius at Susa, sixth century B.C. From Dowlatshahi 1979, 61.

4.62   Man's shoulder or waist cloth, Sumba. From Fischer 1979, pl. 27, Lawrence Moss Collection. Photo by G. Prince.

4.63 Schematic *p'm11*

p'm11

In class *p'm11* the color reversals occur across alternate vertical mirror axes (Figure 4.63). Depending on the visual juxtaposition of the motifs, the mirror axes may seem to be between motifs, as in Figure 4.64, or may alternately bisect and lie between motifs, as in Figure 4.65.

Such a color change can also be seen on a fragment of a Peruvian strap (Figure 4.66). In this case, the band has been divided into panels with *pmm2* symmetry and then filled with motifs to yield *pm11* symmetry. Even though these rectangular panels alternate colors and would if undecorated have *p'mm2* symmetry, the symmetry assignment for the pattern as a whole can only be the two-color class of *p'm11* because the motifs in the panels reduce the symmetry.

4.64 Ceramic design, San Ildefonso Pueblo. From Chapman 1970, pl. 131f. Redrawn by the University of Wisconsin Cartographic Lab.

4.65 Ceramic design, San Ildefonso Pueblo. From Chapman 1970, pl. 109j. Redrawn by the University of Wisconsin Cartographic Lab.

4.66 Carrying strap fragment, pre-Columbian Peru (California Academy of Sciences, San Fransico, no. 389-2479). Photo by C. Thomas.

4.67   Schematic *pm'11*

pm'11

The second two-color class of *pm11* is *pm'11*, where the color reversals occur across all vertical mirror axes (Figure 4.67).

A San Ildefonso ceramic design (Figure 4.68) shows this alternation, as do the birds on a band on a Cree side pocket (Figure 4.69), and a Pueblo kilt pattern (Figure 4.70). However, on another kilt pattern (Figure 4.71), the small white hooks inserted in the center of the stepped triangles reduce the whole pattern symmetry to *p111*. In this example, even though the coloring of the stepped triangles is class *pm'11*, the presence of the hook permits only translation.

4.68   Ceramic design, San Ildefonso Pueblo. From Chapman 1970, pl. 109i. Redrawn by the University of Wisconsin Cartographic Lab.

4.69   Detail, Cree side pocket (Lewis Henry Morgan Collection, Rochester Museum and Science Center, no. 70.89.15). Photo by D. Washburn.

4.70   Embroidered kilt design, Awatovi kiva mural. From Tanner 1976, fig. 3.30b.

4.71   Embroidered kilt design, Awatovi kiva mural. From Tanner 1976, fig. 3.30d.

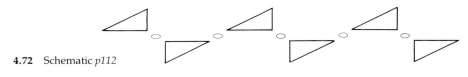

4.72 Schematic *p112*

p112

Class *p112* admits only translations and twofold rotations (half-turns). The rotation centers are marked by small ovals in our schematic drawings, as in Figure 4.72. We illustrate a number of examples to familiarize the user with this symmetry.

A number of San Ildefonso patterns illustrate how this motion class can be generated from common design elements. Figure 4.73 shows a twofold motif repeated twice, the minimum number of transformations necessary for a one-dimensional pattern. However, note that the centers are filled with a two-dimensional pattern that will not admit twofold rotation, so a classification of the symmetry of the entire pattern must be *p111*. Figure 4.74 shows the band design field subdivided into parallelograms which by themselves have *p112* symmetry. The added motifs retain this *p112* symmetry.

Finally, a parallelogram paneled pattern from San Ildefonso in Figure 4.75 appears to be two-color, but careful inspection reveals that any twofold motion, either inside the panels or from one panel to the next, leads to color superposition, not color reversal.

Interlocking hooks, frets, and spirals are elements that lend themselves to arrangement by twofold rotation. Such examples are found on several bands of a bottle from the Ica Valley (Figure 4.76), a Mesa Verde black-on-white bowl from the American Southwest (Figure 4.77), and a Mexican pre-Columbian cylindrical stamp (Figure 4.78). Note that in all three of these patterns the negative

4.73 Ceramic design, San Ildefonso Pueblo. From Chapman 1970, pl. 99g.

4.74 Ceramic design, San Ildefonso Pueblo. From Chapman 1970, pl. 138i.

4.75 Ceramic design, San Ildefonso Pueblo. From Chapman 1970, pl. 138c. Redrawn by the University of Wisconsin Cartographic Lab.

4.76 Ceramic jar, Ica 4, Peru (Lowie Museum of Anthropology, University of California, Berkeley, no. 4-4828)

4.77 Mesa Verde black-on-white bowl, Pueblo III, Anasazi tradition (Colorado State Historical Society, Denver, no. 0314). Photo by D. Crowe.

4.78   Cylindrical clay stamp, Mexico. From Enciso 1953, 21.

4.79   Wood cup, Kuba, Zaire. Courtesy of the Trustees of the British Museum.

4.80   Black-on-red bowl, Maricopa, by Mary Juan (California Academy of Sciences, San Francisco, no. 370-284). Photo by C. Thomas.

and positive (the background and the design) have the same symmetry structure.

Two other spiral examples appear incised in a wooden drinking cup from the Kuba, Zaire (Figure 4.79), and painted on a twentieth-century bowl from the Maricopa Indians, Arizona (Figure 4.80).

P112 patterns can be found in paneled *pmm2* layouts. For example, a section of a Maori rafter (Figure 4.81) shows how diagonal division of a rectangular panel produces a pattern having only rotational symmetry.

We also discuss here several common *p112* pattern situations whose classifications may be puzzling. The

4.81   Painted wood rafter, Maori. From Hamilton 1896, no. 6.

first is the center pattern on a carved wood box from Norway (Figure 4.82). Although at first it appears to have both horizontal and vertical reflection axes, the overlapping of the lines does not admit either of these symmetries. In fact, the only motions which this pattern admits, in addition to translation, are half-turns. (It may help to actually rotate this picture 180° to see that the overlaps are in the same position.)

The second is a pattern on a prehistoric Pueblo burden basket (Figure 4.83) which appears to be two-dimensional and two-color. Actually, it is only a one-dimensional, one-color *p112* pattern. The key is to consider the symmetry of the major band units—the black hooks which clearly have *p112* symmetry. The two rows of checked hooks pendant from the banding lines which interlock with the black units, taken together, also have *p112* symmetry. There are no color reversals because the checked hooks always superimpose only upon other checked hooks, and the black hooks always superimpose only upon the black hooks, even though they appear to be interlocking with units of alternate colors.

A final potentially puzzling pattern (Figure 4.84) admits only twofold rotation, even though the separate units have sixfold rotational symmetry. Any rotations other than 180° would move the band design off the single line axis. (Sixfold rotations are admissible in two-dimensional patterns, but not in band patterns.)

4.82   Carved wood box, Setesdal. Norway. From Arneberg 1951, pl. 31, no. 3.

4.83   Burden basket design, Pueblo III, Anasazi tradition. From Tanner 1976, fig. 2.31.

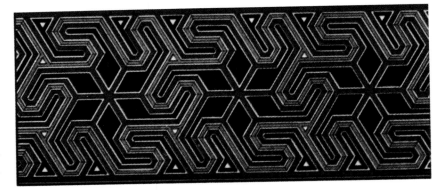

4.84   Carved wood, Arabic. From Prisse d'Avennes 1978, 5.

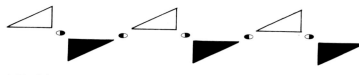

4.85   Schematic *p112'*

p112'

Class *p112'* has color reversals around all twofold centers. We mark such color reversing centers by black-white ovals in schematic drawings, as in Figure 4.85.

It is easily seen on the central motifs in a San Ildefonso pattern (Figure 4.86) where both the gray and black units inside the parallelogram panels, as well as the units in the adjacent panels, alternate colors. A band of interlocking spirals on a tile pavement from Antioch (Figure 4.134, below) also has *p112'* color reversal. Two pre-Columbian Peruvian examples, one a fragment of cloth (Figure 4.87) and the other the center band on a vessel from Nazca (Figure 4.88) have series of interlocking stepped units in color reversal. (The upper and lower bands of the Nazca vessel have color symmetry *p'111*, not *p112'*. In rotations about the twofold centers of the underlying pattern the black and white together superimpose upon the gray background areas, but black or white alone does not, and there is no half-turn which interchanges black and white; therefore there is no color reversal around the rotation centers.)

Figure 4.89 shows a Maori rafter pattern structured and colored by *pma'2'*. However, careful inspection reveals that the small single hooks in the pattern do not allow mirror reflection. Thus, only half-turns are admitted by the complete pattern and, with color reversals, it is again *p112'*.

4.86   Ceramic design, San Ildefonso Pueblo. From Chapman 1970, pl. 138j. Redrawn by the University of Wisconsin Cartographic Lab.

4.87   Fragment, textile border, pre-Columbian Peru (California Academy of Sciences, San Francisco, no. 389-2513). Photo by C. Thomas.

4.88   Ceramic vessel, Nazca, Peru. Permission of The Fine Arts Museums of San Francisco (no. 70.25.49). Photo by C. Thomas.

4.89   Painted wood rafter, Maori. From Hamilton 1896, no. 12.

4.90   Schematic *p'112*

p'112

The second color class for *p112* is *p'112*, shown schematically in Figure 4.90. Color reversals occur here on alternate twofold centers.

Class *p'112* can be easily seen on a San Ildefonso pottery design (Figure 4.91) where the color reversal occurs only between the parallelogram-shaped units, not within them. This popular color class can also be seen on the glazed wall tiles of the palace of King Assurnasirpal at Nimrud (Figure 4.92), and on a Chilean pottery design (Figure 4.93).

Three Maori rafter patterns illustrate how different underlying structures can have the same color symmetry because of differences in coloring and added design elements. Figure 4.94a shows how a rectangular paneled *pmm2* pattern becomes a *p'112* pattern when the interlocking spirals in the panels are colored. Figure 4.94b shows a *pma2* pattern which, when colored, can no longer admit vertical reflection. The whole pattern can only be a colored class of *p112*. Figure 4.94c shows a pattern where both the paneled structure and the basic four-part design layout in the panels have *pmm2* symmetry. However, careful inspection reveals that the small single curved hooks on the sides of the panels do not admit reflection. A half-turn interchanges these hooks and since this rotation also reverses the gray and black sections of the design, this pattern is class *p'112*.

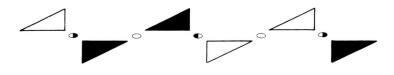

4.91   Ceramic design, San Ildefonso Pueblo. From Chapman 1970, fig. 97k. Redrawn by the University of Wisconsin Cartographic Lab.

4.92   Glazed wall tile, Palace of Assurnasirpal at Nimrud. From Speltz 1915, pl. 10. Redrawn by C. Sudekum.

4.93   Ceramic design, Chile. From Gutierrez n.d., no. 112.

4.94a   Painted wood rafter, Maori. From Hamilton 1896, no. 19.

4.94b   Painted wood rafter, Maori. From Hamilton 1896, no. 13.

4.94c   Painted wood rafter, Maori. From Hamilton 1896, no. 22.

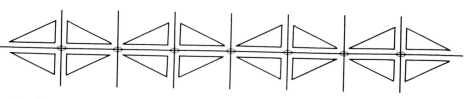

4.95   Schematic *pmm2*

pmm2

In this class there is a central mirror axis running the length of the band, as well as the vertical mirror axes perpendicular to this axis. There are half-turns about all points of intersection of these mirror axes. All these are marked in the schematic drawing in Figure 4.95. We have seen that this is the structure of rectangular band panels and, as such, it is frequently the underlying symmetry of a design whose symmetry is subsequently reduced by elaboration of the motifs.

Figure 4.96 shows a series of San Ildefonso ceramic designs of class *pmm2*. Figures 4.96a and b show designs for which both the underlying structure and the whole design are of class *pmm2*. Figure 4.96c, however, has *pmm2* structure in the diamond units; this is reduced to *pm11* by the added elements which do not admit horizontal reflection. The design in Figure 4.96d is a *pmm2* paneled band which has been reduced to *p112* symmetry by the diagonals added to the panels. Figure 4.96e is a similar *p112* pattern except that the units in alternate panels reverse colors. However, it is not the colored class *p'112* because, although the adjacent panels change colors, the alternating units also alternate positions, so that superposition occurs only on units of the same color and shape. In effect, the motif of this design consists of two adjoining panels, not one.

Figure 4.97 shows class *pmm2* on a northwest California coast basket.

4.96a   Ceramic design, San Ildefonso Pueblo. From Chapman 1970, pl. 99b.

4.96b   Ceramic design, San Ildefonso Pueblo. From Chapman 1970, pl. 96c.

4.96c   Ceramic design, San Ildefonso Pueblo. From Chapman 1970, pl. 96f. Redrawn by the University of Wisconsin Cartographic Lab.

4.96d   Ceramic design, San Ildefonso Pueblo. From Chapman 1970, pl. 132k.

4.96e   Ceramic design, San Ildefonso Pueblo. From Chapman 1970, pl. 132j.

4.97   Twined basket, Northwest coast, California (California Academy of Sciences, San Francisco, no. 370-759). Photo by C. Thomas.

4.98 Section, calumet pipe stem, Sioux (Lewis Henry Morgan Collection, Rochester Museum and Science Center, no. 70.89.97). Photo by D. Washburn.

Figure 4.98 shows this class on a calumet pipe stem. Figure 4.30 (above) shows this *pmm2* symmetry on the upper and lower bands of a Tlingit basket. Sometimes the motifs are alternated but they still retain the *pmm2* structure, as on a Maori rafter (Figure 4.99) or a pre-Columbian strap from Peru (Figure 4.100).

The tumpline strap from the village of Macusani, Peru (Figure 4.101), is a good example of a situation where the weaving technique has raised the warps and wefts differently. Thus, although the green and white colors are reversed on the two sides, the symmetry on both sides is identical, class *pmm2*.

4.99 Painted wood rafter, Maori. From Hamilton 1896, no. 10.

4.100 Carrying strap fragment, pre-Columbian Peru (California Academy of Sciences, San Francisco, no. 389-2441). Photo by C. Thomas.

4.101 Section, belt by Herminia Ramos, Macusani, Peru (California Academy of Sciences, San Francisco, no. 514-153). Photo by C. Thomas.

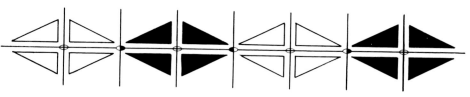

4.102 Schematic *p′mm2*

p′mm2

In this coloring of *pmm2* reflection across the central axis of the band preserves colors and reflection across alternate axes perpendicular to it reverses colors (Figure 4.102). Half-turns about the points of intersection of these (color-reversing) axes with the central axis reverse colors.

San Ildefonso patterns show both arrangements of this color alternation. In Figure 4.103 the colors reverse across axes between the motifs, whereas in Figure 4.104 the colors reverse across axes which bisect the motifs.

A Maori rafter pattern (Figure 4.105) shows nested ovals which change color according to class *p′mm2* symmetry. But the coloring of the small triangles along the borders, between the ovals, is not consistent with the *p′mm2* symmetry of the ovals. The triangles reverse colors by translation and thus reduce the whole pattern to class *p′112* symmetry.

On a Cheyenne pouch (Figure 4.106) only the two inner rows of triangles on either side of the crosses change colors. Figure 4.107 is the other side of the calumet pipe stem shown in Figure 4.98 (above). On this side both the motif and the panel background change colors.

4.103 Ceramic design, San Ildefonso Pueblo. From Chapman 1970, pl. 132p. Redrawn by the University of Wisconsin Cartographic Lab.

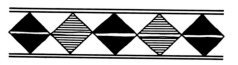

4.104 Ceramic design, San Ildefonso Pueblo. From Chapman 1970, pl. 96d. Redrawn by the University of Wisconsin Cartographic Lab.

4.106 Detail, beaded pouch, Cheyenne. (California Academy of Sciences, San Francisco, no. 376-7). Photo by C. Thomas.

4.105 Painted wood rafter, Maori. From Hamilton 1896, no. 11.

4.107 Reverse side of Figure 4.98

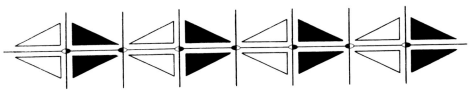

4.108   Schematic *pm'm2'*

pm'm2'

The two-color class *pm'm2'* has color
reversals across every mirror axis perpendicular to the central mirror axis,
but not across that central axis. Every
half-turn reverses colors (Figure 4.108).

We can see clear examples in a San
Ildefonso ceramic design (ignoring the
spheres along the bottom of the pattern) (Figure 4.109) and on the wide
band along the border of a plaited mat
from the Marshall Islands (Figure
4.110).

4.109   Ceramic design, San Ildefonso
Pueblo. From Chapman 1970, pl. 95b.
Redrawn by the University of Wisconsin
Cartographic Lab.

4.110   Plaited mat, Majuro, Marshall
Islands. Courtesy of the Trustees of the
British Museum (no. 1938-10-1.60).

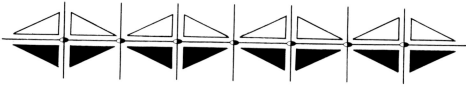

4.111   Schematic *pmm'2'*

pmm'2'

In class *pmm'2'* the color reversals occur across the central mirror axis, but not across any of the mirror axes perpendicular to it. Every half-turn reverses colors (Figure 4.111).

This is easily seen on the San Ildefonso ceramic design in Figure 4.112 and on a contemporary Peruvian carrying cloth from Cuzco (Figure 4.113).

4.112   Ceramic design, San Ildefonso Pueblo. From Chapman 1970, pl. 132q. Redrawn by A. Pertschuk.

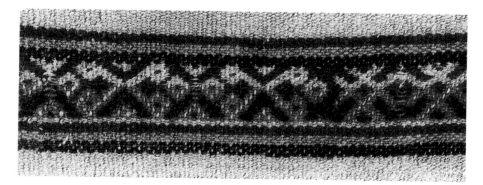

4.113   Detail, carrying cloth, Cuzco, Peru (California Academy of Sciences, San Francisco, no. 280-51). Photo by C. Thomas.

4.114   Schematic *p'ma2*

p'ma2

When the colors reverse across the central axis as well as on alternate axes perpendicular to it, the color class is *p'ma2* (Figure 4.114). Half-turns around alternate rotation centers (axis intersection points) also reverse colors.

A simple example of this class can be easily seen on a San Ildefonso pattern in Figure 4.115. The center band of a Germantown Navajo blanket

4.115   Ceramic design, San Ildefonso Pueblo. From Chapman 1970, pl. 95o. Redrawn by A. Pertschuk.

(Figure 4.116) is another interesting case. Although obviously woven with great care, the color reversals are not quite perfect for any one symmetry class. Another Navajo blanket pattern (Figure 4.117) clearly shows this alternation in colors if we consider only the upper and lower rows of triangles. The symmetry of the entire pattern is not, however, *p'ma2* because the black zigzag overlaps a white zigzag in the center and reduces the whole design to *p'112* symmetry.

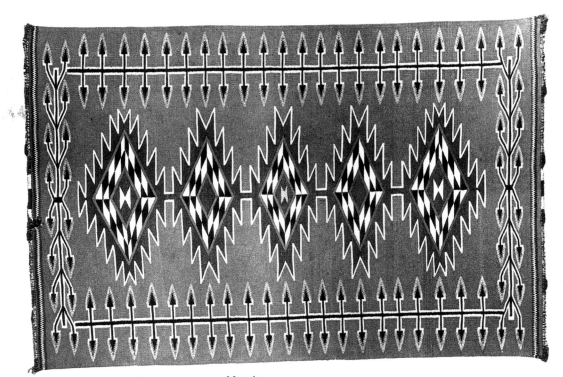

4.116   Germantown rug, Navajo (California Academy of Sciences, San Francisco, no. 370-654). Photo by C. Thomas.

4.117   Redrawn section of Navajo blanket. From Sides 1961, pl. 47e.

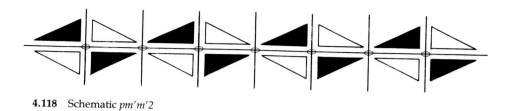

4.118   Schematic *pm'm'2*

pm'm'2

If color reversals occur across all mirror reflection lines, then the color class is *pm'm'2* (Figure 4.118). No half-turns reverse colors.

An example is found on the two bands on either side of the central band on a Kuba raffia cloth (Figure 4.119).

4.119   Raffia cloth, Kuba, Zaire (Musée Royal de l'Afrique Centrale, Tervuren, Belgium, no. 50.24.172)

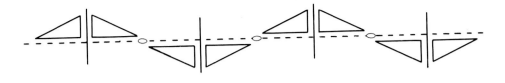

4.120   Schematic *pma2*

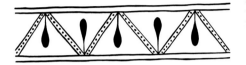

4.121   Ceramic design, San Ildefonso Pueblo. From Chapman 1970, pl. 3d.

pma2

In this symmetry class there is a glide reflection axis, but not a mirror axis running the length of the pattern. There are mirror reflections in lines perpendicular to the glide axis, and half-turns about points halfway between the mirror axes (Figure 4.120). In this drawing, and hereafter, a dashed line represents the glide axis.

This is a very frequently occurring pattern class. Perhaps its simplest and most common motif is the zigzag, such as is seen elaborated on a San Ildefonso ceramic design in Figure 4.121. Other common designs with this structure are found on the main band of a dress hat from Northwestern California (Figure 4.122), on the main body band of a Santo Domingo Pueblo jar (Figure 4.61), on an ivory inlaid silverware case from Japan (Figure 4.123), and on an Arabic border design (Figure 4.124).

There are numerous ways to reduce the *pma2* symmetry by elaborations. Two San Ildefonso Pueblo ceramic designs show how added elements can cause symmetry reduction to *p111* (Figure 4.125) and *pm11* (Figure 4.126).

Certain colorings of the *pma2* structure may reduce the symmetry to that of another structure class. For example, the Ojibwa beaded sash in Figure 4.127 has as its main design element a zigzag (*pma2*) which has been colored on alternate "legs" so that the striped portion moves into the plain portion with color reversals only by glide reflection, but there are no longer any mirror reflections. The resulting class is *p1a'1*.

4.122   Twined hat, Northwest coast, California (California Academy of Sciences, San Francisco, no. 48-14). Photo by C. Thomas.

4.123   Traveling chopstick case, Japan (California Academy of Sciences, San Francisco, no. 389-2000). Photo by C. Thomas.

4.124   Wall mosaic, Arabic. From Prisse d'Avennes 1978, 3.

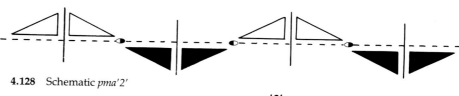

4.128   Schematic *pma'2'*

pma'2'

In this coloring of *pma2* (Figure 4.128) the glide reflections reverse colors and half-turns reverse colors, but colors are preserved across all mirror axes.

A San Ildefonso ceramic design (Figure 4.129) is a simple example, as are two patterns from Peru: a fragment of a pre-Columbia Ica Valley pottery design (Figure 4.130), and the middle band on a contemporary coca bag from Macusani (Figure 4.131). A

4.125   Ceramic design, San Ildefonso Pueblo. From Chapman 1970, pl. 131k.

4.129   Ceramic design, San Ildefonso Pueblo. From Chapman 1970, pl. 131o. Redrawn by the University of Wisconsin Cartographic Lab.

4.126   Ceramic design, San Ildefonso Pueblo. From Chapman 1970, pl. 131q.

4.130   Ceramic design, Ica 6, Ica Valley, Peru. From Menzel 1976, pl. 26, no. 311.

4.127   Beaded sash, Ojibwa. From Lyford 1953, pl. 75. Redrawn by A. Pertschuk.

4.131   Coca bag, Macusani, Peru (California Academy of Sciences, San Francisco, no. 514-142). Photo by C. Thomas.

Maori rafter pattern (Figure 4.132), an Islamic border pattern (Figure 4.133), and the inside border of a tile pavement from the House of the Drunken Dionysus at Antioch (Figure 4.134) are other easily identified examples.

4.132 Painted wood rafter, Maori. From Hamilton 1896, no. 14.

4.133 Border design, Islamic. From Gombrich 1979, fig. 103.

4.134 Tile pavement, House of the Drunken Dionysus, Antioch. From Levi 1947, pl. 7b.

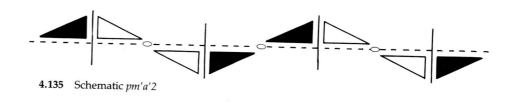

4.135   Schematic *pm'a'2*

pm'a'2

Color class *pm'a'2* (Figure 4.135) has color reversals across mirror axes and along the glide axes, but no color reversals around the rotation centers.

The San Ildefonso ceramic design (Figure 4.136) is a clear example, as is a Maori house rafter pattern (Figure 4.137). In the latter example the design field has first been subdivided into rectangular panels. In each panel there is no color reversal around the rotation center, but there is color reversal across the vertical reflection line which also serves as the panel divider.

4.136   Ceramic design, San Ildefonso Pueblo. From Chapman 1970, pl. 131e. Redrawn by A. Pertschuk.

4.137   Painted wood rafter, Maori. From Hamilton 1896, no. 25.

4.138   Schematic *pm'a2'*

pm'a2'

Color class *pm'a2'* (Figure 4.138) has color reversals across all mirror axes and around the rotation centers, but the colors are preserved in the glide reflections.

This symmetry is found on one section of a tapa cloth from Fiji (Figure 4.139) and on a design by the Auetö Indians of Brazil (Figure 4.140).

4.140   Fish scale design, Auetö Indians, Brazil. From Boas 1927, fig. 79c. Redrawn by C. Sudekum.

4.139   Section of a tapa, Matuku, Fiji. Courtesy of the Field Museum of Natural History, Chicago (no. 135438).

4.141   Schematic *p1a1*

p1a1

The only symmetry of this class is glide reflection along the central axis of the band. There are no mirror reflections or half-turns.

A simple San Ildefonso ceramic design (Figure 4.142) illustrates this symmetry, although not quite perfectly as do a detailed series of leaves on a block print from India (Figure 4.143) and a curvilinear motif in carved wood from Norway (Figure 4.144). A bag from Peru (Figure 4.145) shows two vertically oriented bands of design with pairs of animals facing first left, then right, then left, then right in perfect *p1a1* symmetry. The two incised bands on a wood jar from Zaire (Figure 4.146) have the common *pma2* zigzag structure but the addition of the slanted lines parallel to one of the sides of the triangles formed by the zigzag reduces the symmetry of the fully elaborated pattern to glide reflection. This particular pattern is very common and appears in many media, especially incised ceramics and other carved materials.

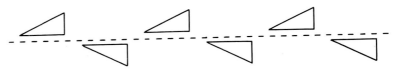

4.142   Ceramic design, San Ildefonso Pueblo. From Chapman 1970, pl. 4f.

4.143   Block print, India. From Lewis 1924, pl. 5.

4.144   Carved wood border, Hallingdal, Norway. From Arneberg 1951, pl. 25

4.145   Wool bag, Peru (California Academy of Sciences, San Francisco, no. 389-2442). Photo by C. Thomas.

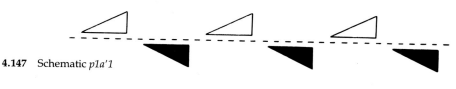

4.147   Schematic *p1a'1*

p1a'1

There is only one two-color class for *p1a1*, class *p1a'1*, where the glide reflection interchanges the two colors (Figure 4.147).

In Figures 4.148 and 4.149 San Ildefonso ceramic designs show this color reversal sequence between the upper and lower rows of isosceles triangles. Note that in both designs the triangles alone form *pma2* designs, but the elaboration inside the triangles reduces the symmetry to *p1a1*, and then the coloring produces the symmetry class *p1a'1*.

Examples are seen around the border of a Navajo blanket (Figure 4.150) and on a Maori rafter (Figure 4.151).

4.148   Ceramic design, San Ildefonso Pueblo. From Chapman 1970, pl. 132a. Redrawn by the University of Wisconsin Cartographic Lab.

4.149   Ceramic design, San Ildefonso Pueblo. From Chapman 1970, pl. 131p. Redrawn by the University of Wisconsin Cartographic Lab.

4.151   Painted wood rafter, Maori. From Hamilton 1896, no. 23.

4.146   Wood container, Zaire (California Academy of Sciences, San Francisco, no. 389-1438). Photo by C. Thomas.

4.150   Border, "Eye Dazzler" blanket, Navajo (California Academy of Sciences, San Francisco, no. 370-697). Photo by C. Thomas.

Tray, late Ming dynasty, China (Avery
Brundage Collection, Asian Art Museum of
San Francisco, no. B62 M14)

5 Two-Dimensional Patterns

5.1 Flow Charts for the Two-Dimensional Patterns

IN THIS CHAPTER we present flow charts for classifying one-color and two-color, two-dimensional patterns. The general discussion in Section 4.1, although directed mainly to the use of the one-dimensional flow chart in Table 4.2, applies as well to the flow charts in this chapter. Refer to Chapter 3, especially Section 3.5, and to Chapter 4, Section 4.1, to review the concepts of *preserve colors, reverse colors,* and *consistent with color,* which are used in these flow charts.

While one-dimensional patterns only admit one kind of rotation (180°) or no rotations, two-dimensional patterns fall into five categories based on rotation: those admitting 60°, 90°, 120°, and 180° rotations, and those admitting no rotations at all. For this reason, both of the flow charts in this chapter have five branches, one for each of the five kinds of rotation. Both flow charts first ask the user to determine the kind of rotation present in the pattern. The flow chart for one-color patterns is in Table 5.1. The flow chart for two-color patterns (Table 5.2) has been subdivided and each branch (Tables 5.2a–e) appears in a different section of this chapter. One-color patterns can be classified using only Table 5.1; this table should be self-explanatory with the explanation in Chapter 4 and the following discussion of "smallest rotation." For two-color patterns, start with Table 5.2. The initial question, "What is the smallest rotation consistent with color?" directs the user to the branch of the flow chart for the kind of rotations admitted: none (Table 5.2a), 180° (Table 5.2b), 120° (Table 5.2c), 90° (Table 5.2d), and 60° (Table 5.2e). A pattern that admits more than one kind of rotation must be classified according to its *smallest rotation.* For example, a *p6m* pattern (which admits rotations by 60°, 120°, and 180°) will appear in the 60° branch of the flow chart (Table 5.2e), not the 120° or 180° branch.

The meaning of certain crucial terms must be understood before the user classifies two-dimensional patterns that admit 90° rotations. First, in Table 5.2c a question asks, "Is there a *twofold center* which preserves colors?" Some patterns that admit 90° rotations have two kinds of half-turn centers. For example, in a checkerboard (cf. Figure 3.1, above) the midpoint of the edge of a square is a true *twofold center.* There are also half-turns about the point where four squares meet, but this is *not* called a twofold center; that term is reserved for centers admitting *only* half-turns and no other rotations. Thus, for a checkerboard the answer to the question "Is there a twofold center which preserves colors?" is "no," because half-turns about two-fold centers always *reverse* colors (even though half-turns about fourfold centers, such as the points where four squares meet, preserve colors).

Second, in the same table there are questions about *closest* fourfold centers, or fourfold centers and *closest* twofold centers. These questions mean exactly what they say. It is imperative that the user examine centers which really are *closest to each other,* since otherwise it is easy to get a wrong answer.

In Section 5.1 we will key out one example of each of the sixty-three classes

Table 5.1   Flow chart for the seventeen one-color, two-dimensional patterns

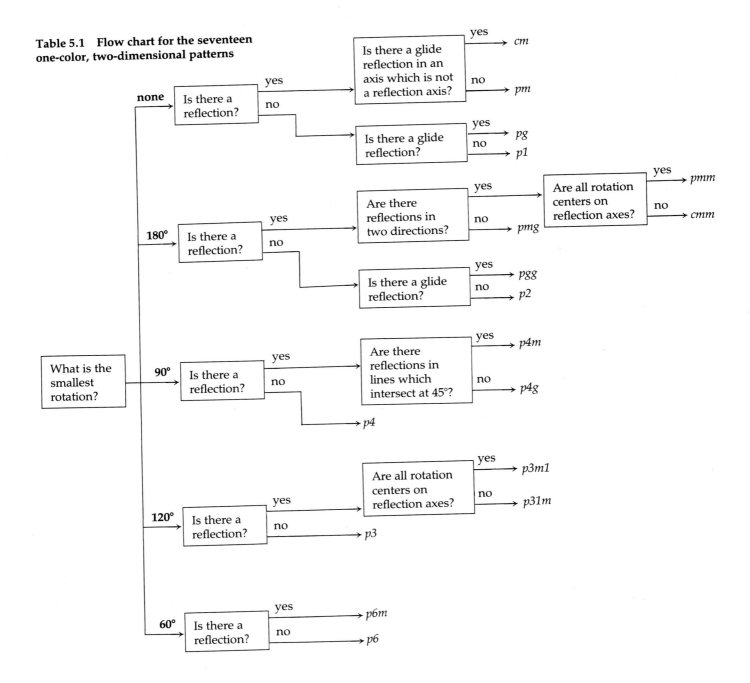

**Table 5.2 The five branches of the
flow chart for the sixty-three one-color
and two-color, two-dimensional patterns**

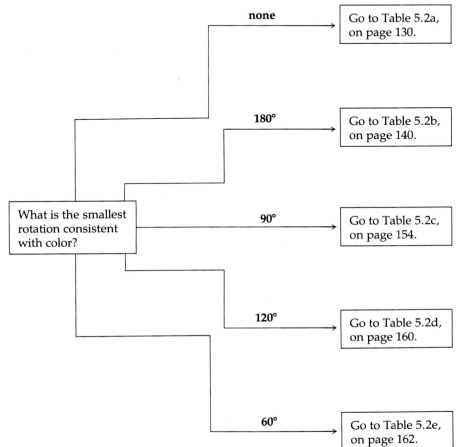

of two-color, two-dimensional patterns, using the flow chart. The reader will
need to follow this section with the correct branch of the flow chart in hand at
every step. In Section 5.2 we will examine other examples of each class.

Let us begin with the simplest two-dimensional patterns, those whose only
motions are translations. In our sample pattern (Figure 5.1), the main section
of a loincloth in Chancay style from Peru, there are no rotations. The user can
thus answer "none" to the first question, "What is the smallest rotation con-

sistent with color?" We now move to Table 5.2a. To the next question, "Is there a reflection consistent with color?" and to the third question, "Is there a glide reflection which preserves color?" we can answer "no" because there are no mirror or glide reflections in the pattern. We can see that all the rodents are the same color; this means a "no" answer to the question, "Is there a translation which reverses colors?" Finally, because we have already determined that no glide reflections are present in the pattern, we can answer "no" to the last question and arrive at the classification of *p1*.

Table 5.2a   Flow chart branch for the two-dimensional patterns admitting no rotations consistent with color

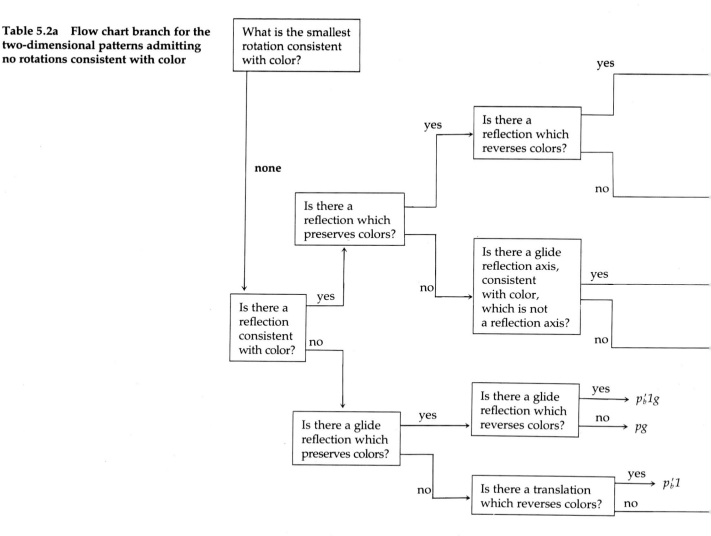

5.1 *p1* Loincloth, Chancay style, A.D. 1200–1500, Peru (The Textile Museum, Washington, D.C., no. 1960.6.7)

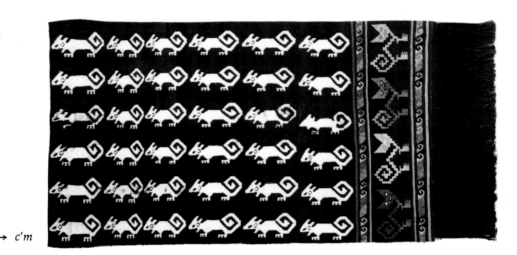

Is there a translation, along a reflection axis, which reverses colors?
→ yes → $c'm$
→ no → p'_b1m

Is there a translation which reverses colors?
→ yes → Is there a translation, along a reflection axis, which reverses colors?
  → yes → p'_bm
  → no → p'_cm
→ no → Is there a glide reflection axis, consistent with color, which is not a reflection axis?
  → yes → cm
  → no → pm

Is there a translation which reverses colors?
→ yes → p'_cg
→ no → cm'

Is there a translation which reverses colors?
→ yes → p'_bg
→ no → pm'

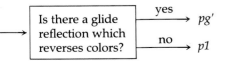

Is there a glide reflection which reverses colors?
→ yes → pg'
→ no → $p1$

5.2 $p_b'1$ Detail, sleeve of woman's dress, early twentieth century, Kicevija, Yugoslavia (Institute of Folklore, Skopje, Yugoslavia, no. 318)

Examining a dress sleeve from Yugoslavia (Figure 5.2), we have to answer "yes" to the question, "Is there a translation which reverses colors?" The hooks alternate colors along both vertical and horizontal axes, so a translation which moves each horizontal row to the next one below (or above it) reverses all colors. Likewise a translation which moves each vertical row to the next one to the right (or left) of it reverses all colors. The classification is $p_b'1$.

Let us remain at the bottom of this chart and examine one- and two-color patterns admitting glide reflections. On the Peruvian tunic of Figure 5.3 we see, on either side of the central seam, a series of birds arranged by glide reflection. (There is approximate mirror reflection across the seam but we restrict our attention to one side.) We answer "yes" to the question, "Is there a glide reflection which preserves colors?" because all the birds are the same color. So, the answer to the final question is "no" because we just determined that there were no color reversals in the pattern. The classification is *pg*. (The single *g* of the notation reminds us that there are glides in only one direction; in this case the birds move vertically along the glide axes.)

For *pg* there are two colored classes, *pg'* and $p_b'1g$. If we examine a beaded apron from Botswana (Figure 5.4), we see that there are no rotations or mirror reflections. To the question, "Is there a glide reflection which preserves colors?" we must answer "no" because the black triangle units all move along the vertical glide axes, such as G, into white units while white diamonds move to black diamonds, and vice versa. We also answer "no" to the question, "Is there a translation which reverses colors?" because, if we follow a series of black units or white units, they all preserve their colors. Since we found glide reflections that reversed colors, we answer "yes" to the last question and so arrive at the classification *pg'*.

5.3 *pg* Tunic, A.D. 1200–1500, Central
Coast Peru (The Textile Museum,
Washington, D.C., no. 1960.6.3)

5.4 *pg'* Beaded apron, Mbukushu,
Botswana. Redrawn by D. Crowe.

We examine another Peruvian textile in Figure 5.5a, which we have redrawn in Figure 5.5b. Again, since there are no rotations or mirror reflections, we come to the question, "Is there a glide reflection which preserves colors?" We see that there is a vertical glide axis, J, which preserves colors. Thus, along J black shape *a* moves to black *b*, to black *c*, to black *d*, and so forth. Likewise, white shape 1 moves to white 2, to white 3, to white 4, and so forth. So the answer to the question is "yes." But we can also answer "yes" to the next question, "Is there a glide reflection which reverses colors?" because we see that along another glide axis, K, black shape *a* glides to white 2, which then glides to black *c*, then to white 4 and so on. This response leads us to the classification of $p_b'1g$.

5.5a $p_b'1g$ Fragment, textile, Late Intermediate, Central Coast Peru. Permission of the Fine Arts Museums of San Francisco (no. 74.3.95).

5.5b Textile fragment, redrawn from Fig. 5.5a

Still examining patterns with no rotations, let us now move to those that admit mirror reflections, where we can answer "yes" to the question, "Is there a reflection consistent with color?" There are two one-color classes described by this set of questions, *pm* and *cm*, with five and three colored classes respectively.

A Coptic textile (Figure 5.6) illustrates our study of *pm* patterns. Examining the color arrangement we see that all clovers are in white spaces, and these rows alternate with dark rows of heart-shaped units. So all the mirror reflections across vertical axes such as J, through the centers of the clovers, and across axes such as K, through the hearts, are consistent with color because they preserve colors. Thus, we answer "yes" to the first two questions and "no" to the third.

We must now determine whether there is a translation which reverses color. Moving either horizontally or vertically, the clovers remain the same color, so we can answer "no" to this question and move to the final question, "Is there a glide reflection axis, consistent with color, which is not a reflection axis?" The answer here is "no," since all glide axes pass vertically through the centers of the clovers or hearts. These axes are already mirror reflection axes. The classification is thus *pm*. (The single *m* of the notation reminds us that there are mirror reflections, in one direction only, and that there are no separate glide axes.)

5.6 *pm* Textile, Coptic. From Gerspach 1975, 44.

5.7 *p'ₐm* Marble floor, twelfth-thirteenth century, Church of Santa Maria in Cosmedin, Rome. From Speltz 1914, pl. 52, no. 6. Redrawn by A. Pertschuk.

Let us examine a colored *pm* pattern. In this drawing of the marble mosaic floor in the Church of Santa Maria in Rome (Figure 5.7) we see that mirror reflection axes such as J, through the apexes of the large triangles, as well as those such as K, between them, preserve colors. There are no mirror reflection lines which reverse colors, so we arrive at the question, "Is there a translation which reverses colors?" To this we answer "yes," because vertical movement of the triangles leads to alternations in color. The answer to the final question, "Is there a translation along a reflection axis which reverses colors?" is "yes," since we can apply the same test as we did for the previous question to see the color reversals. The classification is *p'ₐm*.

5.8 p'_b1m Detail, velvet on silk. From Day 1904, fig. 219.

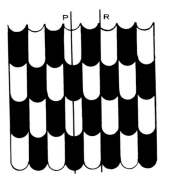

5.9 $c'm$ Detail, Egyptian design. From Stevens 1980, fig. 22.4a.

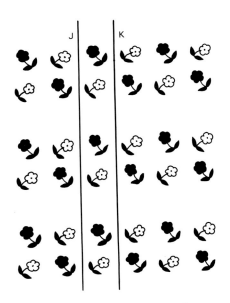

5.10 pm' Quilt. "Forget-Me-Not." Adapted from Edwards 1975, no. 61. Redrawn by A. Pertschuk.

For the next colored pm pattern let us examine a motion class where there are both color reversals and color preservations across mirror axes. In a section of velvet on silk cloth (Figure 5.8) we see that a vertical mirror reflection axis down through the white ornament (panel on the left) preserves colors, while a mirror axis between this section and the adjacent series of black ornaments reverses colors. This brings us to the question, "Is there a translation, along a reflection axis, which reverses colors?" This must be answered "no," because the only reflection axes are vertical. Translations in the vertical direction do not reverse colors. Thus the classification is p'_b1m.

Suppose, however, that we examine a design, such as one from ancient Egypt (Figure 5.9), which has both color-preserving mirror reflection axes such as P and color-reversing mirror reflection axes such as R. Moreover, the units are arranged so that translations along reflection axes reverse the colors. This arrangement results in a $c'm$ pattern.

More complex are patterns such as the quilt in Figure 5.10, where the mirror reflections are across vertical lines, such as J or K, and none of them preserves color. We must consider whether there is a glide reflection axis consistent with color that is not a mirror reflection axis. The answer to this question is also "no," since there are no glide reflections at all. This is because the rows are paired so that any glide reflection which would move a white flower to the next black flower above it would move the next black flower below it to the space between the flowers. Finally, we must answer "no" to the last question, "Is there a translation which reverses colors?" because translation in both horizontal and vertical directions will always preserve the colors: the black flowers move into black flowers, and likewise, the white flowers move into white flowers. The classification is pm'.

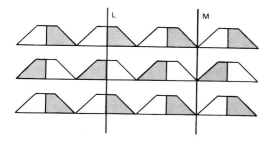

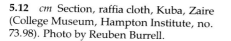

5.11 $p_b'g$ Invented design

5.12   *cm* Section, raffia cloth, Kuba, Zaire (College Museum, Hampton Institute, no. 73.98). Photo by Reuben Burrell.

The last colored *pm* pattern has color reversals everywhere, as in this invented pattern (Figure 5.11). Lines L and M are mirror lines across which colors reverse, but there are no mirror reflections which preserve color and no glide axes which are not reflection axes. And, because there are color reversals everywhere, translations vertically reverse the colors to give us the classification $p_b'g$.

The other group of one- and two-color plane patterns which are based on mirror reflections has the units arranged in an *offset* distribution. That is, each row of motifs is obtained from the row next to it by a glide reflection rather than by a simple mirror reflection. This leads to differing coloring arrangements along the mirror and glide axes.

For the one-color pattern *cm*, exemplified here on a Kuba raffia cloth (Figure 5.12), we know that since there are no color reversals, any mirror reflections, such as across line M, or translations must preserve the colors. This brings us to the final question, "Is there a glide reflection axis, consistent with color, which is not a reflection axis?" We answer "yes" to this question because, since the units are offset, there is a glide axis, such as line G, between any two vertical rows of units. (The reflection axis passes through the center of each unit.) The classification is *cm*. (The single *m* is a reminder of the mirror axes, in one direction only.)

5.13 $p'_c m$ Sampler, Berlin woolwork, nineteenth century, American (Helen L. Allen Textile Collection, The University of Wisconsin, Madison, no. EAE-690)

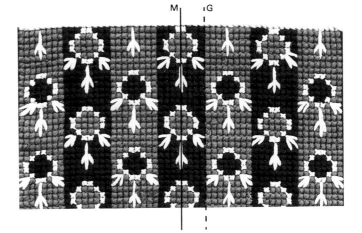

There are three colorings of *cm*. If we examine the colorings of a nineteenth-century sampler (Figure 5.13), we see that the reflection axes, such as line M, all pass through the flower units and preserve colors. Since the units are offset there is no reflection axis which reverses colors. The next question, "Is there a translation which reverses colors?" is answered "yes," because a diagonal translation reverses colors. However, these diagonal translations are not along reflection axes, and hence the answer to the last question is "no" and the classification is $p'_c m$. Notice that in this example there are glide axes, such as G, but they are not needed for the flow chart classification.

Suppose we examine colored patterns of *cm* that have no mirror reflection axes which preserve color. A stunning example is found on a tiling from the site of Timgad (Figure 5.14). Here the colors reverse along the glide axes, which lie halfway between the mirror reflection axes. For the next question, "Is there a translation which reverses colors?" the answer is "no," since all translations preserve colors. The classification is *cm'*.

An invented pattern (Figure 5.15) shows the colored *cm* pattern $p'_c g$. Although there are mirror reflections which are consistent with color, in lines like U and V, there are no mirror reflections which preserve colors. Since there is a glide axis (G) halfway between reflection axes that is not a reflection axis, we are left with the final question, "Is there a translation which reverses colors?" Inspection of the pattern shows that horizontally or vertically the colors are preserved by a translation, but diagonally they are reversed. Thus, the classification is $p'_c g$.

5.14   *cm'* "Tête de Meduse," mosaic tiling from site of Timgad. From Germain 1969, pl. 39.

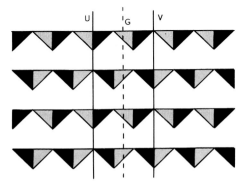

5.15   *p'$_c$g* Invented design

We move next to an entirely different branch of the flow chart, which keys out patterns containing twofold rotations. These patterns have 180° rotational symmetry in addition to translations, mirror reflections, and glide reflections. We begin again, answering "180°" to the question, "What is the smallest rotation consistent with color?"

Table 5.2b   Flow chart branch for the two-dimensional patterns whose smallest rotation consistent with color is 180°

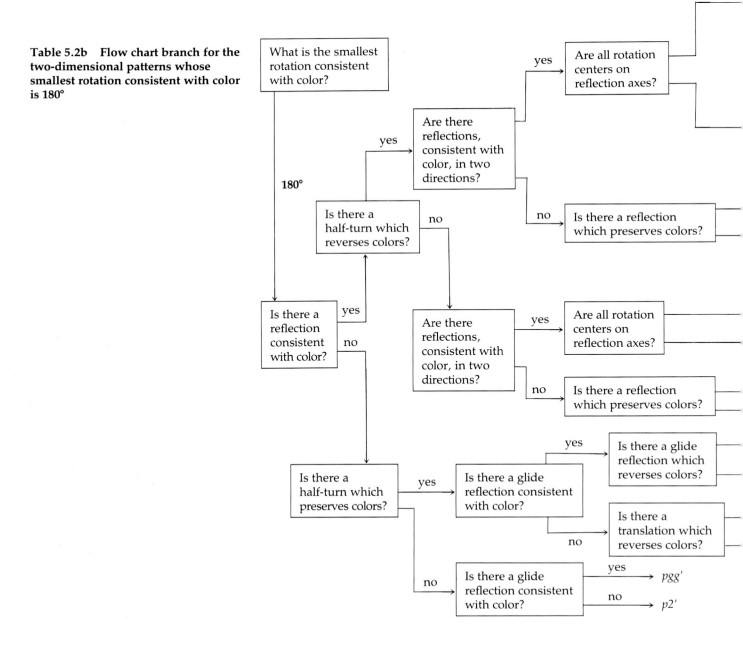

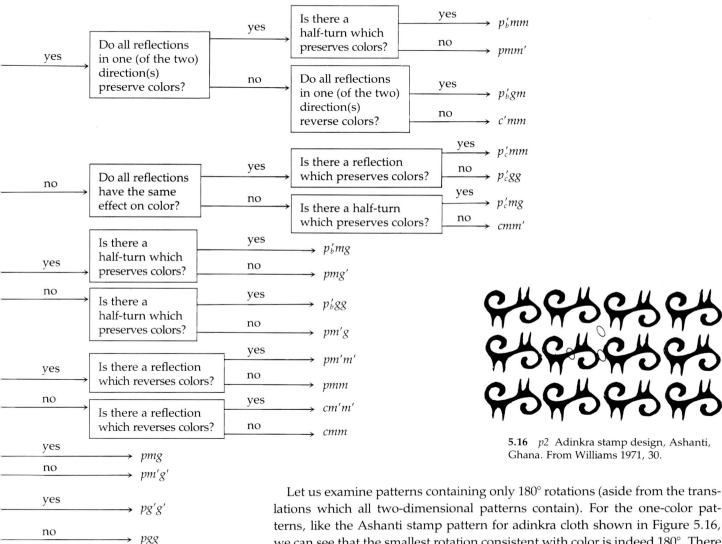

5.16 *p2* Adinkra stamp design, Ashanti, Ghana. From Williams 1971, 30.

Let us examine patterns containing only 180° rotations (aside from the translations which all two-dimensional patterns contain). For the one-color patterns, like the Ashanti stamp pattern for adinkra cloth shown in Figure 5.16, we can see that the smallest rotation consistent with color is indeed 180°. There are rotation centers in the center of each two-ended spiral unit, as well as between these units. Three of these are marked by small ovals in Figure 5.16. Because there are no mirror reflections, we move to the third question, "Is there a half-turn which preserves colors?" The answer is an easy "yes" because all the units are the same color. We answer "no" to the next question because there are no glide reflection axes in this pattern and "no" to the last question because there are no translations which reverse the colors. The classification is *p2*. (The 2 serves as a reminder of the half-turns.)

5.17 $p_b'2$ Shoulder bag, Huichol, Mexico (School of American Research Collections in the Museum of New Mexico, no. 9628/ 12). Photo by A. Taylor.

Suppose we examine a $p2$ pattern that is colored. A good example appears on a Huichol shoulder bag (Figure 5.17). Again, there are no mirror reflections. To the question, "Is there a half-turn which preserves colors?" we can answer "yes," because a rotation about the center of any double-hooked black or white unit moves the upper black hook into the lower black hook. (There are also rotations which reverse colors, but they are not relevant to this particular question.) Since there are no glide axes in this pattern, the answer to the next question is "no." The final question asks if there is a translation which reverses colors. Since there is a diagonal translation which moves black to white (and vice versa), a "yes" answer gives the classification $p_b'2$.

On another example, a pre-Columbian Peruvian bag from Nazca (Figure 5.18), the black hooks (or white hooks) do not by themselves have rotational symmetry. Therefore, there can be no rotations which preserve colors; all rotation centers are between black and white hooks and all reverse colors. This means that we answer "no" to the question about the presence of color preservations and move to the last question, "Is there a glide reflection consistent with color?" This is easily answered because there are no glide axes in this pattern. Thus the classification is $p2'$.

5.18 $p2'$ Small bag, Nazca, pre-Columbian Peru (California Academy of Sciences, San Francisco, no. 303-22). Photo by C. Thomas.

Let us now turn to patterns admitting glide reflections as well as twofold rotations. A one-color example, here illustrated by a Japanese coverlet (Figure 5.19), is easy to key out. Each four-stepped white unit has 180° rotations and these preserve colors. There are no mirror reflections. The glide axes run horizontally and vertically between the rows of units. Since all the glide reflections preserve colors, a "no" answer to the last question gives the classification pgg. (The double g in the symbol records glide reflections in the two directions.)

There are two colorings for class pgg. The design on a pre-Columbian Peruvian textile (Figure 5.20) has 180° rotations (half-turns) and glide reflections. All the half-turns reverse colors because the white hooks interlock and rotate

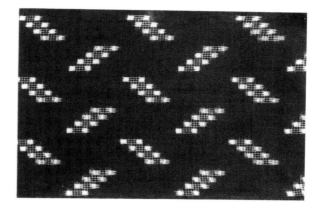

5.19 *pgg* Detail, Japanese coverlet, twentieth century (Helen L. Allen Textile Collection, The University of Wisconsin, Madison, no. W.Re.J.2344)

5.20 *pgg′* Fragment, small bag, Late Intermediate, Central Coast Peru. Permission of The Fine Arts Museums of San Francisco (no. 74.3.39).

with the black hooks. The last question, "Is there a glide reflection consistent with color?" is answered "yes." Along the vertical glide axes black hooks move into black hooks and white hooks into white hooks, preserving colors. Along the horizontal axes, however, glide reflections lead to color reversals. The classification is *pgg′*.

An invented pattern (Figure 5.21) illustrates the second coloring of *pgg*. In this pattern there are half-turns around the center of each black unit and white unit, as well as around each corner point. Two such centers are marked in the figure with small ovals. Although four units meet at each corner, it is clear that the shapes, regardless of their color, can only be superimposed by a 180° turn. There are no mirror reflection axes. Half-turns preserve colors: rotations around the points between units moves a black unit to black and a white unit to white, while rotation around the center of a unit moves its lower corner to the upper corner with no color change. Glide axes, marked by dashed lines in the figure, run vertically and horizontally, and glide reflections in either direction consistently reverse colors. The classification is *pg′g′*.

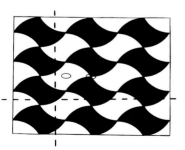

5.21 *pg′g′* Invented design. Redrawn by A. Pertschuk.

5.22 *pmg* Ceramic scoop, Mohave (California Academy of Sciences, San Francisco, no. 252-33). Photo by C. Thomas.

5.23 *pm'g'* Invented design

There is another series of patterns, *pmg*, based on glide reflections and mirror reflections as well as 180° rotations. For this series we can answer "yes" to the question, "Is there a reflection consistent with color?" If we examine a Mohave scoop (Figure 5.22) we see that reflection across any vertical mirror axis passing through the center of the black triangular areas preserves the colors. The next question, "Is there a half-turn which reverses colors?" must be answered "no" since all the design units are the same color. Since the mirror axes pass in only one direction through the design (in the orientation of this example, they pass vertically), we must answer "no" to the next question. Since we have already determined that all design units are the same color, the last question is answered "yes," giving a classification of *pmg*. (The *m* and *g* remind us of the mirror axes and glide axes, always perpendicular to each other, in *pmg* patterns.)

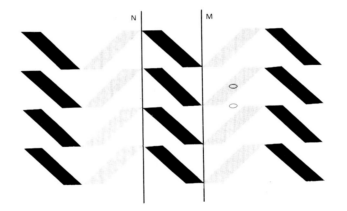

There are five motion classes which describe the colorings of *pmg*. One, as seen on this invented pattern (Figure 5.23), has mirror reflection lines, such as M and N, which pass between the angled bars. Reflections across all these axes reverse colors. Hence the answer to the question, "Is there a reflection consistent with color?" is "yes." To the question, "Is there a half-turn which reverses colors?" we answer "no," since the 180° rotation centers are at the midpoint of each bar and between bars of the same color (one of each is marked with a small oval), and these preserve colors. Since there are mirror reflections in only one direction (vertical in this example) we answer "no" to the next question, and "no" to the final question because it is apparent that all mirror reflections lead to color reversals. The classification is *pm'g'*.

5.24 *pm′g* Fragment, textile, pre-Columbian Peru (California Academy of Sciences, San Francisco, no. 389-2555). Photo by C. Thomas.

5.25 *p′₁gg* Beaded apron, Okavango, Botswana. From Williams 1971, 61.

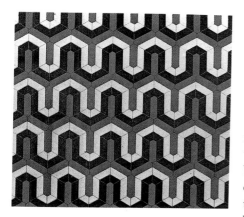

5.26 *pmg′* Wall mosaic, fourteenth century, Arabic. From Prisse d'Avennes, 1978, 9.

Many designs, particularly those on textiles, have no background space between the unit motifs and this necessitates careful scrutiny to determine the symmetries and color changes present. If we examine a pre-Columbian textile fragment from Peru (Figure 5.24) we see that this pattern is more complex than previous examples we have examined. In this pattern we can see that 180° rotations change colors in the pairs of interlocking white and black stepped units. There are also vertical mirror reflection axes; across these the stepped units reverse color. Both the rotations and the mirror reflections are consistent with color and so we may move to the third question, "Is there a half-turn which reverses colors?" The answer is "yes," as we have already determined. There are no horizontal mirror reflections, and so the answer to the next question is "no." Since none of the mirror reflections prerserves colors, the next question is answered with a "no." We again answer "no" to the last question, "Is there a half-turn which preserves colors?" and arrive at the classification *pm′g*.

Another colored *pmg* design is redrawn from a beaded apron from Botswana (Figure 5.25). To the question, "Is there a reflection consistent with color?" we answer "yes." In this example, mirror reflections across horizontal axes such as H, which bisect the black-white diamonds, consistently interchange the two colors. There are half-turns which reverse colors because a rotation around points such as A moves the black triangles to the white triangles. The next question requires careful inspection: "Are there reflections, consistent with color, in two directions?" We have already determined that there are horizontal mirror reflection axes and that across these axes the colors reverse. We are also tempted to see mirror reflection axes bisecting the diamonds vertically, but the small parallelograms bordering the diamonds are not symmetrical across such axes. Hence mirror reflections are not present in both directions in this case and we answer "no" to that question. The horizontal reflections all reverse colors, so we answer "no" to the next question. The final question asks, "Is there a half-turn which preserves colors?" Since the diamond units are staggered, there are half-turn centers at points such as B around which the colors are preserved. The classification is *p′₁gg*.

A fourth coloring of *pmg* is seen on a fourteenth-century Arabic wall mosaic (Figure 5.26). In this pattern there are mirror reflections across vertical axes which pass through the centers of the high points and low points along each row of crenelated lines. These reflections are consistent with color because there are no color changes anywhere across these axes. To the question, "Is there a half-turn which reverses colors?" we answer "yes," because a rotation of a black bottom segment in a line moves it to an white upper segment. To the next question about reflections in two directions we answer "no," since only vertical mirror reflections are present. We also answer "yes" to the next question because we found that all the reflections preserve colors. Since no half-turn preserves colors, a "no" answer to the final question leads us to the classification *pmg′*.

The last coloring of *pmg* is exemplified by one of the most frequently occurring two-dimensional patterns—a series of zigzags. It can be considered to be a coloring of *pmg* if the distance between zigzags is equal to their width, which makes the background serve as the alternating color. We see this on a Sonoran weaving (Figure 5.27).

5.27 $p'_b mg$ Throw rug, Mayo. By Julia Mendoza, Bacabachic, Sonora (A. Abrams, Phoenix).

We know from one-dimensional *pma2* patterns that single zigzags have both vertical reflections and 180° rotations. In this example we first check to see if the reflections and rotations are consistent with color. The answer is "yes" to both: reflections across suitable vertical axes preserve colors, half-turns at points within a zigzag preserve the colors, and half-turns at points between white and black zigzags reverse the colors. Since zigzags admit mirror reflections in only one direction, the next question is answered "no." But since these reflections do not reverse the colors, the next answer is "yes." This leads us to the final question, "Is there a half-turn which preserves colors?" We have seen that half-turns around centers within a zigzag line preserve the colors of that line and all others, so the answer is "yes." The classification is $p'_b mg$.

The next large category of patterns includes those admitting both horizontal and vertical mirror reflections as well as 180° rotations. These are the *pmm* patterns. There are five color classes.

Let us begin by looking at the one-color class, *pmm*, as illustrated by an Ashanti stamped cloth (Figure 5.28). Each set of four attached spirals can only

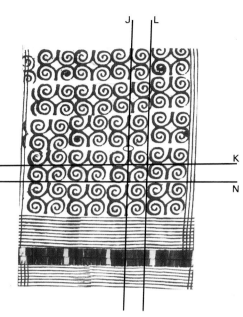

5.28 *pmm* Section, adinkra cloth, Ashanti (University of Denver, no. DU3775). Photo by D. Crowe.

5.29 *c'mm* Section, Ibo cloth, Akwete, Nigeria (Coll. K. Kent). Photo by D. Crowe.

admit half-turns; that is, a 180° turn is necessary to superimpose the two inward facing spirals and vertical divider on top to the same elements on the bottom of the set. We see further that there are mirror axes which run through the diamond centers of the motifs both horizontally (such as K) and vertically (such as J), as well as mirror axes running between the motifs both horizontally and vertically (such as N and L). Since all spiral sets are the same color, there are no color reversals along either the reflection or rotation axes. Thus, we answer "yes" to the first question, "no" to the second, and "yes" to the third.

The fourth question, "Are all rotation centers on reflection axes?" may need some careful examination of the pattern. We have already shown that there is 180° rotation about the center of each white diamond unit at the intersection of vertical and horizontal reflection axes. There are also rotations about points between the sets of spirals, one of which is marked on line J, but these too are on reflection axes which pass vertically and horizontally between the units. Thus, we answer "yes" to this question and move on to the final question, "Is there a reflection which reverses colors?" Since this is a one-color pattern, the answer is "no" and the classification is *pmm*. (The double *m* records the mirror axes in the two perpendicular directions.)

Among the easiest two-color *pmm* patterns are rectangular checkerboards. (Ordinary square checkerboards are colorings of *p4m*, not *pmm*.) On the West African cloth example (Figure 5.29), in order to answer the question, "Is there a reflection consistent with color?" we see that the mirror axes pass through the centers as well as between the blocks of color. Across mirror axes which pass through these centers the colors are always preserved; across mirror axes which pass between the units the colors are always reversed. So, along any one of these axes, there are consistent color preservations or color reversals. To the next question, "Is there a half-turn which reverses colors?" we answer "yes," because half-turns around the midpoints between the units reverse the colors in the checkerboard arrangement. The next two questions are both answered "yes" because there are reflections, consistent with color, in two directions, and each rotation center is on one of the reflection axes that run through and between the units.

The next question may be tricky. "Do all reflections in one (of the two) direction(s) preserve colors?" At first it may seem that we should answer "yes," since a mirror axis through the center of any unit will preserve color. But if we examine a mirror axis in the same direction which passes between the units, the colors will change, so we must answer "no." The final question asks, "Do all reflections in one (of the two) direction(s) reverse colors?" We found that, in either direction, some axes reverse and some axes preserve colors. Thus, since colors are not reversed across all axes in any one direction, we answer "no." The classification is *c'mm*.

In some colored *pmm* patterns, alternate rows of units change colors. Let us examine such a case, an Egyptian tomb ceiling pattern (Figure 5.30). Notice in this case that although the black units are the same shape as the striped and white units, there are twice as many of the black as either striped or white units. Hence, there is no motion which takes all blacks to striped or all blacks to white, and we must treat the black as background. That is, this is a two-color pattern whose two colors are striped and white.

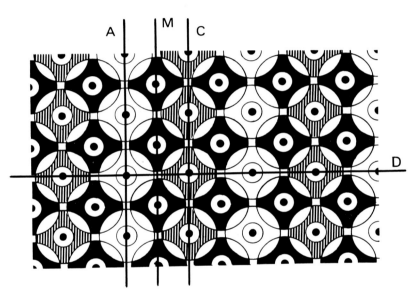

5.30 *p'ₙmm* Tomb ceiling, Egypt. From Jones 1856, pl. 10, no. 2. Redrawn by A. Pertschuk.

Notice also that the underlying uncolored pattern here has a checkerboard appearance so that the colored pattern might at first be thought to have four-fold rotational symmetry. However, the only rotations consistent with this particular coloring are indeed half-turns, which confirms that we are in the correct (180°) section of the flow chart. It is a common error, when using the flow charts, to give a hasty wrong answer to this initial question concerning smallest rotation and thereby make a false identification of a pattern.

Returning to our examination of Figure 5.30, in this case we can answer "yes" to the question, "Is there a reflection consistent with color?" because the striped and white are consistently preserved across vertical mirror axes through the units, such as A and C, and consistently reversed across vertical mirror axes between the units, such as M. There are half-turns (between the units) which reverse colors. There are reflections consistent with color in two directions because vertical and horizontal mirror axes through the units, such as A and D, preserve colors. As in all *pmm* patterns the rotation centers are all on reflection axes, so we answer "yes" to that question. This takes us to the question, "Do all reflections in one (of the two) direction(s) preserve colors?" Since *all* reflections across the horizontal axes—those which run both through and between the design units—preserve colors, we answer "yes." And we answer "yes" to the final question, "Is there a half-turn which preserves colors?" because half-turns around the center of each unit will preserve the color. The classification is $p_b'mm$.

Another colored class of *pmm* is found on a ribbon blanket (Figure 5.31). Here vertical mirror axes through and between the units all preserve colors, while horizontal axes through and between the units all reverse colors. Thus, there are reflections consistent with color in both directions. There are half-turns in the center of each unit, as well as between the units, which reverse the colors. We have already answered the third question about reflections in two directions with a "yes," so we move to the next question, "Are all rotation centers on reflection axes?" As in all *pmm* patterns, the twofold rotation centers lie on the mirror axes, so we answer "yes." Our next decision is whether all reflections in one direction preserve colors. We have seen that mirror reflections across vertical axes all preserve colors so the answer is "yes." Finally, inspection of all half-turns (both about the centers of the units and about points between the units) shows that they all reverse colors. Hence no half-turn preserves colors. This "no" response gives the classification *pmm'*.

We illustrate a rarely occurring colored *pmm* class with an invented drawing in Figure 5.32. Here the background is white. All vertical reflections, whether

5.31 *pmm'* Section, ribbon blanket, Woodland Indians, Great Lakes (California Academy of Sciences, San Francisco, no. 370-687). Photo by C. Thomas.

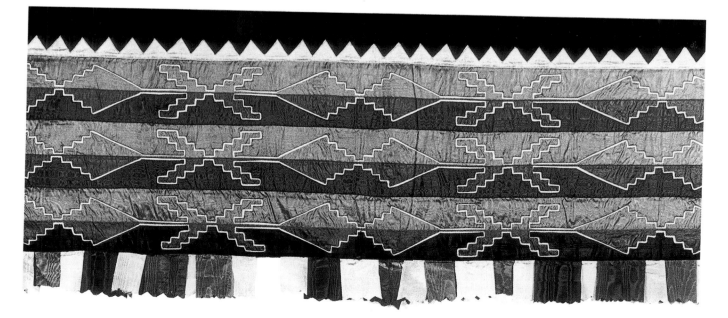

5.32 *p'ₜgm* Invented design

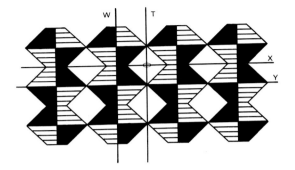

within the units, such as across line W, or between them, such as across line T, change colors, so the mirror axes are consistent with color. (Across all vertical mirror axes the colors change; across alternate horizontal mirror axes the colors are changed or preserved.) Half-turns around the centers of the white diamonds reverse the colors (one half-turn is marked). There are reflections consistent with color in two directions. All rotation centers are on mirror axes. We answer "no" to the question whether all reflections in one direction preserve colors, because we have seen that colors are preserved across the horizontal axes through an hourglass unit, such as X, but are reversed across horizontal axes between such units, such as Y. Finally, we answer "yes" to the last question because all vertical mirror axes have color reversals across them. The classification is *p'ₜgm*.

The final color class of *pmm* is illustrated by a quilt design (Figure 5.33). Here the pattern consists of the dark and white triangles making up the points of the stars. (The light gray triangles and white diamonds around the stars are background.) At first, because the units are hexagonal stars, the user may think that this is a *p6m* pattern. This is not the case because the units are not packed in a hexagonal grid, but in a *pmm* grid. Inspection shows that all reflections in the underlying pattern are consistent with color because all colors change across all mirror reflection axes, such as A, B, C, and D. But all half-turns (between stars, as well as around the centers of stars or diamonds) preserve colors, so the answer to the second question is "no." The third question is answered "yes," as we have already seen that reflections in both directions change colors. Because all the rotation centers are on mirror reflection axes we move to the final question, "Is there a reflection which reverses colors?" Since we have seen that all reflections reverse colors, our "yes" answer gives us the classification *pm'm'*.

The final pattern type in this section of the flow chart is *cmm* and its colored classes. The distinguishing symmetry characteristic of *cmm* patterns (as compared with *pmm*) is that some rotation centers are *not* on reflection axes. In many cases this is immediately apparent because the design units are offset from row to row so that two adjacent rows are related by glide reflection (and not by mirror reflection). The rotation centers lying on these glide axes are not on any mirror reflection lines.

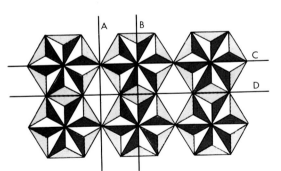

5.33 *pm'm'* Quilt design. From Edwards 1975, 23. Redrawn by D. Crowe.

5.34 *cmm* Section, raffia cloth, Kuba, Zaire (College Museum, Hampton Institute, no. 11.1673). Photo by Reuben Burrell.

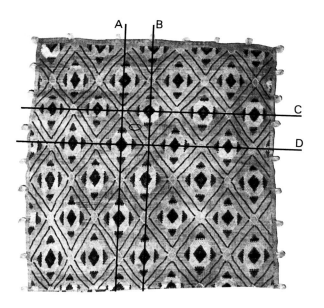

A clear example of a one-color *cmm* pattern is found on a Kuba raffia cloth (Figure 5.34). Here all the reflections, such as across lines A, B, C, and D, are consistent with color, because the units are all the same color. Likewise, there are no half-turns which reverse colors, for the same reason. There are reflections consistent with color in two directions, again because all colors are identical. Since there are twofold rotation centers, such as the one marked, which are not on mirror reflection axes, we answer "no" to the question, "Are all rotation centers on reflection axes?" Our last decision again requires a "no" answer, for there are no reflections in a one-color pattern which reverse colors. The classification is thus *cmm*. (Again the double *m* records the mirror axes in two perpendicular directions.)

There are five color classes of *cmm*. The easiest to see is a sort of diamond checkerboard where alternate horizontal and vertical rows change color. Here we see this class on a Chilean pattern (Figure 5.35). When we check whether there are reflections consistent with color, we see that all vertical mirror axes, such as A and B, preserve the colors. Likewise horizontal mirror axes, such as C and D, will do the same. Our "yes" answer takes us to the next question, "Is there a half-turn which reverses colors?" The answer is "yes" since a turn around the midpoint of the zigzag boundary between two diamond units (one is indicated) will lead to color reversal. We answered the next question in our first examination of the pattern because we found that, yes, all vertical and horizontal mirror axes preserved the colors. We just saw that not all rotation centers were on reflection axes, because the centers which led to a color reversal were between such axes. We also found that all mirror reflections preserve colors, so our "yes" answer to this question leads us to the final question, which is answered "yes" for the same reason. The classification is $p'_c mm$.

5.35 $p'_c mm$ Design on grave at Tacna, Chile. From Gutierrez n.d., no. 156.

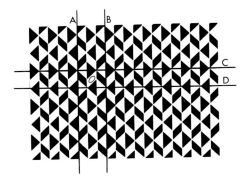

5.36 *p′c̷mg* Allover pattern. From Hornung 1975, pl. 25.

The next color class of *cmm* has a dizzying sequence of color reversals (Figure 5.36) which requires careful inspection to key out correctly. Checking for reflections consistent with color, we see that all vertical reflection axes, such as A and B, reverse colors and all horizontal reflection axes, such as C and D, preserve colors. Half-turns around the centers of the squares (i.e., between white and black triangles) reverse colors, so we answer "yes" to that question. We proceed to reconfirm that there are reflections in two directions that are consistent with color. In typical *cmm* fashion, there are rotation centers (at the midpoints of the black, or white, parallelograms as indicated) which are not on reflection axes, so we answer "no" again. We have already answered "no" to the next question, "Do all reflections have the same effect on color?" because we saw that vertical reflections reverse the colors but horizontal reflections preserve the colors. To the final question "Is there a half-turn which preserves colors?" we can answer "yes," since rotation around the parallelogram centers preserves colors. Thus the classification is *p′c̷mg*.

We turn to some dexterous basket weaving from Africa (Figure 5.37) to illustrate our next two-color class of *cmm*. When we check for mirror reflections consistent with color, we see that colors are preserved across vertical axes which bisect the isosceles triangles, and colors are reversed across the horizontal mirror axes which pass along the bases of these triangles. So, on both horizontal and vertical mirror axes, the reflections are consistent with color. We answer "yes" to the question whether half-turns reverse color, because all 180° turns around the centers between triangles or at their vertices reverse colors. Since

5.37 *cmm′* Basket, Central Africa (Musée Royal de l'Afrique Centrale, Tervuren, Belgium, no. 59.21.342)

we have already affirmed the next question, we move on to the question, "Are all rotation centers on reflection axes?" Here the answer is "no," as it is for all *cmm* patterns. To the question, "Do all reflections have the same effect on color?" we answer "no," because we have already seen that vertical mirror axes preserve color while horizontal mirror axes reverse color. We also answer "no" to the last question, "Is there a half-turn which preserves colors?" because we found that all half-turns everywhere reverse the colors. The classification is *cmm'*.

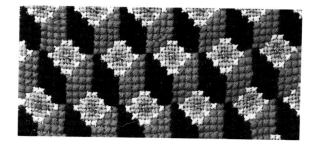

5.38 *cm'm'* Sampler, Berlin woolworks, mid-nineteenth century, American (Helen L. Allen Textile Collection, The University of Wisconsin, Madison, no. EAE-916)

A mid-nineteenth-century sampler (Figure 5.38) exemplifies an even more complex coloring of *cmm*. Note first that the lighter diamonds are background in this pattern. In the section shown, we can easily see that both horizontal and vertical mirror reflection axes bisecting the background diamonds reverse the other two colors everywhere, so the answer to the first question is "yes." Half-turns which reverse colors are not present anywhere, so the answer to the next question is "no." Moving through the next question which we have already answered affirmatively, we come to an easy question, "Are all rotation centers on reflection axes?" The rotation centers at the midpoints of the black and gray design units are *not* on reflection axes, which leads us to the final question about color reversals by reflections, whose answer is "yes." The classification is thus *cm'm'*.

The last coloring of *cmm* is perhaps the most complex and we show a pattern found on a palm wine calabash from West Africa (Figure 5.39). The horizontal and vertical mirror reflections all reverse colors and so are consistent with color. (Two of each are indicated.) Thus we may answer "yes" to the first question. Half-turns about the midpoints of the diagonals between the diamond units (one of which is shown) reverse colors, so we may answer "yes" to the next question. We have already seen that there are reflections consistent with color in two directions, so the answer to the third question is "yes." Since the half-turns which reverse colors are not on reflection axes, we must answer "no" to the question, "Are all rotation centers on reflection axes?" Since all reflections reverse colors, and thus none preserve colors, the classification is *p'_cgg*.

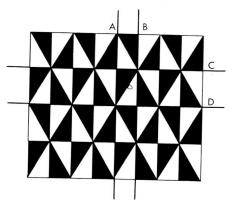

5.39 *p'_cgg* Palm wine calabash, West Africa. From Bossert 1955, pl. 9, no. 17. Redrawn by C. Sudekum.

We now move to the branch of the flow chart which treats patterns whose smallest rotations consistent with color are quarter-turns, or *fourfold rotations*. This means that the pattern must make four quarter-turns, superimposing upon itself at each 90° rotation, before returning to its original position. There are three one-color classes admitting rotations of this kind: *p4*, *p4m*, and *p4g*. (Although a 90° rotation center obviously also admits 180° rotations, we will for purposes of classification use *twofold center* to refer to rotation centers that allow only half-turns and not quarter-turns.)

Table 5.2c   Flow chart branch for the two-dimensional patterns whose smallest rotation consistent with color is 90°

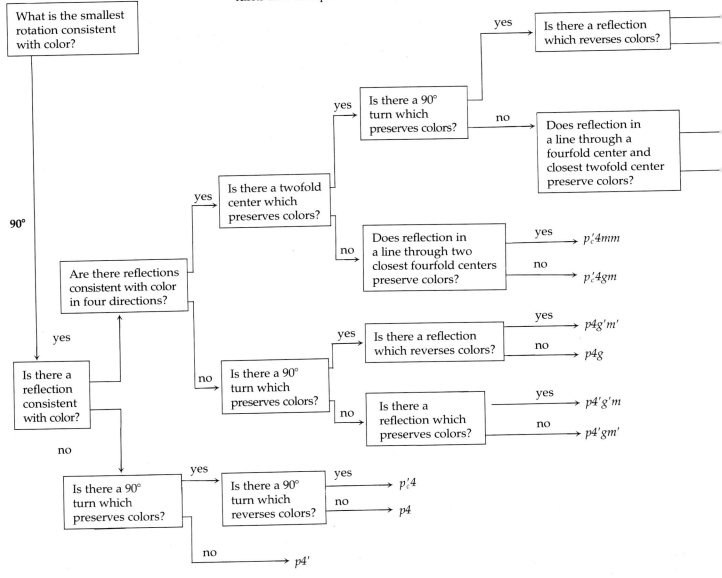

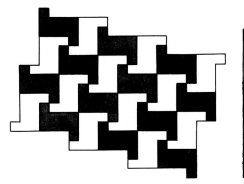

5.41 *p4'* Invented design

5.42 *p$_c$'4* Pattern derived from chess-board. From Christie 1929, fig. 73.

yes
⟶ *p4m'm'*

no
⟶ *p4m*

yes
⟶ *p4'mm'*

no
⟶ *p4'm'm*

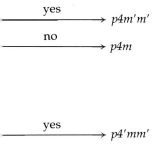

5.40 *p4* Painted ceiling, Eighteenth Dynasty, Egypt. From Christie 1929, fig. 40.

We first consider how to key out those patterns containing fourfold rotations but no reflections. A painted Egyptian ceiling of the Eighteenth Dynasty (Figure 5.40) illustrates this case. To determine that this pattern contains fourfold rotations, we look for unit parts that must be rotated four times, and we see them in the circular units with four extensions which, when turned four times, return to their original positions. The next question, "Is there a reflection consistent with color?" must be answered with a "no," since there are no mirror reflections in the pattern. We answer "yes" to the next question, "Is there a 90° turn which preserves colors?" because all units are the same color, so any quarter-turn of the pattern will preserve colors. We must answer "no" to the last question, since no color reversals occur. The classification is *p4*. (The 4 records the quarter-turns.)

Suppose, however, that we find patterns where the fourfold units change colors when rotated. There are two such arrangements. In the first (Figure 5.41) we begin by moving down the chart to the question, "Is there a 90° turn which preserves colors?" In this pattern the fourfold centers are located where the four short right angle turns of each rectangular unit join and where the corners of each unit join. Quarter-turns about any of these points reverse colors. Thus, we can answer "no" to this question, and the classification is *p4'*.

Alternatively, the units which rotate around fourfold centers may themselves admit fourfold rotation. In the example in Figure 5.42 each unit possesses a fourfold center in its center which preserves colors. Thus, our "yes" answer to the question whether there is a 90° turn which preserves colors takes us to the opposite question, "Is there a 90° turn which reverses colors?" The answer is again "yes," since it is easy to see that the colors are reversed at the junction of every four units. The classification is *p$_c$'4*.

The *p4m* patterns are based on both fourfold rotations and mirror reflections. We will begin to examine how to key out these with the one-color pattern, *p4m*, as exemplified on a Huichol bag (Figure 5.43). We can answer "yes" to the first two questions because the pattern is one-color, and therefore all vertical, horizontal, and diagonal mirror reflections preserve colors. To the questions whether there are 180° and 90° centers which preserve colors we must answer "yes," since this is a one-color design. And finally, for the same reason, there are no color reversals across reflection axes. The classification is thus *p4m*. (The *4* and *m* record the existence of quarter-turns and mirror axes.)

Perhaps the most common of the colored *p4m* patterns is the square checkerboard, here shown on a Maori feather robe (Figure 5.44). The vertical and horizontal reflection lines which pass through and between the squares yield mirror reflections consistent with color. If they bisect the square, they preserve the colors; if they pass between the squares they reverse the colors. Since each

5.43   *p4m* Shoulder bag, Huichol, Mexico (California Academy of Sciences, San Francisco, no. 472-56). Photo by C. Thomas.

5.44   *p'4mm* Feather robe, Maori, New Zealand. From Hamilton 1896, pl. 11, fig. 5.

square is all one color, there are reflections consistent with color in four directions: horizontal, vertical, and diagonal in two directions. There are no twofold centers which preserve colors because the only twofold centers are found between the squares and they reverse colors. The last question, "Does reflection in a line through two closest fourfold centers preserve colors?" is a bit tricky but we must answer "yes." The reason is that two closest fourfold centers are the center of a square and one of its corners. The line through these two points is a diagonal of the square, and colors are indeed preserved by reflection across such a diagonal. We arrive at the classification p'_c4mm.

Another pattern based on a checkerboard is found in an inlaid marble floor from fourteenth-century Italy (Figure 5.45). To the question, "Is there a reflection consistent with color?" we answer "yes," because any mirror axis which passes vertically or horizontally through the center of the circles, such such as J or K, leads to color reversals everywhere. However, across all diagonal mirror axes, such as L or M, there are color preservations everywhere. Thus, across any given mirror axis, there are reflections consistent with color, and there are such mirror axes in four directions.

To the question, "Is there a twofold center which preserves colors?" we answer "yes," because all twofold centers, such as the two indicated, are in the middle of the oblongs between the circles. On 180° rotation about these points, the white quarters superimpose on the white quarters and the black quarters superimpose on the black quarters. We must then answer the following question with a "no," since all 90° turns reverse colors. For the last question we note that no vertical or horizontal reflection lines pass through any twofold centers. Thus to examine the effect of a mirror reflection through a fourfold center and closest twofold center, we must look at the diagonal lines such as L and M. Reflections in these lines preserve colors. Our "yes" answer gives us the classification $p4'mm'$.

We show a second coloring of $p4m$ in Figure 5.46. Here the white diamonds are background. Reflections across the vertical and horizontal axes, such as lines A and B, reverse colors, but reflections across the diagonal axes, such as C or D, preserve colors. Thus colors are consistent across all reflection axes and we can answer "yes" to the first question. Additionally, there are reflections in four directions and so we can answer "yes" to the next question also. The twofold centers, one of which is marked on line B, are at the centers of the white diamonds. Any half-turn about one of these centers preserves colors. Our "yes" answer to this question leads us to ask, "Is there a 90° turn which preserves colors?" We find fourfold centers at the junction of all black and gray units and around all these points the colors are reversed. Our "no" answer leads us to the question, "Does reflection in a line through a fourfold center and closest twofold center preserve colors?" In this pattern such lines run horizontally, or vertically, through the centers of the diamonds. Reflection across such lines reverses colors, so our answer is "no." Thus the classification is $p4'm'm$.

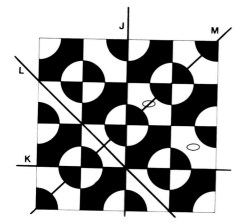

5.45 $p4'mm'$ Inlaid marble, fourteenth century, Italy. From Stevens 1980, fig. 34.5b.

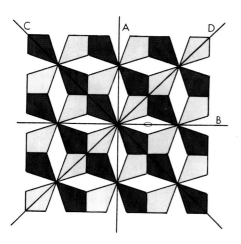

5.46 $p4'm'm$ Invented design.

5.47 *p4m'm'* Inlaid tile. From Day 1904, fig. 53.

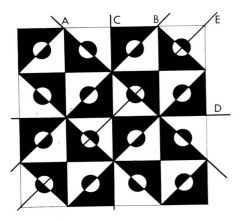

5.48 *p'₄gm* Paving tiles, fourteenth century, France. From Stevens 1980, fig. 34.5a.

5.49 *p4g* Block stamp design for printing cotton, nineteenth century, India. From Christie 1929, fig. 259.

Another coloring of *p4m* appears in a tiling (Figure 5.47). To determine whether there is a reflection which is consistent with color, we see that reflection axes which pass vertically, horizontally, and diagonally reverse the colors. Thus there are color consistencies across all the mirror reflection lines. We have also determined that there are mirror reflections consistent with color in four directions. Our "yes" answer to this last question leads us to the question, "Is there a twofold center which preserves colors?" There are twofold centers between horizontal or vertical pairs of rosettes, and we can see that these preserve color so we answer "yes." For our next question, "Is there a 90° turn which preserves colors?" we examine the fourfold centers in the centers of the rosettes and see that a quarter-turn will preserve the colors. White triangles move to white triangles and black triangles move to black triangles. Thus our "yes" answer leads us to the final question, "Is there a reflection which reverses colors?" Since we have seen that all mirror reflections reverse the colors, our "yes" answer leads us to the classification *p4m'm'*.

Another tiling illustrates the last coloring of *p4m* (Figure 5.48). We see here a checkerboard whose squares have each been divided by diagonals such as A and B, across which colors are reversed. The presence of circles on these diagonals reverses colors again but does not change the symmetries of the pattern as a whole. All mirror reflections across these diagonals—as well as across the vertical and horizontal axes such as C and D, between the squares—reverse colors. Thus we can answer "yes" to the first question, that indeed there is a reflection consistent with color. We have also seen that there are reflections consistent with color in four directions, so our "yes" answer to that question leads us to the next question, "Is there a twofold center which preserves colors?" The twofold centers are located in the centers of the circles and inspection shows that a twofold rotation will reverse the colors so that our answer must be "no." This leads us to the last question, "Does reflection in a line through two closest fourfold centers preserve colors?" Following a mirror reflection axis either horizontally (line D) or vertically (line C) through two junction points of four squares reveals that the colors are always reversed, thus giving us a "no" answer and the classification *p'₄gm*. Note that you cannot answer this question by inspection of the mirror axes, such as E, that run diagonally (in the orientation of this example) because such axes would pass through a fourfold center, then a twofold center, and then a fourfold center. The question only asks about closest fourfold centers, and only those fourfold centers along horizontal and vertical mirror axes are closest in this pattern.

The following patterns contain fourfold rotations as well as glide and mirror reflections. The one-color class, *p4g*, is easy to see in an Indian blockprint (Figure 5.49). Since it is a one-color pattern, we can answer "yes" to the first question about color consistencies and move to the next question to determine whether there are reflections consistent with color in four directions. In the orientation of the example we see that there are mirror reflection axes which

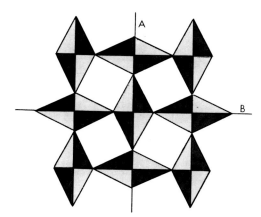

5.50 *p4g'm'* Invented design.

5.51 *p4'g'm* Painted design, Eighteenth Dynasty, Egypt. From Christie 1929, fig. 358.

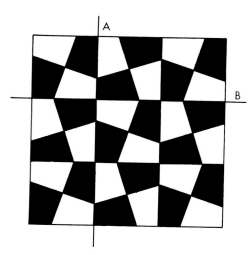

5.52 *p4'gm'* Invented design.

run horizontally and vertically, but not diagonally, so that there are reflections in only two, not four, directions. Our "no" answer leads us to the question, "Is there a 90° turn which preserves colors?" The answer is an easy "yes"—the center is at the corners where four units meet. We move to the last question, "Is there a reflection which reverses colors?" Again, there are no color reversals since the pattern is one-color and we answer "no," arriving at the classification *p4g*. (The 4 and *g* record the quarter-turns and glide reflections.)

Our first coloring of *p4g* is seen in an invented pattern (Figure 5.50) where the units of Figure 5.49 are replaced by diamonds bisected horizontally and vertically by mirror reflection axes, such as A and B. Reflections across both these axes always lead to color reversals so we may say that there are mirror reflections consistent with color. Again, as in Figure 5.49, we find that we must answer "no" to the question about reflections consistent with color in four directions, because there are reflections in only two directions. To the question, "Is there a 90° turn which preserves colors?" we answer "yes," since fourfold rotation around the center of each white square preserves colors. Since we found that all mirror reflections reverse colors, the classification is *p4g'm'*.

A wall decoration from the Eighteenth Dynasty in Egypt (Figure 5.51) illustrates a second coloring of *p4g* with dark horizontal hourglass figures and light vertical hourglass figures. Horizontal and vertical reflection axes through the hourglass figures always preserve colors, so we may answer "yes" to the first question. As in the preceding pattern, there are reflections in only two directions so we answer "no" to the next question and proceed to ask, "Is there a 90° turn which preserves colors?" Here we see that the fourfold center is located at the center of each spiral which joins four hourglass figures. Since 90° rotation about such a center takes the light vertical figures to the dark horizontal ones, and vice versa, it is clear that the answer is "no," and we move to the last question, "Is there a reflection which preserves colors?" We have already seen that all mirror reflections preserve colors, so the answer is "yes" and the classification is *p4'g'm*.

The last coloring of *p4g* is shown in an invented design in Figure 5.52. Here we see that the vertical and horizontal mirror reflection axes such as A and B, which pass between the squares, all consistently reverse colors. Thus reflections are consistent with color and we can answer "yes" to the first question. Again we answer "no" to the second question because there are reflections in only two directions, not four. To the question, "Is there a 90° turn which preserves colors?" we answer "no," because a quarter-turn around the center of each square produces color reversal. To the last question, "Is there a reflection which preserves colors?" we again answer "no," because we have already found that all mirror reflections reverse colors. The classification is *p4'gm'*.

Table 5.2d   Flow chart branch for the two-dimensional patterns whose smallest rotation consistent with color is 120°

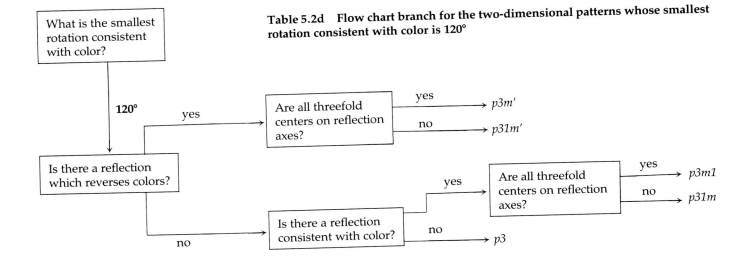

The next branch of the flow chart keys out patterns containing threefold rotations. In the one-color form, *p3*, as exemplified in a thirteenth-century Persian tiling (Figure 5.53) it is easy to see the threefold centers at the meeting point of three rotating bent lines. There are also threefold centers at the corners of the hexagons. There are no mirror reflection lines, so the answer to the first two questions must be "no" and this brings us to the end of the chart, with the classification *p3*. (The *3* records the threefold rotations.)

There can be no two-color classes of *p3*, since a two-color decoration on a threefold design would not admit any rotations consistent with color.

There are two one-color pattern arrangements based on threefold rotations and mirror reflections (see Figures 5.54 and 5.55). In such patterns there are, of course, no color reversals, so we may answer "no" to the first question and "yes" to the second question. We come to the critical question—whether all the threefold centers are on reflection axes. Examination of Figure 5.54 shows that the mirror axes pass through the threefold rotation centers in the middle of each trefoil as well as at the juncture of three trefoils. That is, all threefold rotation centers lie on lines like A and B. The classification for this pattern is *p3m1*.

Suppose, however, that we have a pattern such as Figure 5.55, where the threefold centers are in the center of the trefoils and at the curvilinear juncture of three such trefoils. Reflection axes such as A and B pass through the threefold center in the center of the trefoil. However, there is also a threefold center (marked by a small triangle) at the curvilinear junction halfway between lines A and B. It is not on any reflection axis. Hence, the answer to the last question is "no" and the classification is *p31m*.

There is one colored pattern each for patterns *p3m1* and *p31m* and these also are distinguished by whether all the threefold centers are on the reflection axes.

5.53   *p3* Tiling, thirteenth century, Persia. From Christie 1929, fig. 354.

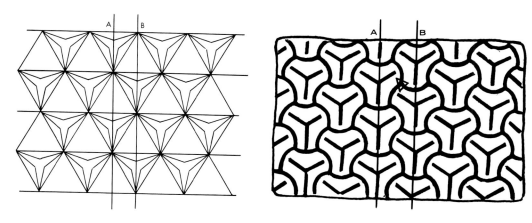

5.54   *p3m1* Invented design

5.55   *p31m* From Christie 1929, fig. 356

5.56   *p3m′* Invented coloring of Japanese design. Adapted from Wade 1982, no. 269. Redrawn by A. Pertschuk.

In Figure 5.56 we see a pattern which has the threefold centers in the center of the trefoils as well as in the center of the background black hexagons and where three trefoils meet. Mirror axes passing through these points reverse the colors in the trefoils so the answer to the first question is "yes." Additionally all rotation centers are located on these reflection lines and so the answer to the last question is "yes." The classification is *p3m′*.

In Figure 5.57 we see a pattern where the mirror axes all lead to color reversals so the answer to the first question is again "yes." However, there are threefold centers located in the centers of the small white background triangles which are not on mirror axes, as well as in the centers of the large colored triangles which are on mirror axes. Thus the answer to the last question is "no" and the classification is *p31m′*.

5.57   *p31m′* Invented design

Table 5.2e   Flow chart branch for the two-dimensional patterns whose smallest rotation consistent with color is 60°

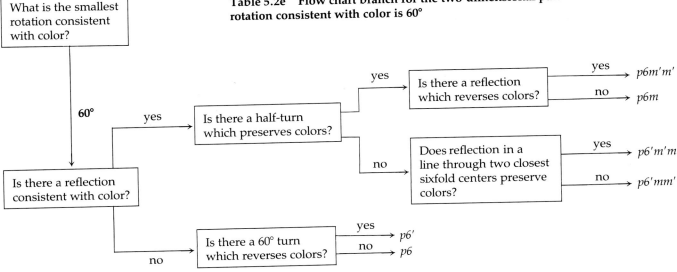

5.58   *p6* Lattice design, A.D. 1900, Shanghai, Kiangsu, China. From Dye 1974, fig. C10b.

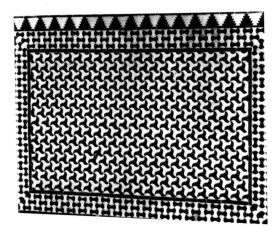

The last group of two-dimensional patterns is based on sixfold rotations. Each rotation moves the units 60°. There are two classes of one-color arrangements: those with only rotations, *p6*, and those with both reflections and rotations, *p6m*.

Those based only on rotations are easily keyed out because we may answer "no" to the question whether there are reflections consistent with color. A one-color example is shown on a Chinese lattice pattern (Figure 5.58), which admits sixfold rotation about the center of each circle. The classification is *p6* because the 60° turns do not reverse the colors. (The *6* of the notation records the sixfold rotations).

If, however, the 60° turns do reverse the colors, as in this tiling from Spain (Figure 5.59), the classification is *p6'*. In this case the sixfold centers are located where six threefold units join. Inspection of these centers reveals that the black and white units alternate colors.

Sixfold patterns with mirror and glide reflections have a single one-color form, *p6m*, and three two-color forms. The one-color form, shown here in a Chinese lattice pattern (Figure 5.60), clearly shows the six directions for mirror reflection. There are three reflections in lines through pairs of opposite vertices of the larger hexagon, and three reflections in lines which are perpendicular bisectors of opposite sides of the larger hexagon. We may answer "yes" to the first question, because there are reflections and they are consistent with color

5.59   *p6'* Wall tile, Hall of the Ambassador, Alcazar, fourteenth century, Seville. From Gombrich 1979, fig. 104.

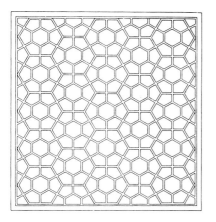

5.60 *p6m* Lattice design, A.D. 1850, shop in Shaohing, Chekiang, China. From Dye 1974, fig. C9b.

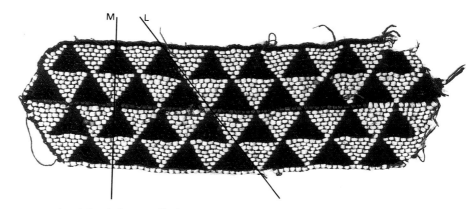

5.61 *p6'mm'* Beaded strap, Chokwe, Angola (California Academy of Sciences, San Francisco, no. 276-52). Photo by C. Thomas.

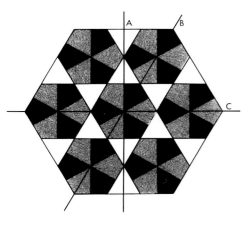

5.62 *p6'm'm* Invented design

5.63 *p6m'm'* From Burnside 1911, 417. Redrawn by D. Crowe.

(because the pattern is one-color). To the question, "Is there a half-turn which preserves colors?" we answer "yes," because the twofold centers between any two hexagons do not change colors in this one-color pattern. Similarly, there are no reflections which reverse colors, so the classification is *p6m*. (As always, the *6* and *m* record the sixfold rotations and mirror axes.)

Turning to the three ways of coloring *p6m* we may easily key them out. The beaded strip from the Chokwe of Angola (Figure 5.61) illustrates a case where there is a reflection which preserves colors, for example, in line M. Thus, we can answer "yes" to the first question. The next question asks, "Is there a half-turn which preserves colors?" This pattern admits half-turns only about the midpoints of the sides of the triangles, and all such turns reverse colors, so we must answer "no." Finally, if a mirror axis, such as line L, passes through two closest sixfold rotation centers, the colors will be reversed across the axis. (Sixfold rotation centers are located where six equilateral triangles meet). Thus the answer to the third and last question is "no," and the classification is *p6'mm'*.

The invented pattern in Figure 5.62 has mirror reflection axes, such as line A, which pass through the white (background) triangles, and mirror reflection on these axes always reverses colors. It also has mirror reflection axes such as B and C, which do not pass through the white triangles, and across which colors are always preserved. Thus we answer "yes" to the first question. There are sixfold rotations about the centers of the colored hexagons, threefold rotations about the centers of the white triangles, and half-turns about the corner points where any two hexagons meet. These half-turns will reverse colors. Therefore the answer to the next question, "Is there a half-turn which preserves colors?" is "no." The last question asks, "Does reflection in a line through two closest sixfold centers preserve colors?" The answer is "yes," but this is only apparent if you examine lines like B and C (*not* lines like A), where the sixfold centers are closest to each other. The classification is *p6'm'm*.

Patterns such as Figure 5.63, which has color reversals across all mirror axes but color preservations about the 180° rotation centers (at the midpoints of the sides of the hexagonal units) are classified as *p6m'm'*.

5.2 Examples of One-Color and Two-Color, Two-Dimensional Patterns

This section contains many examples of each of the two-dimensional pattern classes, both one- and two-color. In contrast to the preceding section, where the emphasis was on the flow chart analysis of the patterns, the main purpose of this section is to provide a multitude of examples which the reader can compare with patterns found in the field. In a few cases we were unable to find any "real life" patterns, but in each case there is at least one invented example and a schematic, computer-drawn example of that class.

On the computer-drawn schematics, we have indicated reflection axes (solid lines); glide reflection axes (dashed lines); half-turn centers (small ovals, colored black-white if there is a color change by a half-turn about that point); 120° rotation centers (small equilateral triangles); quarter-turn centers (small squares, colored black-white if there is a color change on quarter-turns about that point); and 60° rotation centers (small hexagons, colored black-white if there is a color change by 60° rotations about that point).

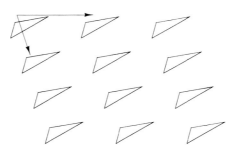

5.64   Schematic *p1*

5.2.1 Patterns with No Rotations

p1

The *p1* patterns are the simplest of the two-dimensional patterns. That is, they involve no other isometry than the translation of (usually asymmetrical) units along multiple axes. Two such translation vectors are marked in Figure 5.64 and in all subsequent schematic drawings. Very often the axes are perpendicular to each other, as in a checkerboard, but this is not necessary (see, for example, Figure 5.64).

Although a plain grid of squares has symmetry *p4m* and a plain grid of rectangles has symmetry *pmm*, such structures are reduced to *p1* symmetry when the elements inside the squares or rectangles are asymmetrical. The *p1* motion class frequently results when fields of figurative rather than geometric images are depicted. For example, the birds in the square grid on the Coptic textile in Figure 5.65 or the whales in the rectangular grid on the Chilkat blanket in Figure 5.66 reduce the whole pattern symmetry to *p1*.

5.65   Textile fragment, Coptic (The Brooklyn Museum, gift of Captain John C. Cooney, no. 45.77.1)

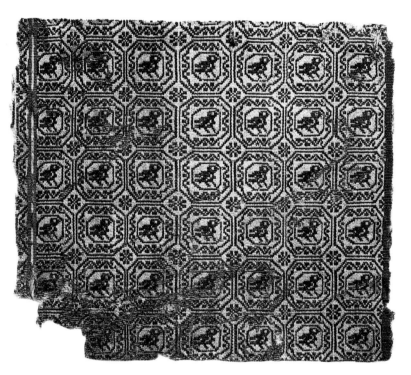

5.66   Blanket, Chilkat, Tlingit. Courtesy of the Field Museum of Natural History, Chicago (no. 19571).

5.67 "Ngula" (pressed camwood powder), Kuba, Zaire (Musée Royal de l'Afrique Centrale, Tervuren, Belgium, no. 53.74.7179)

5.68 Sleeping mat, Yombe (Musée Royal de l'Afrique Centrale, Tervuren, Belgium, no. 29.929)

The Kuba artifact in Figure 5.67 shows that the natural axes of a pattern may run diagonally, and may not be at right angles to each other. The Yombe woven sleeping mat (Figure 5.68) is a somewhat less regular example because the added squares technically cancel the *p1* symmetry. The general layout is, however, *p1*.

Other *p1* patterns are more subtle. For example, the Thousand Lamas plaque from Tibet (Figure 5.69) at first appears to be a *pm* pattern, with vertical mirror reflection axes passing through the center of each of the seated lamas. Closer inspection reveals that because the arms and legs of each lama are crossed, the vertical reflection is cancelled and the lamas can only be superimposed by translation.

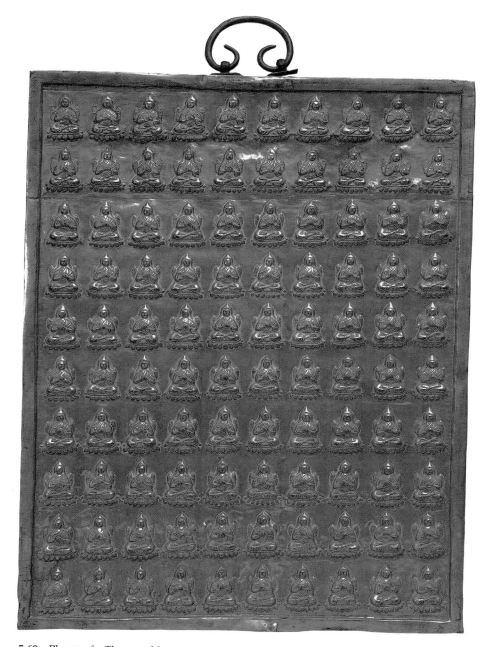

5.69   Plaque of a Thousand Lamas,
eighteenth century, Tibet (Avery Brundage
Collection, Asian Art Museum of San
Francisco, no. B60 S202)

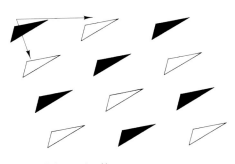

5.70   Schematic p'_b1

p'_b1

There is only one coloring for two-dimensional patterns which admit no motions other than translation. This class, p'_b1, is presented in Figure 5.70. Here the color reversals occur as the pattern is translated horizontally or along a (nearly vertical) diagonal. Depending on the orientation of a pattern, color reversals may be said to occur in the vertical, horizontal, or diagonal directions.

An example of this color class where the color reversals occur on one diagonal, but not on the other diagonal, is found on several wide bands of a pre-Columbian Peruvian poncho (Figure 5.71). On the nineteenth-century American quilt (Figure 5.72) color reversals occur diagonally but not horizontally or vertically.

We also illustrate here several examples of patterns which appear to have other symmetries in addition to translation. However, careful examination and keying out of these designs with the flow chart shows that their colorings allow only translation.

5.71   Section, poncho, Late Intermediate, Central Coast Peru. Permission of the Fine Arts Museums of San Francisco (no. 1974.3.107).

5.72   Presentation quilt, 1891, American (Wisconsin State Historical Society, no. 1974.1.35)

5.73   Pattern adapted from the Alhambra. From Christie 1929, fig. 349.

For example, the simplified version of a tiling pattern from the Alhambra in Figure 5.73 appears at first to have sixfold centers at each of the tips of the triangular units. However, any attempt to rotate the units around such a center does not result in consistent color alternations. In fact, because white units occur twice as frequently as black or dotted units, they cannot alternate consistently with either the black or dotted units. We treat the white units as background. Given this, we have black and dotted triangles which only alternate colors by translation along a diagonal axis. There are no rotations which reverse the colors consistently. On the flow chart for two-dimensional patterns the answer to the question, "What is the smallest rotation consistent with color?" is "none." Answering "no" to the subsequent questions about mirror and glide reflections, we see that only translations are left to reverse the colors.

A tiling from the Palazzo di Teodorico at Ravenna (Figure 5.74) appears to be some coloring of a *cm* pattern (as Figure 5.73 appeared to be, but was not, a coloring of *p6*). Let us key this example out on the flow chart to show why it has only $p_b'1$ symmetry. We choose the same flow chart section since there are no rotations. The next question, "Is there a reflection consistent with color?" is the critical one. The only reflection lines of the underlying pattern pass vertically through the semicircular units. However, reflection in such a line preserves the colors of the units it bisects, and interchanges the colors of some of the immediately adjacent units. Hence the answer to the question is "no." The next question asks, "Is there a glide reflection which preserves colors?" The only glide axes of the original pattern run vertically, halfway between the reflection lines just examined, and any glide reflection preserves some colors but reverses other colors. Thus we must answer "no" to this question and proceed to the final question, "Is there a translation which reverses colors?" The answer is "yes" since suitable movement of the units horizontally or vertically results in color reversals.

5.74   Tile mosaic, Palazzo di Teodorico, Ravenna, Italy. From Berti 1976, pl. 33, no. 37.

5.75   Fragment, textile, pre-Columbian Peru (Los Angeles County Museum of Natural History, no. L.2100.A.13.63.438)

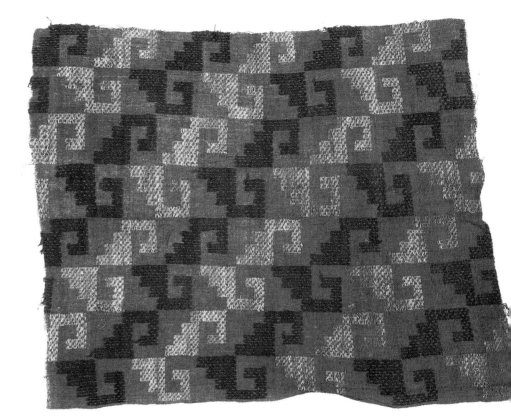

Our final example is a Peruvian textile (Figure 5.75) whose underlying pattern has glide reflections but whose coloring has reduced the symmetry to $p_b'1$. To determine which section of the flow chart to use, first note that the gray units occur twice as often as black or white units; gray is therefore the background. There is no rotation which moves the black units to the white units, so we must use the section of the flow chart for patterns with no rotations. Inspection also shows us that there are no mirror reflection lines, so we proceed to the question, "Is there a glide reflection which preserves colors?" We can see the horizontal glide axes, but the hooked figures do not change colors *consistently* along these axes; for example, a glide reflection will move the black hooks in one row to the black hooks in the adjoining row, but the same motion also causes color reversal between the rows above and below. There are also vertical glide axes, but again, colors do not change consistently along them. So we must answer "no" and proceed to the last question, "Is there a translation which reverses colors?" We can see that consistent color reversals do occur as the hooks are simply translated along the horizontal axes, and so we answer "yes," giving us the classification $p_b'1$.

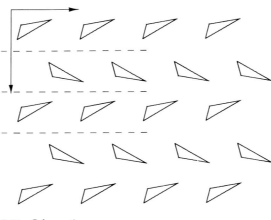

pg

This pattern class, with its two color classes, admits only glide reflections in one direction. The individual design units are asymmetrical and are moved along their axes by glide reflections. In Figure 5.76 these glide reflection axes are horizontal and are marked by dashed lines.

5.76   Schematic *pg*

An easy example is on an Indian blockprint (Figure 5.77) where the men and birds alternate the direction they face as they move along the vertical glide axes. Another example is found on a Kuba raffia cloth (Figure 5.78). Here the hooked units clearly move vertically along glide axes.

The *pg* class is popular for textile patterns. In Figure 5.79 we see it used on a detail of a mid-eighteenth-century French velvet panel. In this case both black and white flowers are moving along vertical glide reflection axes.

Finally we illustrate a *pg* pattern which is more difficult to detect on a detail of a woman's mourning shawl from Gualaceo, southern Ecuador (Figure 5.80). The ikat process has faithfully transferred the black and white leaf-shaped units which have *pm* symmetry of the structure and *cʳm* symmetry of the colored design. However, the small white stems which descend to one side of the black units (which are placed on the left for two rows, before they shift to the right) cancel any mirror symmetries and admit only the glide reflection *pg* motion.

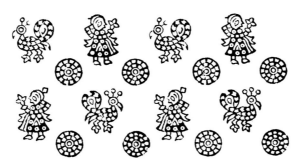

5.77   Block print design, India. From Lewis 1924, pl. 13, fig. 2.

5.78   Section, raffia cloth, Kuba, Zaire (Musée Royal de l'Afrique Centrale, Tervuren, Belgium, no. R.G.27757)

5.79   Detail, gold embroidered silk velvet panel, ca. 1750, France (Los Angeles County Museum of Art, gift of Miss Bella Mabury, no. M.55.20.2)

5.80   Detail, woman's ikat mourning shawl, ca. 1930, Gualaceo, Ecuador (Coll. D. Penley, San Francisco). Photo by D. Penley.

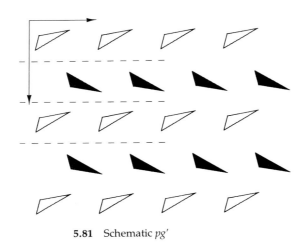

5.81 Schematic *pg'*

5.82 Pillow cover, twentieth century, American. Redrawn by A. Pertschuk.

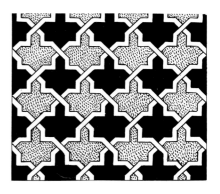

5.83 Detail, textile, Middle Horizon, South Coast, Peru (California Academy of Sciences, San Francisco, no. 389-2367). Photo by C. Thomas.

5.84 Pattern derived from Persian tiles. From Christie 1929, fig. 310.

pg'

In this coloring of *pg* (Figure 5.81), color reversal occurs along the glide axes.

This is easily seen on a pillow cover (Figure 5.82). Horizontal rows of swans alternate the directions they face. Swans in each horizontal row are the same color, so colors are reversed along the vertical glide axes. An older example is seen on a detail of a pre-Columbian burial wrapping from Peru (Figure 5.83). Here alternate horizontal rows of small birds face alternate directions. Each horizontal row is the same color, but they reverse colors as they move along the vertical glide axes which pass between the diamonds. A difficult pattern is shown in Figure 5.84 where the units appear to be arranged in colored *cm* symmetry, class p'_cm. However, the bordering white strips of the units overlap and thus cancel the *cm* structure. The only symmetry which will superimpose these units is glide reflection along vertical axes. Since the units alternate colors along the glide axes, the classification is *pg'*.

$p_b'1g$

This coloring of *pg* has color reversals along alternate glide axes moving in the same direction. In Figure 5.85 the colors reverse along the upper and lower glide axes, but not along the middle one.

This can be seen on a Samoan tapa cloth (Figure 5.86a) which has solid black and solid red right triangles on a background of patterned triangles (see redrawing, Figure 5.86b, for black and gray triangles respectively). The glide axes are horizontal. Some, like C, are between the rectangular units and some, like D, are through the centers of the rectangular units. Along axes like C, black units glide to black units and gray units to gray units. Along axes like D, the colors reverse.

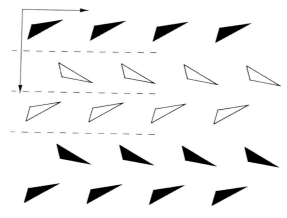

5.85   Schematic $p_b'1g$

5.86a   Tapa, Samoa. Courtesy of the Field Museum of Natural History, Chicago (no. 38811).

5.86b   Redrawn from Figure 5.86a

pm

5.87   Schematic *pm*

The *pm* patterns have mirror reflection axes in one direction only. Although these axes are often vertical, as in Figure 5.87, or horizontal, other orientations are possible. In our schematic figures we have marked mirror reflections by solid lines. In actual occurrences of *pm* patterns, the two parts are not normally separated, as in Figure 5.87, but form a single bilaterally symmetrical unit.

5.88   End of loincloth, Late Intermediate (A.D. 900–1476), Central Coast, Peru. Courtesy of the Museum of Fine Arts, Boston. Ross Collection (no. 10.268).

A complex *pm* pattern is seen on a pre-Columbian textile from the Central Coast of Peru (Figure 5.88). In this case the underlying pattern is a series of square units with *p4m* structure. However, when the "faces" are inserted in the middle of each square, the symmetry is reduced to *pm*. That is, because the faces only allow reflection in vertical mirror axes, the horizontal mirror reflections of the squares have been cancelled. (Actually, we can only consider this pattern to be a *pm* design if we ignore the narrow bands of *p112* frets that border each square. These bands should be described separately.)

In the upper two rows on a Samoan tapa (Figure 5.89) the striped isosceles triangles are each bisected by a vertical mirror axis through their apexes. The mirror axes run both vertically through the triangles as well as vertically between the rows of triangles. (In the lower section of the tapa, the stripes seem to alternate colors inside each triangle and between adjacent triangles, but this color alternation is not consistent throughout.) Another example with this same vertical orientation is seen on the uppermost band of design on a ceramic drum from Algeria (Figure 5.90). The irregularities from hand painting do not obscure the obvious *pm* symmetry of this pattern.

5.89   Tapa, Samoa. Courtesy of the Field
Museum of Natural History, Chicago (no.
39659).

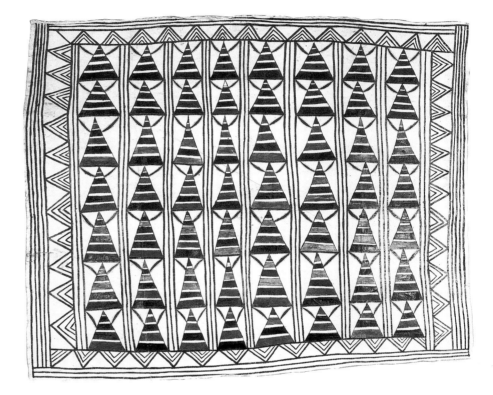

5.90   Ceramic drum, Algeria (Lowie
Museum of Anthropology, University of
California, Berkeley, no. 5-12914)

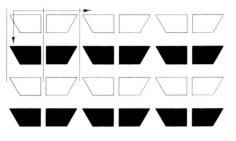

5.91 Schematic *p'ₐm*

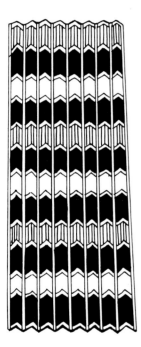

5.92 Detail, wood pillar, Eighteenth and Nineteenth dynasties, Thebes, Egypt. From Speltz 1915, no. 8. Redrawn by A. Pertschuk.

p'ₐm

This coloring of *pm* has rows of single-colored units running in one direction (which happens to be horizontal in all our examples). Thus there are no color reversals across the mirror axes. Reversals occur as the units are translated along the mirror axes (Figure 5.91).

This type of coloring appears on an early Egyptian decoration (Figure 5.92). At first it may appear to be a three-color design, but careful inspection reveals that the black units appear twice as often and are therefore considered as background. The units in any given horizontal row are one color. Color reversals occur as the units arer translated vertically. Another example may be seen on a Nez Perce corn husk bag (Figure 5.93a, redrawn in Figure 5.93b), where each horizontal row of hourglass figures is the same color. Although it may appear at first that this pattern also has horizontal reflection axes, the rectangles are "behind" only the top of each hourglass figure, and thus the whole unit does not admit horizontal reflection.

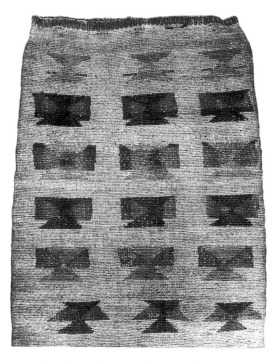

5.93a Corn husk bag, Nez Perce, Idaho (California Academy of Sciences, San Francisco, no. 370-443). Photo by C. Thomas.

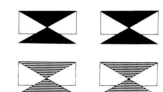

5.93b Detail of Figure 5.93a. Redrawn by A. Pertschuk.

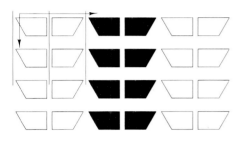

5.94   Schematic $p_b'1m$

$p_b'1m$

Similar to class $p_b'm$ is coloring $p_b'1m$ (Figure 5.94), except that here the colors are preserved as the units translate along the mirror axes. Color reversals occur in the other direction, across alternate mirror axes.

A clear example is found on the lower section of a Basketmaker bag from northeast Arizona (Figure 5.95). Here the colors are preserved vertically, but are reversed horizontally across alternate mirror axes.

Another example is on a Tapa cloth panel (Figure 5.96), on which hanging black and white triangles are suspended over two-pronged shapes of the opposite colors. The arrangement of white and black triangles is the same as that of the gray and black of the previous example, but instead of the neutral background of the Basket-maker bag, we have complementary shapes whose colors make them an integral part of the pattern.

5.95   Woven bag, Basketmaker, Northeast Arizona. From Tanner 1976, fig. 3.14a.

5.96   Section of a tapa (Rijksmuseum Kröller-Müller, Otterlo, The Netherlands)

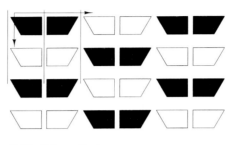

5.97   Schematic *c′m*

5.98   Wall panel, Museum of the Count of Biscari, Catania, Sicily. From Speltz 1914, pl. 22. Redrawn by C. Sudekum.

c′m

In this coloring of *pm* the colors are reversed across alternate mirror axes which run in one direction (vertical in Figure 5.97). Additionally, the colors are reversed as the units are translated in this same direction or perpendicular to it.

A clear example is a decoration from the Museum of the Count of Biscari at Catania, Sicily (Figure 5.98). Color reversals occur across alternate vertical mirror axes and in translations in two directions. Another interesting example is found on a wool sampler from mid-nineteenth-century America (Figure 5.99) where the mirror axes are diagonal.

5.99   Sampler, Berlin Woolworks, mid-nineteenth century, American (Helen L. Allen Textile Collection, University of Wisconsin, Madison, no. EAE-137)

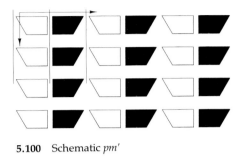

5.100   Schematic *pm'*

5.101   Cloth swatch, France. From Persoz 1846(4), no. 301. Photo by the Los Angeles County Museum of Art.

pm'

In this coloring of *pm* (Figure 5.100) reversal occurs across all the mirror reflection axes. There are no color reversals as the units are translated in either direction.

This is most easily seen on a cloth swatch from a mid-nineteenth-century treatise on textiles (Figure 5.101). Colors are reversed across mirror axes which run vertically (in the orientation here), both bisecting and passing between V-shaped units.

Another example is found on a late nineteenth-century jar from Acoma Pueblo (Figure 5.102). Here the mirror reflection axes run vertically and separate two mirror halves of each isosceles triangle; one side is solid, the other hatched. (We ignore the black ovoid units between each solid/ hatched triangle.)

5.102   Polychrome jar, ca. 1870, Acoma Pueblo, New Mexico. Courtesy of the School of American Research Collections in the Museum of New Mexico (no. 8073/12). Photo by A. Taylor.

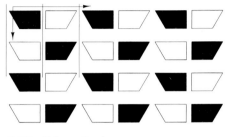

5.103   Schematic $p_b'g$

$p_b'g$

In this *pm* coloring the colors reverse across all mirror axes as well as by translations along the mirror axes (Figure 5.103).

A beautiful example of this color class appears on the main field of design of a Chancay-style breechcloth from the central coast of Peru (Figure 5.104). In the upper area of each rectangle the stepped corner triangles alternate colors as they reflect across all vertical mirror axes and as they translate vertically along these axes.

5.104   Panel, loincloth, Chancay style, A.D. 1200–1500, Peru (The Textile Museum, Washington, D.C., no. 1960.6.2)

cm

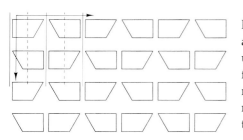

5.105   Schematic *cm*

In *cm* patterns (Figure 5.105) there are again mirror reflections, but since the units of design are offset, glide reflection axes are introduced between mirror reflection axes. (Mirror axes are marked by solid lines and glide reflection axes are marked by dashed lines.)

A straightforward example is on the tenon base of a bronze Persian gargoyle (Figure 5.106). (On the neck is a

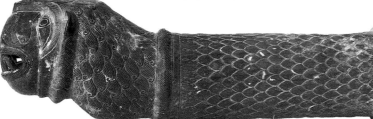

5.106   Bronze gargoyle, Persia (Avery Brundage Collection, Asian Art Museum of San Francisco, no. B61 B10+)

simulated mane arranged in a *p1* net.) A very similar pattern is the hemispherically shaped incised design on the robe of a Japanese netsuke (Figure 5.107). The *cm* arrangement is frequently seen on decorated fabrics and wallpaper such as this mid-nineteenth-century wallpaper designed and hand painted by Owen Jones (Figure 5.108). Mirror reflection axes pass vertically through each circular floral unit; vertical glide axes run between the floral units.

The wood carving from the Bamum tribe, Cameroon, is a reminder that sculptured artifacts often have repeated patterns (Figure 5.109). The mirrors axes pass vertically through the centers of the faces.

5.108   Hand printed wallpaper, 1874, designed by Owen Jones (Victoria and Albert Museum, London)

5.107   Netsuke, Japan (California Academy of Sciences, San Francisco, no. 429-44). Photo by C. Thomas.

5.109   Wood vessel, Bamum, Cameroon (Musée Royal de l'Afrique Centrale, Tervuren, Belgium, no. R.G.68.7.109)

$p'_c m$

Of the three colorings of *cm*, perhaps this class occurs most often. There are no color reversals across the mirror reflection axes. Color reversals occur along the glide axes which pass vertically (in the schematic drawing, Figure 5.110) halfway between the mirror axes.

This arrangement appears on a stylized floral pattern (Figure 5.111) where the vertical rows alternate black and white units. Here, moving vertically along the glide axes, the white units move into black units, then black units move back into the white units, and so forth. A similar arrangement is seen on a late nineteenth-century American pillow cover (Figure 5.112), where blue and red flowers change colors along vertical glide axes.

Another example is a very simple floor tiling (Figure 5.113) which is a coloring of a *p6m* grid. Note that the mirror axes are on the diagonal in this orientation.

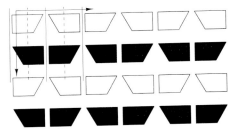

5.110   Schematic $p'_c m$

5.111   Design adapted from velvet and satin hanging, sixteenth century, Italy. From Christie 1929, fig. 248.

cm'

In this coloring of *cm* color reversals occur across the mirror axes, and also as the units are moved by glide reflections (Figure 5.114).

For example, consider a slightly deceptive pattern on a nineteenth-century sampler (Figure 5.115). We can see that the upper half of each square is black, the lower half gray. The mirror axes pass *horizontally*, with color reversals across them. (No vertical reflection exists here since there is a dark line along only the right edges of two sides of each square unit.) The glide axes in this pattern are also horizontal, and glide reflections along them interchange the upper and lower colors of the square units.

The Byzantine floor tiling (Figure 5.116) has a complex three dimensional appearance, but careful inspection shows the *cm'* coloring of this

5.112   Sampler, pillowcase cover, late nineteenth century, American. Courtesy of the Margaret Woodbury Strong Museum, Rochester (no. 80.481). Photo by H. Bickelhaupt.

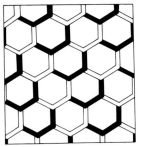

5.113   Floor tile, San Giovanni in Laterano, Rome. From Watt 1848, fig. 4. Redrawn by A. Pertschuk.

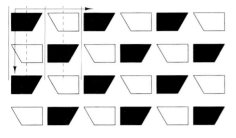

5.114   Schematic *cm'*

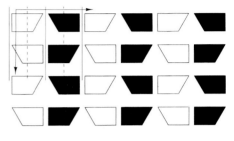

5.118   Schematic $p'_c g$

pattern. The mirror reflection and glide reflection axes run diagonally from upper left to lower right. The two colors which reverse are "striped" and white. All the rest is background.

A somewhat distorted example is on a fragment of a Hawaiian tapa (Figure 5.117). For exact superposition, each of the triangles should be perfectly isosceles in shape. Here, due to the irregular shape of the triangles, the mirror line which bisects each triangle does not pass exactly from mid-base to apex. Nevertheless, the intention of the artist seems to be clear: color reversals occur across vertical mirror reflection axes and along vertical glide axes.

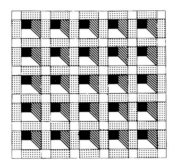

5.116   Marble floor mosaic, Byzantine. From Speltz 1914, pl.5, no. 6. Redrawn by A. Pertschuk.

$p'_c g$

This coloring of *cm* has color reversals across the mirror axes but not along the glide reflection axes (Figure 5.118).

In our invented example (Figure 5.119) the units are bisected by vertical mirror axes across which the colors are reversed. However, movement along vertical glide axes between the units preserves colors.

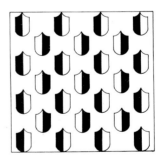

5.119   Invented design by D. Crowe. Redrawn by A. Pertschuk.

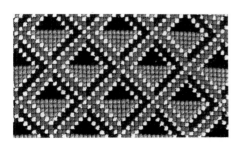

5.115   Sampler, Berlin woolworks, 1881, American (Helen L. Allen Textile Collection, The University of Wisconsin, Madison, no. EAE-690)

5.117   Tapa, Hawaii (Bishop Museum, Honolulu, no. D2400)

5.2.2 Patterns with 180° Rotations

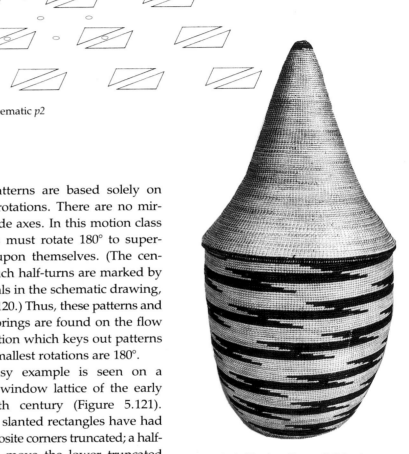

5.120   Schematic *p2*

p2

These patterns are based solely on twofold rotations. There are no mirror or glide axes. In this motion class the units must rotate 180° to superimpose upon themselves. (The centers of such half-turns are marked by small ovals in the schematic drawing, Figure 5.120.) Thus, these patterns and their colorings are found on the flow chart section which keys out patterns whose smallest rotations are 180°.

An easy example is seen on a Chinese window lattice of the early nineteenth century (Figure 5.121). Here the slanted rectangles have had their opposite corners truncated; a half-turn will move the lower truncated corners to the upper truncated corners.

5.122   Coiled basket, Burundi (Musée Royal de l'Afrique Centrale, Tervuren, Belgium, no. 41588)

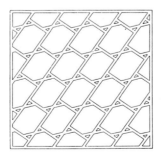

5.121   Lattice from painting. A.D. 1825, China. From Dye 1974, Y13.

The problem of differentiating the design and the background (also called the ground) often arises, particularly where identity in shape of the design and background may confuse the color classification. If the shape of the design is different from the shape of the background, it is a one-color pattern. If the units and the background are the same shape, then it is a two-color pattern.

We attempt to clarify this problem with two examples on baskets, since it is possible to count the rows of coils or the twining stitches and thereby accurately test for identity in shape. On a Burundi basket (Figure 5.122) there are seven coils of white background for every four coils in each black parallelogram unit. Likewise, on the quiver (Figure 5.123), the white space between the double rows of elongated black zigzags is much wider than the units themselves. For this reason, both of these are examples of the one-color pattern *p2*.

We frequently encounter patterns where the symmetry of the underlying structure is different from the symmetry of the elaborated design. The design symmetry is often reduced or changed because of motif elaborations and colorings. The underlying symmetry of the design structure on this Acoma Pueblo jar (Figure 5.124) is *p4m*. (Despite the slight distortion due to the globular shape of the jar, we consider the underlying structure to be a grid of squares). However, the artist added diagonal lines in half the squares and triangular spirals in the other half. The diagonals and the spirals cancel the vertical and horizontal reflections of the *p4m* structure, and the spirals further cancel all the diagonal reflections. Thus the symmetry of the final design, after all element elaborations are added, is *p2*.

5.124   Ceramic jar, ca. 1950, Acoma Pueblo, New Mexico (California Academy of Sciences, San Francisco, no. 370-24) Photo by C. Thomas.

5.123   Twined basket quiver, Klamath/ Modoc, Oregon/California (California Academy of Sciences, San Francisco, no. 389-565). Photo by C. Thomas.

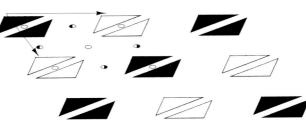

5.125   Schematic $p'_b 2$

$p'_b 2$

In this color class of $p2$ (Figure 5.125) the color reversals occur around alternate half-turn centers. (In our schematic drawings, ovals indicating such color reversing centers are colored half black and half white.) It is most easily seen on patterns where units having twofold symmetry alternate colors among rows.

On an Achomawi hat (Figure 5.126) and on a pre-Columbian Ica Valley vessel (Figure 5.127) the colors reverse as the units translate horizontally but are preserved as they translate vertically.

On the Javanese batik (Figure 5.128) colors reverse as the units translate diagonally from upper left to lower right but are preserved as they translate in the other diagonal direction, lower left to upper right. Also diagonally arranged, but less apparent because of the curvature of the basket, is the $p'_b 2$ coloring of a Tlingit rattle-top basket (Figure 5.129).

5.126   Twined basket hat, Achomawi, California (California Academy of Sciences, San Francisco, no. 370-779). Photo by C. Thomas.

5.127   Ceramic dish, Ica 3c, Chulpaca, Peru (Lowie Museum of Anthropology, University of California, Berkeley, no. 4-4285)

5.128   Detail, Cotton batik, Surakarta, Java. From Fischer 1979, 46, no. 21 (Coll. Beverly Latin). Photo by G. Prince.

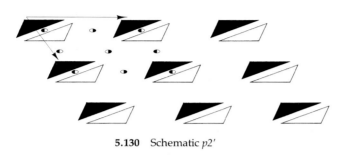

5.130   Schematic *p2′*

p2′

This coloring of *p2* has color reversals around all twofold rotation centers (Figure 5.130).

These *p2′* patterns are found, for example, in half of the rectangles on a twentieth-century Acoma Pueblo jar (Figure 5.131). Each of these rectangles has been subdivided into smaller rectangles and these have been divided diagonally and one of the halves colored black. A half-turn superimposes each black right triangle onto a white right triangle, thus reversing the colors.

5.131   Black-on-white ceramic bowl by Lucy Lewis, ca. 1960, Acoma Pueblo, New Mexico (Museum of New Mexico, no. 49555/12). Photo by A. Taylor.

5.129   Twined basket, Tlingit (California Academy of Sciences, San Francisco, no. 91-33). Photo by C. Thomas.

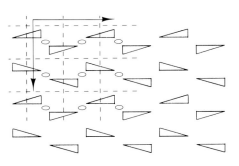

5.132   Schematic *pgg*

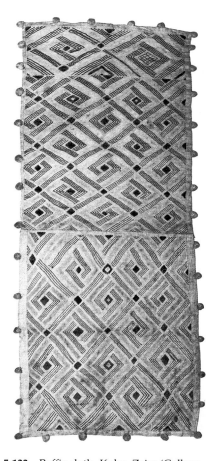

5.133   Raffia cloth, Kuba, Zaire (College Museum, Hampton Institute, no. 11.1654). Photo by Reuben Burrell.

pgg

This pattern and its two colorings have glide axes at right angles to each other (Figure 5.132). There are twofold rotation centers between (but not on) the glide axes and in many examples they are at the centers of, as well as between, the design units.

This motion class is easy to see on a Kuba raffia cloth (Figure 5.133). A 180° turn about the center of a black square moves one hooked line into another. There are also twofold centers between any two horizontally placed or vertically placed sets of hooked units. The glide axes run both vertically and horizontally between the rows of hooked lines. (We note the irregularity of the center row of open squares as opposed to the other rows of solid squares, but have chosen this pattern because of its simplicity.)

When ordinary over-under weaving (class *p4g*) is distorted in one direction, the resulting pattern is *pgg*. This is illustrated by the long striped parallelograms of the Yombe palm leaf mat of Figure 5.134. If these were rectangles, meeting at right angles, the pattern would be *p4g*. As it is, there are half-turns about the center of each striped parallelogram as well as about the centers of the rhombuses between them. The glide axes run horizontally and vertically between, but not through, these centers. (We are ignoring the slightly irregular designs in these rhombuses.)

We illustrate class *pgg* with two other patterns from the American Southwest which have hooked lines moving in opposite directions on alternate glide axes. The easiest to see

5.134   Mat, Yombe (Musée Royal de l'Afrique Centrale, Tervuren, Belgium, no. 53.74.1326)

5.135 Ceramic pitcher, Little Colorado white ware, Arizona (Museum of Northern Arizona, no. 1116/A.1146). Photo by D. Crowe.

5.136 Wool rug, ca. 1940, Navajo (California Academy of Sciences, San Francisco, no. 370-570). Photo by C. Thomas.

is on a Little Colorado white ware pitcher (Figure 5.135). A more elaborate version, which contains the minimum number of axes for a two-dimensional pattern, is on a Navajo rug (Figure 5.136). A single glide axis runs vertically up the center of the rug, although six glide axes run horizontally between the sets of double hooks. Presumably, since the pattern is not truncated except by the edge of the rug, two more vertical glide axes would run up the two side edges.

On the Navajo rug the interlocking hooks are of different colors. This is a one-color pattern, however, because the two hooks are different shapes. Black hooks can only superimpose on other black hooks and white hooks on white hooks. (Also noted, but overlooked in classification, is the imperfection in one hook in the center of the rug. It lacks the second bend that is present on all the other hooks.)

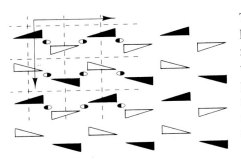

5.137   Schematic *pgg'*

5.138   Detail, raffia cloth, Kuba, Zaire (College Museum, Hampton Institute, no. 11.1658). Photo by Reuben Burrell.

pgg'

There are two colorings of *pgg. Pgg'* has color reversals along glide axes moving in one direction, which is vertical in Figure 5.137, and color preservations along the glide axes moving in the other direction. Color reversals also occur around all half-turn centers.

Two almost identical designs show this coloring clearly: a Kuba raffia cloth (Figure 5.138) and each of the three vertical bands on a Peruvian bag (Figure 5.139). On each the triangular units move along vertical glide reflection axes and maintain their colors. Colors are reversed along the horizontal glide axes.

On a Zapotec wall frieze (Figure 5.140) the recessed part of the carving is the reverse (in shape and color) of the raised pattern, and the recessed and raised areas are interchanged by glide reflections in both diagonal directions. It is easier to see the *pgg'* by turning the pattern 45° so the glide axes appear to be vertical and horizontal, as in the preceding examples.

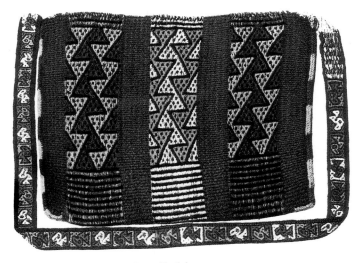

5.139   Wool bag, Peru. From Perleberg n.d. Photo by S. Middleton.

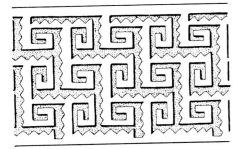

5.140   Incised wall mosaic, Zapotec, Mexico. From Appleton 1950, pl. 52.

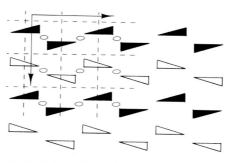

5.141   Schematic *pg′g′*

5.142   Invented design

5.143   Tapa, Samoa. From Bossert 1955, pl. 30. Redrawn by C. Sudekum.

pg′g′

The second coloring of *pgg* does not have color reversals around the two-fold rotation centers, but there are color reversals along the glide axes running in both directions (Figure 5.141).

An easy case to see is the common weaving pattern drawn in Figure 5.142. There are half-turns about the center of each rectangle. A more complex version appears on a Samoan tapa cloth (Figure 5.143). It appears to be a three-color design, but the white occurs twice as frequently and so is background. It also appears similar to the *pmg* zigzag patterns, but here the black parallelograms can only move along glide axes into the dotted parallelograms.

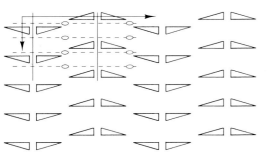

5.144   Schematic *pmg*

pmg

This pattern has both mirror reflections—which are vertical in Figure 5.144—and twofold rotations. Glide reflection axes pass between the units, perpendicular to the mirror axes. Rotation centers lie on the glide axes, midway between mirror axes. The most recognizable form of this pattern is a series of zigzags.

This pattern is seen on the wide band around the center of a basketry casket from the Lower Congo (Figure 5.145). The mirror axes run horizontally, bisecting the V-shaped units. Glide axes run vertically; half of them run between the open ends of the V-shaped units, and the other half run through the closed ends. There are half-turns about points on the glide axes, midway between units. About these centers, the central row of units rotates 180° into the upper or lower row.

5.145   Basket casket, Lower Congo (Musée Royal de l'Afrique Centrale, Tervuren, Belgium, no. 35654).

Another example of this pattern, also a discontinuous zigzag, is found on a Samoan tapa cloth (Figure 5.146). We orient this section of the cloth here so the mirror axes run vertically between the slanted black oval units. Each oval unit can rotate 180° about a point at its center; additionally, a twofold center halfway between two ovals in the same vertical column rotates one to the other.

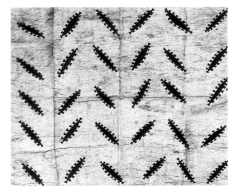

5.146   Detail, tapa, Samoa (California Academy of Sciences, San Francisco, no. 437-1). Photo by C. Thomas.

Another example is on a mosaic pavement from Ravenna (Figure 5.147). The mirror reflection lines are oriented vertically. Although there are two colors in the mosaic, this is not a two-color design since the units of different colors have different shapes; i.e., a white unit cannot be superimposed on a gray unit.

A *pmg* pattern with horizontal mirror axes is found on a Hawaiian water gourd (Figure 5.148). Although the rows are spread out, the alignment is

5.148   Water gourd, Hawaii (California Academy of Sciences, San Francisco, no. 458-451). Photo by C. Thomas.

5.147   Mosaic tiling, Palazzo di Teodorico, Ravenna, Italy. From Berti 1976, pl. 34, no. 39.

5.149   Raffia cloth, Kuba, Zaire (College Museum, Hampton Institute, no. 11.1665). Photo by Reuben Burrell.

consistent enough to classify it as a two-dimensional pattern.

A slightly tricky example is the *pmg* pattern on the Kuba raffia cloth in Figure 5.149. In this orientation there are mirror axes running vertically through the midpoints of the angled units. At first there appear to be horizontal mirror axes also. However, careful inspection shows that a line through the black diamonds between two angled units would *not* bisect adjacent angled units with horizontal reflection of the parts. Glide axes run horizontally between the rows of black diamonds. Thus the whole pattern has only *pmg* symmetry.

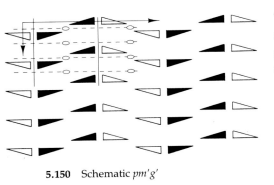

5.150   Schematic *pm'g'*

5.151   Design on bifurcated burden basket, Pueblo III, New Mexico/Arizona. Redrawn by D. Crowe.

pm'g'

These patterns have color reversals across the mirror axes and along the glide axes, but not about the twofold centers (Figure 5.150).

One example appears on a Basketmaker bifurcated basket (Figure 5.151). Here the color reversal does not occur about either the rotation centers between the facing sets of three triangles, or those that lie between the points of the larger, same-colored triangles. Reversals do occur across horizontal mirror axes that run between the bases of the larger triangles, and along the vertical glide axes which run, for example, through the apexes of these triangles.

5.152   Quilt, "Robbing Peter To Pay Paul," ca. 1850, American. Redrawn by A. Pertschuk.

We illustrate also a rather difficult pattern in Figure 5.152 and will use the flow chart to show its *pm'g'* coloring. The pattern, "Robbing Peter to Pay Paul," is a late nineteenth-century American quilt design. It appears to have fourfold rotations about the centers of the large squares, but because quarter rounds occur in only two of the four corners of the small squares, such quarter-turns are not possible. There are, however, half-turns about the centers of these small squares. Thus, we turn to the section of the two-dimensional flow chart where the smallest rotation consistent with color is 180°. We ask, "Is there a reflection consistent with color?" and find that the answer is "yes" because across the horizontal axes bisecting the large squares all mirror reflections reverse colors. No reflections are possible across the vertical axes because the quarter circles in the smaller squares would not superimpose correctly. (Half-turns about the centers of the large squares are impossible for the same reason.) Twofold rotation is only possible about the centers of the small squares and the horizontal rectangular spaces which separate the large squares. In the rotations about these points it is clear that no color reversals occur, and so we answer "no" to the next question. We have already determined that only horizontal reflections are allowed in this pattern, so the answer to the next question is also "no." Finally, the mirror reflections which are present always reverse colors. This leads us to answer "no" to the final question, "Is there a reflection which preserves colors?" and gives us the classification *pm'g'*.

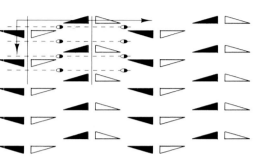

5.153   Schematic *pm'g*

5.154   Section, raffia cloth, Kasai region, Zaire (Musée Royal de l'Afrique Centrale, Tervuren, Belgium, no. R.G.45077)

pm'g

This coloring of *pmg* has color reversals across all mirror axes and around all rotation centers, but there is no color reversal along the glide axes nor as the units translate along the mirror axes (Figure 5.153).

The example we show here, a section of a Kasai region raffia cloth (Figure 5.154), is complex so we key it out using the flow chart. To determine the smallest rotation consistent with color we check to see which points of rotation either reverse all colors or preserve all colors. Although the pattern is composed of squares subdivided by diagonals, the common corner of any set of four squares is not a rotation center because the triangles formed by the diagonal lines do not superimpose when turns are executed. However, a half-turn about the center of a small square will superimpose the triangles correctly, and so we choose the 180° section of the flow chart.

To answer the question, "Is there a reflection consistent with color?" we check along the mirror reflection axes between the squares (vertical in this orientation of the raffia cloth) and find that across any axis, all colors are reversed. Our "yes" answer leads us to the next question, "Is there a half-turn which reverses colors?" Again the answer is "yes" since each 180° rotation will put a black triangular half of a square on a white triangular half. Since there are mirror reflections in only one direction, we answer "no" and move to the next question, "Is there a reflection which preserves colors?" We have already seen that colors always reverse across the vertical mirror axes, so our "no" answer leads us to the final question, "Is there a half-turn which preserves colors?" We have already answered that, in effect, in the second question, so our "no" response leads us to the classification *pm'g*.

Our other example, the Peruvian textile of Figure 5.155, is structurally the same as the preceding example; the stepped units substitute for the triangles of the previous pattern. Color reversals occur across the vertical mirror axes between the stepped units and around the half-turn centers which lie between stepped units of opposite colors. The glide reflections, in horizontal lines through the two-fold centers, all preserve colors.

5.155   Section, cotton textile, pre-Columbian Peru. From Perleberg n.d., pl. 14. Photo by S. Middleton.

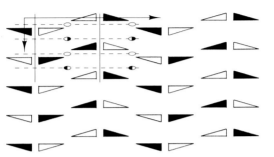

5.156   Schematic *p'ᵦgg*

5.157   Lidded basket, Lower Congo (Musée Royal de l'Afrique Centrale, Tervuren, Belgium, no. 40076)

p'ᵦgg

This coloring of *pmg* has color reversals across all mirror lines, around alternate rotation centers (often between design units of opposite colors), and along alternate glide axes (Figure 5.156).

On a cylindrical basket from the Lower Congo (Figure 5.157), the zigzags seem to move vertically; at each turn the line changes color. Actually, the bends in the zigzags are marked by horizontal mirror reflection axes across which the colors reverse. This same feature is seen on a segment of Hawaiian tapa (Figure 5.158).

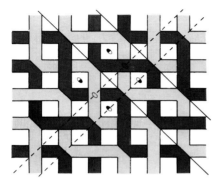

5.159   Rug, Godfather's Pizza Parlor, Madison, Wisconsin. Redrawn by D. Crowe.

5.158   Section, tapa, Hawaii (Bishop Museum, Honolulu, no. 7782)

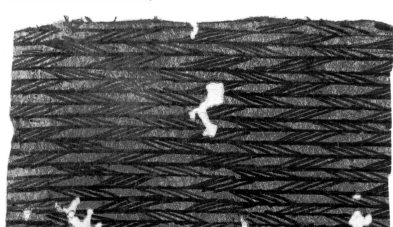

Harder to see is this coloring on a contemporary rug (Figure 5.159). Mirror axes run diagonally from upper left to lower right, diagonally bisecting half of the white squares. Colors reverse along alternate glide axes, which run perpendicular to the mirror axes and bisect the same squares in the opposite direction. Along the remaining glide axes, parallel to the others and bisecting the remaining white squares, colors are preserved. Half-turns about the centers of the latter squares reverse colors, while half-turns about the centers of the Z-shaped figures preserve colors.

pmg'

In this coloring of *pmg* there are no color reversals across the mirror axes, or by translation in any direction. Color reversals occur in all half-turns and all glide reflections (Figure 5.160).

A very clear and typical example of this class is seen on four separate bands of a mid-twentieth-century Navajo rug from the Crystal, Arizona, area (Figure 5.161).

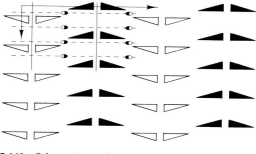

5.160   Schematic *pmg'*

5.161   Rug, vegetal dye, ca. 1957, Crystal, Navajo (California Academy of Sciences, San Francisco, no. 370-672). Photo by C. Thomas.

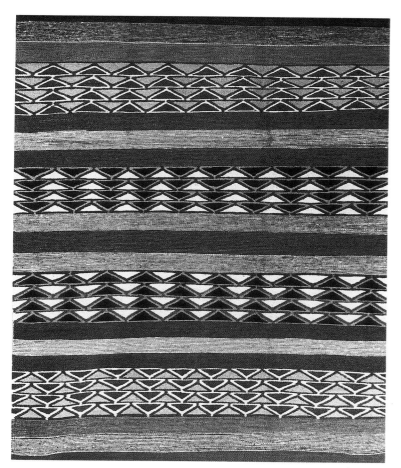

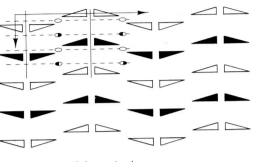

5.162   Schematic $p'_b mg$

$p'_b mg$

This last coloring of *pmg* is perhaps the simplest and easiest to see, with alternating zigzag rows of different colors. In the orientation here, horizontal translations do not change colors, nor do reflections across vertical mirror axes. Half-turns around centers between the rows reverse colors, and vertical translations reverse colors (Figure 5.162).

For example, the banana-fiber skirt from the Caroline Islands (Figure 5.179, below) has two bands of design, one of which is a black-and-white zigzag pattern. We note here that between each of the zigzag lines there is a thinner checked line. Since the checked lines occur twice as often, and since there are differently shaped (i.e., they are thinner), there is no motion which will cause them to exchange with the solid lines. They must therefore be considered background to the black-and-white zigzag pattern, and they do not affect the determination of the color symmetry class. Tiling from a Cairo mosque (Figure 5.163) also displays this color symmetry.

5.163   Tile, Mihrab of Mosque of El-Mu'ayyad, early fifteenth century, Cairo, Egypt. From Christie 1929, fig. 70.

pmm

This pattern class and its five colored forms have two sets of mirror reflection axes, perpendicular to one another. Centers of twofold rotation are located at the intersections of the mirror axes (Figure 5.164). The motifs will often be rectangles or diamonds or ovals, which admit both reflections and half-turns.

This layout is very easy to see in the double-ended hooked units on an Asmat shield (Figure 5.165). The hooked units have centers of twofold rotation about their centers (at the intersection of the mirror axes) as well as on the mirror axes between the units. The rectangles on a Klickitat carrying basket (Figure 5.166) are also easy to see as they are outlined in white imbricated stitching. It may at first seem as if the classification should be *cmm*, since the background rectangles appear to be the same shape as the design. However, careful inspection shows that a brown vertical stripe of cedar bark background separates the *pmm* units, unlike the white imbricated strips joining the *pmm* units along the vertical axes.

A section of a Samoan tapa cloth in Figure 5.167 has large diamond-shaped units. Here the alignment is not quite perfect, but given the stamping technique such irregularities are to be expected. Twofold centers lie at the middle of every diamond figure as well as on the mirror axes between them. A difficult *pmm* pattern is on a Cashinahua carrying basket (Figure 5.168). Tilt the illustration diagonally to see the double T-shaped units laid out in a rectangular grid.

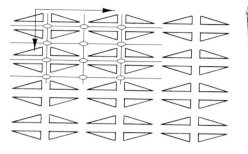

5.164   Schematic *pmm*

5.166   Imbricated carrying basket, Klickitat (California Academy of Sciences, San Francisco, no. 370-876). Photo by C. Thomas.

5.167   Detail, tapa, Samoa (California Academy of Sciences, San Francisco, no. 519-4). Photo by C. Thomas.

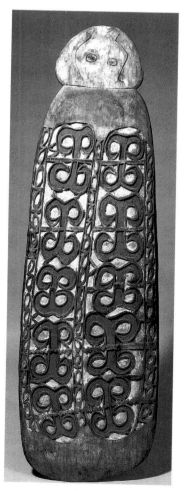

5.168   Plaited basket, "kuki" type, Cashinahua, Peru (Haffenreffer Museum, Brown University, no. 69-10173)

5.165   Wood shield, twentieth century, Asmat, New Guinea. Permission of the Fine Arts Museums of San Francisco (no. 77.42).

Two very deceptive examples of *pmm* patterns, also with diamond-shaped units, are found on Navajo textiles. We discuss them here to highlight some of the important factors to consider when classifying patterns. The first is a mid-twentieth-century rug (Figure 5.169). At first it may appear to be a two-color pattern, but careful scrutiny of the shape of the motifs belies this initial impression. In the center of each dark diamond there is a single hourglass; in the center of each white (background) area there are two hourglass figures connected by two isosceles triangles. There can be no color reversals because these different shapes cannot be superimposed. Given this, we see the pattern as two vertical rows of dark diamonds bisected by a grid of horizontal and vertical mirror reflection axes, with other mirror axes halfway between these. That the pattern continues beyond the solid border is indicated by the partial black units on the white ground which have been truncated. (The solid border is a twentieth-century addition for white consumer tastes. More traditional Navajo blankets, such as the Chief's blanket in Figure 2.16 above, are typified by two-dimensional designs which run right to the borders.)

5.169   Wool rug, ca. 1930, Navajo (California Academy of Sciences, San Francisco, no. 370-638). Photo by C. Thomas.

The second Navajo example is a rug woven in the Tis Nas Pas area of northeast Arizona in the 1930s. We show only a section of this large textile here (Figure 5.170). Again we must examine the shapes of the motifs carefully. It almost appears as if, in this case, the black diamond and the gray (background) diamond are identically shaped but differently colored units, making this a two-color pattern. But close inspection reveals that while the black diamond units are joined along the vertical mirror axis by a small diamond, the gray units are joined by a much broader ground gray area which could only become a diamond if the rows of black units were moved closer together. Here the spacing is just different enough to disallow a two-color classification. It is simply a one-color *pmm* pattern.

5.170 Detail, wool rug, ca. 1930, Tis Nas Pas, Navajo (California Academy of Sciences, San Francisco, no. 370-587). Photo by C. Thomas.

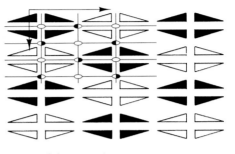

5.171   Schematic *c'mm*

5.172   Panel, textile, Late Intermediate, Central Coast Peru. Permission of the Fine Arts Museums of San Francisco (no. 1974.3.12).

c'mm

There are five colorings of *pmm*. The easiest to detect is class *c'mm*, where units alternate colors in both directions, checkerboard style. Thus, color reversals occur around alternate two-fold centers and across alternate mirror axes (Figure 5.171).

An elaborate version appears on a pre-Columbian Peruvian textile (Figure 5.172), where each rectangle has a figured oval motif in the center. Thus, colors are preserved across the mirror axes bisecting the rectangles, and around twofold centers at the centers and corners of the rectangles. Colors are reversed across mirror axes and around twofold centers between the units.

Another, more complex example is taken from a tiling from the Church of San Lorenzo in Rome (Figure 5.173). Examine the pattern on the diagonal to see the checkerboard alternation of the dotted and hatched elongated diamonds. In this example, all the black figures and the underlying white areas are background. (Although the black diamonds have the same shape as the dotted and hatched units of the pattern, they occur twice as often and therefore cannot exchange with either.)

5.173   Tiling, Church of San Lorenzo, Rome. From Watt 1848, pl. 9, fig. 2. Redrawn by A. Pertschuk.

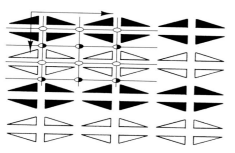

5.174   Schematic *p'$_b$mm*

p'$_b$mm

This coloring of *pmm* has color reversals only across alternate mirror axes in one of the two perpendicular directions (horizontal in Figure 5.174). Color reversals occur only about the twofold centers lying on these alternate axes.

This coloring is shown in a pattern from the ceiling of the tomb of Ay at Tell El Amarna (Figure 5.175). The design has a *p4m* square structural grid but the coloring admits only *p'$_b$mm* symmetry. As in Figure 5.174, colors are preserved across all vertical mirror axes. The color reversals occur across horizontal axes between the units. Although the center flowers have a varying number of petals and thus the mirror axes may not precisely subdivide the flowers, we classify the overall arrangement of colors in this pattern as *p'$_b$mm*.

pmm'

This coloring of *pmm* has color reversals across only one of the two sets of perpendicular mirror reflection axes (horizontal in Figure 5.176). It differs from the previous color class because it also has color reversals around all the twofold centers.

We see an example on a section of a turn-of-the-century Navajo blanket from the Crystal, Arizona, area (Figure 5.177). In this orientation vertical mirror axes bisect continuous T-shaped units as well as pass between them. Colors are reversed across these axes. But colors are preserved across the horizontal mirror axes which bisect, as well as pass between, the T-projections.

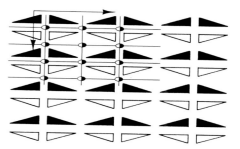

5.176   Schematic *pmm'*

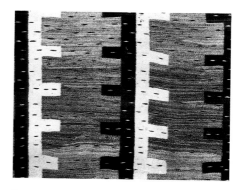

5.177   Detail, wool blanket, ca. 1900, Crystal, Navajo (California Academy of Sciences, San Francisco, no. 370-694). Photo by C. Thomas.

5.175   Detail, painted ceiling, rock tomb Tell El Amarna, Egypt. From Speltz 1915, pl. 5. Redrawn by C. Sudekum.

p$'_b$gm

This color class of *pmm* has color reversals across all of the mirror axes in one direction (horizontal in Figure 5.178) and across half of them in the other direction. Colors are preserved about twofold centers lying on the

latter axes, and are reversed about the others.

On the two end bands on a Caroline Islands banana-fiber skirt (Figure 5.179) we have another case of an apparent three-color pattern. But if we do not consider the checked diamonds, but only the black and white triangles, the rows of two-color diamonds are clear. Viewed from the selvage edge, color reversals occur across all horizontal mirror axes, both inside and between the diamonds. Color reversals occur across only half of the vertical mirror axes: those which separate the diamonds, not those which bisect them. Half-turns about the centers of the diamonds will reverse colors everywhere.

pm'm'

In this *pmm* coloring, colors reverse across all mirror axes, while colors are preserved in all half-turns (Figure 5.180).

A mosaic design from Pompeii (Figure 5.181) and a pattern from Ger-

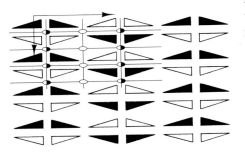

5.178   Schematic *p$'_b$gm*

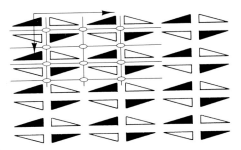

5.180   Schematic *pm'm'*

5.179   Woman's skirt, Fais Island, Caroline Islands. Courtesy of the Peabody Museum of Salem (no. E5569). Photo by M. W. Sexton.

many (Figure 5.182) show how color changes across all mirror axes produce a complex sequence of color reversals. To facilitate classification, first find the points of intersection of the mirror axes. About these twofold centers the colors do not change. Then check for color preservations or reversals across the mirror axes passing through these points. (Note that in the Pompeii mosaic the solid black and white units are all background.)

5.181   Tile mosaic, Pompeii, Italy. From Speltz 1915, pl. 49. Redrawn by A. Pertschuk.

5.182   German design. From Schleifer 1968, pl. 8. Redrawn by A. Pertschuk.

cmm

This structure class is similar to *pmm* except that the units are offset so that glide axes pass midway between the mirror axes in both directions. Additionally, twofold centers are now located on all intersections of mirror axis with mirror axis and glide axis with glide axis (Figure 5.183).

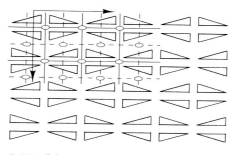

5.183   Schematic *cmm*

The layout is easily seen on the side of a carved wooden container made by the Kuba (Figure 5.184). The units are arranged in a grid which allows horizontal and vertical mirror reflections through each unit and glide axes between the units. If the units were not irregular hexagons, and if their edges were not doubled (as the vertical edges are here), then the pattern would be class *p6m*. But careful inspection shows that these features preclude sixfold rotations.

A shape commonly arranged with *cmm* symmetry is a diamond. Such diamonds are shown in Figure 5.185 on an Iroquois woven sash. Mirror axes pass through the centers of each small diamond both horizontally and vertically, while the glide axes pass midway between them.

5.184   Wooden container, Kuba, Zaire (Musée Royal de l'Afrique Centrale, Tervuren, Belgium, no. R.G.51.31.70)

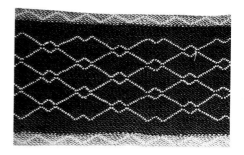

5.185   Section, beaded wool sash, Iroquois, New York. Courtesy of the Museum of the American Indian, Heye Foundation (no. 2/9675).

5.186   Wood pipe, Bamileke (Musée Royal de l'Afrique Centrale, Tervuren, Belgium, no. R.G.64.39.2)

Another shape commonly arranged to yield *cmm* symmetry is the rectangle, here shown on the stem of a Bamileke wood pipe (Figure 5.186). The long axes of the carved rectangular units are aligned vertically. It is easy to see how the mirror axes bisect the units vertically and horizontally and how horizontal glide axes lie between the raised units.

Finally we examine a fifteenth-century glazed bowl from Turkey (Figure 5.187). The *cmm* pattern in the bottom of the bowl at first appears to be two-color, but closer inspection shows that the gray units aligned horizontally are a different shape from the white units aligned vertically. Thus, these two types of units cannot be superimposed. We can choose either the white or gray units to study for classification purposes and consider the other as background. We select the white units for discussion here and note how widely separated they are, compared to the close packing on the Kuba container of Figure 5.184. These distance variations do not affect the symmetry. The offset layout still admits both mirror and glide reflection axes on horizontal and vertical axes. There are rotation centers at the corners and centers of the units; they allow superposition of the pattern with a 180° turn.

5.187   Glazed ceramic plate, fifteenth century, Turkey (The Metropolitan Museum of Art, bequest of Benjamin Altman, 1913, no. 14.40.727)

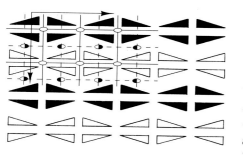

5.188   Schematic $p'_c mm$

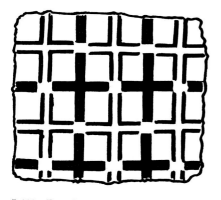

5.189   Detail, vestment in mosaic, twelfth century, Cathedral of Cefalù, Sicily. From Christie 1929, fig. 29.

$p'_c mm$

There are five colorings of *cmm*. In this coloring offset rows of units alternate colors so that no color reversals occur across the mirror axes. Color reversals occur along the glide axes and about the intersections of the glide axes (Figure 5.188). A typical, simple example is a diamond checkerboard. We illustrate four examples.

The first is a pattern from a twelfth-century church vestment (Figure 5.189). This open net makes the symmetry difficult to see. First focus on the black crosses and see that they are aligned in a perfect one-color *pmm* arrangement. The structure becomes colored when white crosses are in-serted into the rectangular spaces between the black crosses. Since the black and white crosses are the same shape, a two-colored *cmm* pattern has been generated.

Perhaps this coloring is easier to see on a late nineteenth-century sampler (Figure 5.190). Horizontal or vertical glide reflection axes move the vertical rows into one another and lead to color reversals. A similar example is on a pre-Columbian Peruvian textile fragment (Figure 5.191). The horizontal glide axes cut through the tips of the light and dark hexagons; the vertical glide axes cut through the right or left sides of these hexagons. A final ex-

5.190   Sampler, Berlin woolworks, 1881, American (Helen L. Allen Textile Collection, The University of Wisconsin, Madison, no. EAE-690)

5.191   Detail, textile, pre-Columbian, Peru. From Perleberg n.d. Photo by S. Middleton.

ample is found on a turn-of-the-century Germantown Navajo rug (Figure 5.192). At first glance it appears to be a one-color pattern, but careful inspection of the stepped squares which form the separate diamonds within the diamond net shows that the offset rows reverse black and white colors.

5.192   Germantown blanket/rug, 1890–1905, Navajo (California Academy of Sciences, San Francisco, no. 370-678). Photo by C. Thomas.

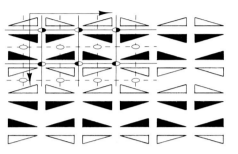

5.193   Schematic $p'_c mg$

5.194   Detail, beaded apron, Mbukushu, Botswana

$p'_c mg$

In this coloring of *cmm*, color reversals occur across only one of the two sets of mirror axes (horizontal in Figure 5.193) and across the glide axes perpendicular to that set. Color reversals occur in half-turns about the intersections of mirror axes but not about the intersections of glide axes.

A section of a woman's beaded apron from the Mbukushu of Botswana (Figure 5.194) illustrates these color changes. In this orientation the horizontal mirror axes bisect the diamonds and reverse the colors. Colors are also reversed by half-turns in the center of the diamonds, but not about the intersection of the glide axes, between the diamonds. The latter points are located in the narrow white and black zigzag spaces which separate the horizontal rows of triangles. A 180° rotation about such a point would move a white triangle into a white triangle or a black triangle into a black triangle, thus preserving colors. Colors are reversed along the vertical glide axes through these points, but not along the horizontal glide axes.

Perhaps more difficult to see is this same pattern type on a section of an inlaid floor from the Baptistery in Florence (Figure 5.195). Here the pattern is spread out, but is essentially the same diamond pattern as on the Botswana apron. The large parallelograms here correspond to the thin parallelograms making up the zigzag in the Botswana example. We will key out this pattern using the flow chart.

There are 180° rotations about the centers of the parallelograms, so we choose this section of the flow chart and look for reflections consistent with

5.195   Inlaid marble pavement, thirteenth century, baptistery, Florence, Italy. From Christie 1929, fig. 201.

color. We can answer "yes" to this question because reflection across a vertical mirror axis through the small diamonds will preserve colors. We can answer "yes" to the next question, "Is there a half-turn which reverses colors?" because rotation around the center of the small diamonds reverses colors. We also answer "yes" to the next question because across vertical mirror reflection axes all colors are preserved and along horizontal mirror axes all colors are reversed. The rows of diamonds are offset, so we must answer "no" to the next question because rotation centers are at the intersection of glide axes (that is, in the centers of the parallelograms). We answer "no" to the next question also, because we have previously seen that some mirror reflections reverse colors and some preserve colors. The final answer is "yes" because we have seen that a half-turn around a parallelogram center preserves colors. Our classification is $p'_c mg$.

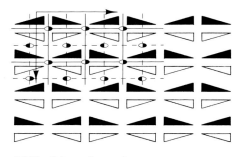

5.196   Schematic *cmm'*

cmm'

For this coloring of *cmm* there are color reversals across the mirror axes in one of the two directions in the grid (horizontal in Figure 5.196) and along the glide axes in that same direction. There are color reversals around all twofold centers on both mirror and glide axes.

Our first example is a beaded African hat (Figure 5.197). Across a vertical mirror axis through the center of a column of white and black diamonds, colors are not reversed. However, reflections across horizontal mirror lines produce color reversals. Color reversals occur about the centers of the diamonds, and at the edges of the diamonds where two diamonds are joined, i.e., at the intersections of glide axes. Color reversals occur along the horizontal glide axes but not along the vertical glide axes.

This same pattern appears on a shield from Cameroon (Figure 5.198), except that when the shield is held, the pattern is turned perpendicular to the example in Figure 5.197. Another similar pattern is on a beaded girdle from East Africa (Figure 5.199) which has vertical columns of *cmm'* patterns separated by columns of one-color diamonds.

5.197   ''Igisingo,'' beaded crown, Tutsi, Rwanda (Musée Royal de l'Afrique Centrale, Tervuren, Belgium, no. R.G.49.21.1)

5.198 Shield, Mambilla, Cameroon (Portland Art Museum, Portland, Oregon, The Paul and Clara Gebauer Collection of Cameroun Art, no. 70.10.87). Photo by A. Monner.

5.199 Beaded girdle, East Africa (Rochester Museum and Science Center, no. AE9129). Photo by D. Washburn.

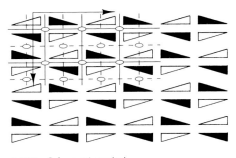

5.200 Schematic *cm'm'*

5.201 Sampler, early nineteenth century, Germany (Helen L. Allen Textile Collection, The University of Wisconsin, Madison, no. EAE-267)

cm'm'

This coloring of *cmm* has color reversals across all mirror reflection axes and along all glide reflection axes, but no color reversals around any two-fold centers (Figure 5.200).

The small parallelograms on an early nineteenth-century German sampler (Figure 5.201) are an example of this coloring. (The flowered diamonds are background here.) Colors reverse across all vertical and horizontal reflection axes and along all glide axes. However, half-turns around the centers of the diamonds do not produce color reversals. Nor are there color reversals at the intersection of the glide axes. In this example such centers are located in the middle of the small parallelograms. This coloring is also present on another very similar design, a mosaic pavement from the Roman site of Timgad in northeastern Algeria (Figure 5.202). If this example is turned 90°, it will match the sampler exactly.

An elegant pre-Columbian Peruvian tunic from the Ica Valley is shown in Figure 5.203. The underlying two-color pattern is a square checkerboard, p'_c4mm. However, the inclusion of diagonal dividers in the squares which angle in two different directions reduces the symmetry to *cm'm'*. These diagonals serve the same symmetry function as the parallelograms in the preceding two examples. Note that the dark diagonals all point the same way, and the light diagonals point the other way, exactly as did the parallelograms in the earlier example.

This classification can be confirmed by using the flow chart to key out the pattern. The diagonal dividers, which themselves have twofold symmetry, direct us to the 180° section of the flow chart. Vertical and horizontal mirror reflections all reverse colors and so are consistent with color. No half-turns, whether about the center of a square or any of its corners, reverse colors. We have found already that reflections consistently reverse the colors in two directions. We know that some rotation centers (those at the centers of the squares) are not on mirror reflection axes, because the presence of the diagonal in each square does not allow mirror reflections down the center of the squares. Finally, we know that all mirror reflections (across axes between squares) reverse colors, so we arrive at the classification *cm'm'*.

5.202   Mosaic tiling, site of Timgad, Algeria. From Germain 1969, pl. 59, no. 176.

5.203   Tunic, Inca style, Ica Valley, Peru (The Textile Museum, Washington, D.C., no. 91.147)

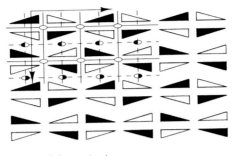

5.204   Schematic $p'_c gg$

5.205   Palm wine calabash, West Africa. From Bossert 1955, pl. 9, no. 17. Redrawn by C. Sudekum.

p'_c gg

This coloring of *cmm* has color reversals across all mirror reflection axes and about rotation centers at the intersection of glide axes. There are no color reversals produced by rotation about twofold centers on mirror reflection axes nor by glide reflection (Figure 5.204).

The pattern redrawn in Figure 5.205 illustrates this colored symmetry as found on a palm wine calabash from West Africa. If we focus on diamonds as the repeating units (although we could also focus on hourglass units), there are color reversals across both the vertical and horizontal mirror reflection axes and around twofold centers on glide axes (the midpoints of the edges of the diamonds). Glide reflections along the vertical and horizontal axes preserve colors. Colors are also preserved by half-turns about the center of each diamond, as the white triangular sections rotate 180° from the lower corner of the diamond to the opposite upper corner.

Another elegant example is on a plaited Samoan basket (Figure 5.206). The flow chart is useful for this difficult example. The first problem in this pattern is to determine the smallest rotation so that we may choose the correct section of the flow chart. It may at first appear that there is a 90° rotation about the center of each step-sided diamond. But careful inspection reveals that the "squares" (each containing one white and one black stepped unit) are not square: four

5.206   Plaited basket, Samoa (California Academy of Sciences, San Francisco, no. 145-162). Photo by C. Thomas.

plaited strips run horizontally and five run vertically. The only rotational symmetry which will move these units is 180° rotation.

In this section of the chart the first question asks, "Is there a reflection consistent with color?" (The "grain" of the plaiting is ignored in this analysis.) The answer is "yes," since reflection in a vertical or a horizontal mirror axis through one of the diamonds reverses colors everywhere. To the question, "Is there a half-turn which reverses colors?" the answer is also "yes," because rotation about the centers between the two stepped units of each square will reverse colors. The next question, "Are there reflections consistent with color in two directions?" was already answered when we found that color reversals occurred consistently across both horizontal and vertical mirror axes. Next, we note that not all twofold centers can be on reflection axes, since we found such a center along the stepped edge of two units in a square and this is not on a mirror axis. Since both horizontal and vertical mirror axes reverse colors, they have the same effect on color. Finally, since there are no reflection axes which preserve colors, the classification is $p'_c gg$.

p4

5.2.3 Patterns with 90° Rotations

This class of patterns has both two-fold and fourfold centers but no mirror reflections or glide reflections. The fourfold centers (indicated by small squares in Figure 5.207 and hereafter) are located at the center of units made up of four rotating asymmetrical parts, and at the common corner of four such units. The twofold centers are located between two fourfold units. (Remember that we use the term *twofold* to describe centers about which the *smallest* rotation is 180°, though of course all fourfold centers necessarily admit half-turns as well.) A variety of examples of this popular pattern class will be illustrated.

Perhaps easiest to see is the fourfold pattern woven into a lidded basket from Fiji (Figure 5.208). In this case the fourfold pattern is composed of four rotating white lathes inside a square of black lathes. Also rectilinear is the fourfold pattern on a painted bridge board from the Celebes (Figure 5.209). (Note that the swastikas all rotate in the same direction. When the swastikas alternate directions the result is generally a *p4g* pattern.) In this

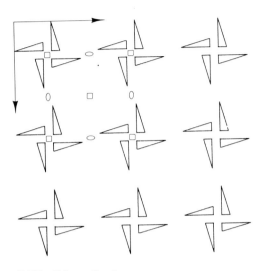

5.207   Schematic *p4*

5.208   Basket with lid, Fiji (California Academy of Sciences, San Francisco, no. 203-1). Photo by C. Thomas.

5.209   Painted bridge board, Celebes. From Bossert 1955, pl. 23. Redrawn by C. Sudekum.

5.210   Mosaic floor, House of the Porticoes, Portico of the Rivers, Antioch. From Levi 1947, pl. 98c.

pattern the fourfold centers are both in the middle of the circles and in the space between four bent arms of the rotating units. The twofold centers are between every pair of interlocked hook ends. Another example of a rectilinear *p4* pattern is found on a mosaic floor at the site of Antioch (Figure 5.210). Here we see two horizontal rows and six vertical rows of swastikas. There are quarter-turns about the center of each swastika and each black X connecting four swastikas. The twofold rotations are centered in the gray lozenge-like units.

The first of several curvilinear examples is another mosaic from Antioch (Figure 5.211), where four spirals leave circular centers and interlock with similar, adjacent units. (The motifs in the circles vary, but we focus here on the underlying structure, which is *p4*.) Fourfold centers are present in the middle of each circular unit and in the middle of each square motif between four rotating circular units.

5.211   Mosaic floor, House of the Phoenix, Antioch. From Levi 1947, pl. 135a.

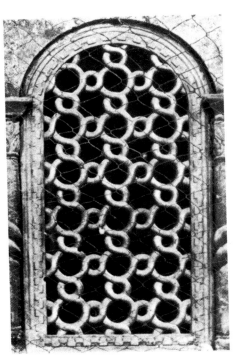

5.212 Stone window, twelfth century, west front, St. Mark's Cathedral, Venice. From Christie 1929, pl. 8.

In a sculptural medium, curvilinear *p4* appears in a twelfth-century window screen on St. Mark's in Venice (Figure 5.212). Although at first the circular motifs (not the chain link fence!) may appear to have *p4m* structure, the overlapping of the spirals as they emanate from the circle cancels any mirror reflections. Another overlapping example is seen on the lining paper of a sixteenth-century English Bible box (Figure 5.213). We note several irregularities in the overlapping sequence of the chain links on the lining paper, but thought this example was so unusual that we could not resist illustrating it. Technically, although the structure of the pattern is *p4*, the symmetry of the whole pattern is reduced to a series of translations along separate band axes because of the variation in floral motifs.

5.213 Woodblock print wallpaper lining a Bible box, late sixteenth century, England (The Metropolitan Museum of Art, Gift of J. Pierpont Morgan, no. 27.114)

p4′

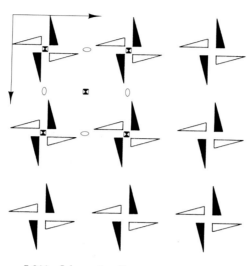

5.214   Schematic *p4′*

This coloring of *p4* has color reversals on 90° rotations about all fourfold centers but not about the twofold centers. We mark such fourfold centers by small black and white squares, as in Figure 5.214.

This coloring is shown on an Arabic pattern (Figure 5.215) where the four rotating sections in each square alternate colors. (The eight-pointed stars do not change color with rotation, and we are ignoring them here. The stars alone form a *p4m′m′* pattern.)

Another famous example of *p4′* is a drawing of lizards by M. C. Escher. The fourfold centers lie at the joins of four feet (Figure 5.216).

5.215   Wall mosaic, seventeenth century, Mosque of Ahmed el-Bordeyny, Egypt. From Prisse d'Avennes 1978, 4. Redrawn by A. Pertschuk.

5.216   "Lizards," M. C. Escher (BEELDRECHT, Amsterdam/V.A.G.A., New York, Collection Haags Gemeentemuseum, The Hague, 1981)

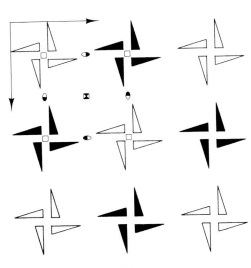

5.217   Schematic $p_c'4$

5.218   Section, quilt, "Virginia Reel," by R. Martin Smith, 1981, Madison, Wisconsin. Photo by D. Crowe.

5.219   Textile pattern, Hagia Triada, Crete. From Petrie 1974, pl. 58. Redrawn by A. Pertschuk.

$p_c'4$

A more common coloring of $p4$ is this arrangement, where each fourfold unit is a single color and color reversals occur on 90° rotations about the fourfold centers where four such rotating units meet. Rotations about the twofold centers also result in color reversals (Figure 5.217).

A very clear example is on a late twentieth-century American quilt (Figure 5.218), in which the fourfold centers which reverse colors are located where the spirals from four fourfold units interlock. (We are ignoring the fact that the black units are connected and the white ones aren't. The overall effect is certainly $p_c'4$.) Another example, a pattern from the Hagia Triada (Figure 5.219), shows how background can be part of the actual pattern. The white fourfold units are the same shape as the black fourfold units and so they rotate in two-color $p_c'4$ symmetry around the fourfold centers in the hatched region.

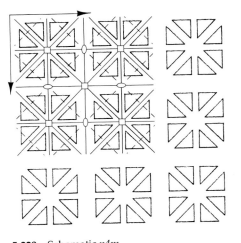

5.220   Schematic $p4m$

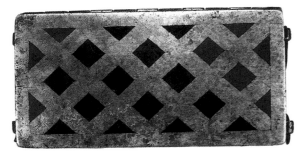

5.221   Brass betel nut box, Philippines (California Academy of Sciences, San Francisco, no. 147-42). Photo by C. Thomas.

p4m

This popular class is commonly found as a grid of squares. There are mirror axes in four directions as well as glide axes in two directions. Fourfold centers are present at the center of each square unit and at the common corner of four such units where four mirror axes intersect. Twofold centers are present at the juncture of two glide axes and two mirror axes; that is, between each pair of square units (Figure 5.220). We illustrate here a wide variety of examples of this frequently used symmetry.

To begin with the simplest examples, we show the lid of an inlaid brass betel nut box from the Philippines (Figure 5.221). Here the squares are oriented diagonally. (In this orientation it is easy to confuse a *p4m* pattern with a *cmm* pattern. The difference is that the non-square diamonds of *cmm* patterns admit reflections in only two directions, and only half-turns; the squares of *p4m* admit reflections in four directions, and 90° turns). Fourfold rotations are present about the centers of each black square as well as at the intersections of the diagonal brass stripes.

An unusual example is found on a head covering (Figure 5.222) where the Kuba have arranged cowrie shells in a *p4m* pattern. The squares are again arranged diagonally, but it is clear that there are fourfold rotations about the point where four cowries meet and about the center of each empty square area.

The bottom of a Persian bowl (Figure 5.223) is divided into squares whose crosses mark some fourfold centers, while the dots at the intersections of the squares mark the others.

5.222 Mask with beads and cowrie shells, Kuba, Zaire (Musée Royal de l'Afrique Centrale, Tervuren, Belgium, no. R.G.24.969)

5.223 Porcelain bowl, Persia (California Academy of Sciences, San Francisco, no. 389-377). Photo by C. Thomas.

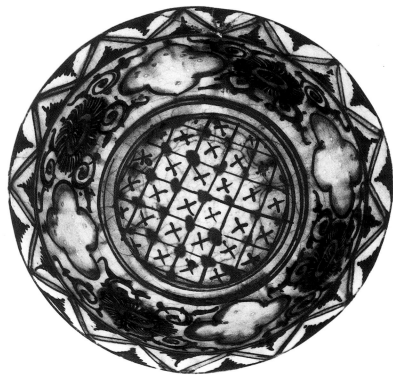

Certain forms of weaving, such as the plaiting on a woven purse (Figure 5.224) allow mirror reflection. Here the orientation of the squares is on the diagonal. It is interesting to note that the weaver, conscious of the overall nature of the pattern, fitted the top to slide over the bottom so that the squares align properly to produce a continuous *p4m* pattern, allowing for slight irregularities.

We now examine several patterns which give the illusion of being quite different from the preceding examples. Because the units appear, in their present orientation, to be offset, it is

5.224 Plaited purse, Oceania (California Academy of Sciences, San Francisco, no. 538-11). Photo by C. Thomas.

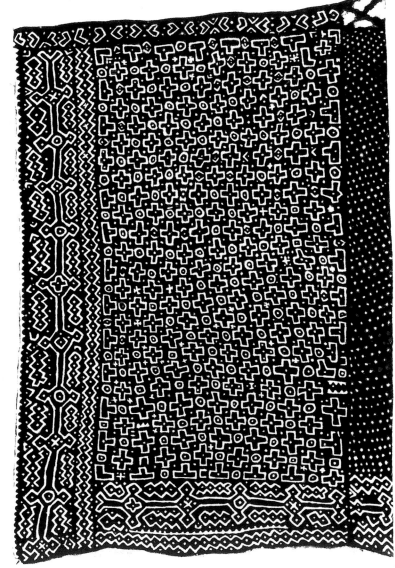

5.225 Section, textile, Bamako market, Mali (Lowie Museum of Anthropology, University of California, Berkeley, no. 5-8795)

5.226 Mosaic floor, House of the Porticoes, Portico of the Rivers, Antioch. From Levi 1947, pl. 99c.

tempting to make the same type of distinction as between *pmm* and *cmm* structures. This would be an erroneous distinction, however, since in fact there are mirror reflection axes in four, not just two, directions. (This illusion of offset layout is seen in the preceding examples of *p4m* patterns as well; for example, in Figure 5.222 the cowrie shell crosses could be described as being offset with the plain squares of the background.)

On a striking textile from Mali (Figure 5.225) the crosses and circles are arranged in a pattern comparable to the cowrie shells and plain squares of the earlier example. There are irregularities which technically cancel the *p4m* symmetry—tiny added elements scattered throughout, and unmatching shapes occasionally substituted for the circles—but the overall intent is clearly a *p4m* pattern.

We turn now to two more examples of seemingly offset layouts which, when viewed on a diagonal, become simple square grids: a mosaic floor from Antioch (Figure 5.226) and a twentieth-century vessel from Acoma

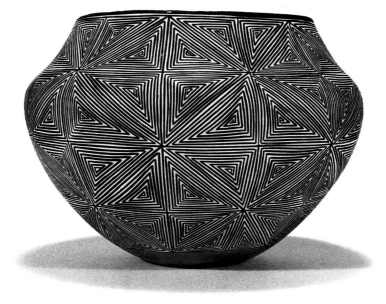

Pueblo, New Mexico (Figure 5.227). This last example is perhaps the most deceptive and difficult to study because of the closely painted parallel line series. (We note some irregularities in the number of turns of the spirals. Indeed, the spirals, strictly speaking, would cancel the reflections and make this a *p4* pattern, but we focus here on the overall *p4m* structure.)

5.227 Ceramic jar by Lucy Lewis, Acoma Pueblo, New Mexico (California Academy of Sciences, San Francisco, no. 370-124). Photo by C. Thomas.

5.228 Schematic p'_c4mm

5.229 Tunic, Inca, Peru (California Academy of Sciences, San Francisco, no. 389-2357). Photo by C. Thomas.

p'_c4mm

There are five colorings of $p4m$. The most common is the square checkerboard (Figure 5.228). In this orientation the color reversals occur across mirror axes running vertically and horizontally between the squares, but not across mirror axes running through the squares, either horizontally, vertically, or diagonally. Glide axes run diagonally, and color reversals occur along them. There are also color reversals around alternate fourfold centers and around all twofold centers. Only a few examples are illustrated since this coloring, once understood and recognized, is so easily identifiable.

It is a well-known pattern on Inca tunics from Peru (Figure 5.229), as well as being found on such diverse objects as a beaded pubic apron from Kenya (Figure 5.230) and sixteenth-century tiles from Seville installed in the Convento Santo Domingo in Lima, Peru (Figure 5.231). (In the latter, the pattern should be viewed on the diagonal. The small ornamented squares are background.)

We do point out that there are patterns with this coloring that will not look like simple square checkboards. We illustrate one example here, as it is fairly complex. It is a late nineteenth-century quilt pattern (Figure 5.232). In this orientation, it is clear that the color reversals occur across alternate vertical and horizontal mirror axes, and not across the diagonal mir-

5.230 Woman's beaded apron, Lumbwa, Kenya (California Academy of Sciences, San Francisco, no. 18-146). Photo by C. Thomas.

ror axes. Turning the pattern on the diagonal, you can see how a glide reflection will shift a black quarter section of a circle into a white quarter section and so forth. The fourfold rotations about the centers of the circles change colors, but those about the centers of squares do not.

5.231   Glazed wall tile from Seville, Spain, sixteenth century, Convento Santo Domingo, Lima, Peru. Photo by D. Washburn.

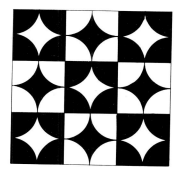

5.232   Quilt, "Robbing Peter to Pay Paul," ca. 1880, American. Redrawn by A. Pertschuk.

5.233   Schematic *p4'mm'*

p4'mm'

This coloring has reversals along all glide axes, across those mirror axes which are parallel to the glide axes, and around all fourfold centers. All rotations about twofold centers preserve colors (Figure 5.233).

The ovals where the circles overlap in a section of a mosaic (Figure 5.234) exemplify this coloring. (The black regions, with their small white circles, are background.) In the orientation here, the glide axes run vertically and horizontally through the centers of the ovals. The user can see how one white oval moves into a checked oval and so forth. The fourfold centers are in the middles of the circles, and at the junctions of four ovals.

5.234   Fresco, Pompeii, Italy. From Speltz 1915, pl. 37, no. 1. Redrawn by A. Pertschuk.

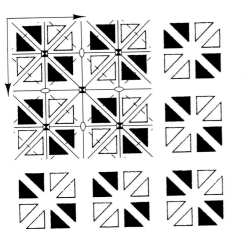

5.235 Schematic *p4'm'm*

p4'm'm

In this coloring, reversals occur across mirror axes in two of the four directions and about all fourfold centers. Reversals do not occur across the glide axes or around the twofold centers. The mirror axes which preserve colors run parallel to the glide axes (Figure 5.235). This contrasts with class *p4'mm'*, where the reverse occurs.

This pattern appears on a section of Kuba raffia (Figure 5.236) oriented diagonally to the edge of the cloth. It is the small black and white squares in the centers of the larger squares which make this a two-color pattern. The large background squares are a straightforward one-color *p4m*. The vertical mirror axes which bisect the small checked squares preserve colors; those on the diagonal (in this orientation) reverse colors. In this view it is easy to see how glide reflection preserves colors; the small white squares move to other white squares and black squares move to black squares. It is

also easy to see how quarter-turns reverse colors.

The next two patterns are not oriented on the diagonal. One is a patchwork quilt (Figure 5.237), with fourfold roations about the centers of the white stars and the points where four stars meet. A section of a stained glass window from France is similarly organized (Figure 5.238).

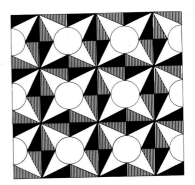

5.237 Quilt, "Compass." From Johnston 1979, 21. Redrawn by A. Pertschuk.

5.236 Section, raffia cloth, Kuba, Zaire (Musée Royal de l'Afrique Centrale, Tervuren, Belgium, no. R.G.28087)

5.238 Stained glass window, Bourges, France. From Dolmetsch 1889, pl. 37. Redrawn by A. Pertschuk.

5.239   Schematic *p4m'm'*

5.240   Quilt, "Le Moyne Star." From Grafton 1975, 23. Redrawn by A. Pertschuk.

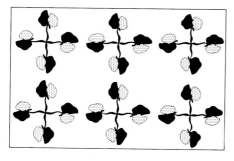

5.241   Quilt, "Sweet Peas." From Edwards 1975, no. 37. Redrawn by C. Sudekum.

p4m'm'

There are color reversals in this coloring across mirror reflection axes in all four directions and along all glide axes. Color is preserved around all fourfold centers and twofold centers (Figure 5.239).

Several quilt patterns favor this coloring. The star pattern in Figure 5.240 clearly shows the color reversals across all mirror axes; that is, across mirror lines which bisect every indented section of each star. A fanciful version is the "Sweet Peas" quilt pattern (Figure 5.241) arranged in the same fashion (although, strictly speaking, the curved stems and slightly larger black petals allow only rotations and no mirror reflections).

Perhaps more difficult to see are the color reversals on this tiling from the Convento Santo Domingo in Lima, Peru (Figure 5.242). Focus here on the circular units inside of which the leaves are bisected by mirror reflection axes which reverse the colors. If the tile section is turned on the diagonal, the color reversals along the glide axes can more easily be seen. (For our purposes, all the rest is background. Note that the one-color aspect of the star-shaped "background" motifs which are found offset to the circular units does not affect the coloring classification.)

5.242   Glazed wall tile from Seville, Spain, sixteenth century, Convento Santo Domingo, Lima, Peru. Photo by D. Washburn.

5.243   Schematic *p'_c4gm*

p'_c4gm

The color reversals in this class occur across the mirror axes parallel to glide reflection axes, as well as across half of the mirror axes in the other two directions. Reversals also occur around all twofold centers and around half of the fourfold centers, but not around the remaining fourfold centers or along glide axes (Figure 5.243).

First we show the occurrence of this pattern on a fragment of mosaic pavement from Timgad (Figure 5.244). This section is oriented so that the vertical mirror reflection lines alternately preserve and reverse colors. The diagonal mirror axes reverse colors. Glide reflections superimpose hourglass units of the same color. Rotations about twofold centers reverse colors. For example, a horizontally oriented black hourglass rotates 180° into a similarly positioned white hourglass.

A twentieth-century example of American floor tiling (Figure 5.245) is oriented here to show the glide axes moving vertically and preserving colors. The fourfold centers in each checkerboard square reverse colors, but fourfold rotations about the centers of the large white squares preserve colors. Half-turns about the corners of the large squares lead to color reversals. (If Figure 5.245 is turned 45°, the pairs of black squares correspond to the black hourglasses of Figure 5.244.)

We turn to a textile example, a mid-nineteenth-century American coverlet (Figure 5.246). Disregarding the black (background) squares, try to focus on the common corner of eight right triangles; a pinwheel effect is visible, with a rotating series of black right triangles alternating with a rotating series of white right triangles. Colors are not reversed around this fourfold center (black wing of pinwheel goes to black, white goes to white), but are reversed around the fourfold center where the right angles of four triangles meet. No color reversals occur along the glide axes (which run vertically and horizontally through the centers of the squares). Again, this corresponds exactly to the Timgad example.

5.244   Mosaic pavement in forum, site of Timgad, Algeria. From Germain 1969, pl. 25.

5.245   Tile floor, David Griffeath residence, Madison, Wisconsin.

5.246   Detail, printed coverlet, mid-nineteenth century, American (Helen L. Allen Textile Collection, The University of Wisconsin, Madison, no. PDUS-315)

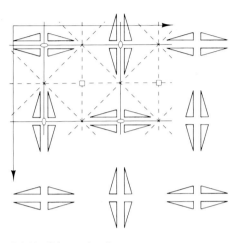

5.247   Schematic *p4g*

p4g

These patterns have glide reflections in four directions, and mirror reflections in two of those directions. Glide axes lie halfway between, and parallel to, the mirror axes, as well as diagonal to the mirror axes. There are twofold rotation centers at the intersections of the mirror axes, and fourfold centers at the intersections of the glide axes parallel to them (Figure 5.247). The design units often appear to be rotating in opposite directions around alternate fourfold centers, in contrast to *p4* patterns where all rotations appear to be in the same direction. This is the pattern of ordinary over-under plaiting, and that prototype can be seen, slightly disguised, in many of our examples.

Several examples clarify this complex symmetry. We first describe a mosaic tiling from Antioch (Figure 5.248). A fourfold center is found where the join of four rotating rectangular units forms a swastika. It is clear that neighboring swastikas turn in opposite directions. Glide axes run

5.248   Mosaic floor, House of the Porticoes, Portico of the Rivers, Antioch. From Levi 1947, pl. 99b.

5.249 Mosaic pavement, site of Timgad, Algeria. From Germain 1969, pl. 59.

vertically and horizontally through these points of fourfold rotation. Another tiling, from the site of Timgad (Figure 5.249), has a very similar arrangement, except that the rectangular units have curvilinear ends.

A Kuba raffia cloth (Figure 5.250) has cut-out areas which show the *p4g* symmetry. We have oriented the cloth so that the two overlapping horizontal rows of pinwheels rotate in oppo-site directions; the top row moves counterclockwise and the bottom row clockwise. Turn the raffia cloth diagonally to see how the triangular quarter sections are reflected across mirror reflection axes. Glide axes parallel to these mirror axes pass through the fourfold centers. Glide axes running vertically and horizontally do *not* pass through fourfold centers, but pass through the triangles themselves.

5.250 Section, raffia cloth, Kuba, Zaire (Musée Royal de l'Afrique Centrale, Tervuren, Belgium, no. 17638)

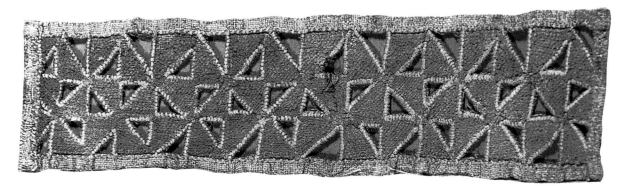

The next two examples show simulated plaiting patterns of the *p4g* type. On another Kuba raffia cloth (Figure 5.251) are what appear to be white bands "woven" in an over-under fashion. The fourfold centers are in the small black squares. Glide axes run through them diagonally, parallel to the mirror axes which run the length of the white rectangles. The Kuba also transferred this type of plaiting image to carved objects, such as the drinking cup in Figure 5.252.

A textile example is seen on the border of a palace hanging from eighteenth-century China (Figure 5.253). The rows of swastikas, which rotate in alternate directions, form the background on which other figures are embroidered.

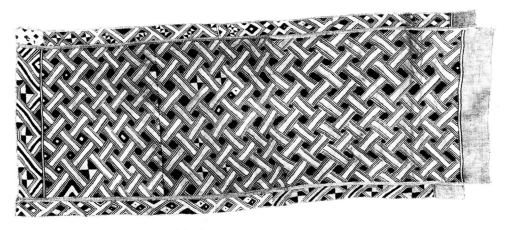

5.251   Raffia cloth, Kuba, Zaire (Musée Royal de l'Afrique Centrale, Tervuren, Belgium, no. R.G.24215)

5.252   Wood cup, Kuba, Zaire (Musée Royal de l'Afrique Centrale, Tervuren, Belgium, no. R.G.56.10.7)

5.253   Detail, palace hanging in embroidered silk, Ch'ing dynasty, eighteenth century China. Courtesy of the Asian Art Museum of San Francisco, The Avery Brundage Collection (no. B60 M41+).

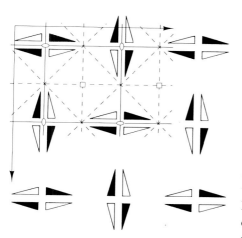

5.254   Schematic *p4g'm'*

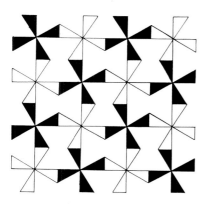

5.255   Suggested by the dust jacket for a geometry book. Redrawn by A. Pertschuk.

p4g'm'

This coloring of *p4g* has no color reversals around the fourfold or twofold centers. Color reversals do occur along all glide axes and across all mirror reflection axes (Figure 5.254).

This is an easy pattern to identify because the one-color fourfold units can stand out clearly as a checkerboard arrangement, except that alternate units rotate in opposite directions. Despite this obvious layout, we have not found an example of this coloring, and present here an example modified from the cover of a geometry textbook (Figure 5.255).

p4'g'm

In this class we see color reversals around the fourfold rotation centers but not around the twofold centers. Colors are preserved across the mirror axes. Colors are reversed along the glide axes which pass between the fourfold centers (diagonal to the mirror axes), but not along the glide axes (parallel to the mirror axes) which pass through them (Figure 5.256).

This arrangement describes two-color over-under plaited patterns such as in the floor tiling in Figure 5.257. Here the fourfold center is in the small white square and the four rectangular parts rotate around it in an offset layout: dark, light, dark, light. Tilting the tiling on the diagonal reveals how the rectangular shapes reverse colors along the glide axes which pass between the fourfold centers.

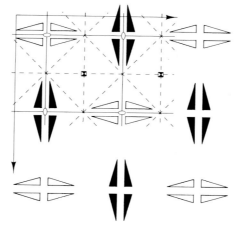

5.256   Schematic *p4'g'm*

5.257   Tile floor, 1887, Science Hall, University of Wisconsin, Madison.

Two early Roman pavement mosaics also show this symmetry. A section of a floor from Ravenna (lower right, Figure 5.258) closely resembles the tiling example except that the rectangles have their sides altered with concave and convex curves. The four-fold center lies where four corners of these curved rectangles meet. Around this point the units alternate: gray, black, gray, black. In this orientation, the units reverse colors along the vertical glide axes, but not along the diagonal glide axes, which pass between the rotating units. Mirror reflections (diagonal in this orientation) do not produce color reversals.

Finally, we examine a *p4'g'm* pattern on a mosaic from Antioch (Figure 5.259). The white and gray diamond units alternate colors about

fourfold centers in the middle of the black squares, very similar to the elements of the mosaic in the preceding example. The pattern is difficult to classify because the eye is at first drawn to the black squares. These background spaces seem to create some type of *p4m* pattern. However, the answer to the second question in

the flow chart, "Are there reflections consistent with color in four directions?" is no; there are no mirror axes in the diagonal. Therefore, even if we begin by analyzing the arrangement of black squares instead of the gray and white diamonds, we must turn to the section of the flow chart which deals with *p4g* patterns.

5.258 Mosaic pavement, Palazzo di Teodorico, Ravenna, Italy. From Berti 1976, pl. 33, no. 37.

5.259 Mosaic floor, House of Narcissus, Antioch. From Levi 1947, pl. 10a.

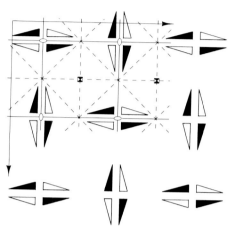

5.260   Schematic *p4'gm'*

p4'gm'

In this coloring of *p4g*, there are color reversals about the fourfold centers but not about the twofold centers. Color reversals occur along the glide axes that pass through the fourfold centers but not along the other glide axes. Color reversals occur across the mirror reflection axes (Figure 5.260).

In our example, an Arabic mosaic (Figure 5.261) identical in element shape and layout but not in coloring to the mosaic in Figure 5.259, a fourfold center is in the center of the white squares, and the black and gray triangles alternate around this point. In the orientation we show here, the mirror axes run vertically and horizontally between the units and lead to color reversals. The glide axes which pass vertically through the fourfold centers lead to color reversals, but the glide axes which pass diagonally between the units do not.

5.261   Mosaic pavement, Egypt. Adapted from Prisse d'Avennes 1978, 7. Redrawn by D. Crowe.

p3

5.2.4 Patterns with 120° Rotations

These patterns have threefold (120°) rotations around centers which are arranged in a grid based on equilateral triangles. These centers are marked by small triangles in the schematic drawings. There are no twofold, fourfold, or sixfold rotations. No mirror or glide reflection axes are present (Figure 5.262). There can be no two-color classes for patterns with *p3* symmetry, since no such coloring would allow any rotations consistent with color.

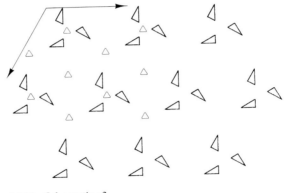

5.262 Schematic *p3*

A classic example is found on a tiled wall at the Alhambra (Figure 5.263). There are threefold centers at the meeting point of each group of three rotating "leaves," and in the center of each six-pointed star. (The original from which this was drawn has, in fact, several colors: green, red, black. It has *p3* symmetry only when all these colors have been made the same, e.g., as redrawn using black in Figure 5.263).

5.263 Tile, Mirador de la Daraxa, Alhambra. Adapted from Grabar 1978, no. 115. Redrawn by A. Pertschuk.

p3m1

There are two pattern classes which incorporate mirror axes, glide axes, and 120° rotations. The critical feature which differentiates *p3m1* patterns from *p31m* patterns is whether the threefold centers all lie on mirror reflection axes. In *p3m1* patterns they do; in *p31m* patterns half of them do and half of them do not. In the schematic drawing of class *p3m1* we see that all the threefold centers are at intersections of mirror lines. Glide axes pass between the mirror axes (Figure 5.264).

This class is seen on a lattice from a shop window from Szechwan (Figure 5.265), where one set of mirror reflection axes runs vertically. Another example is a border pattern on a Persian manuscript (Figure 5.266). Here black hexagons and white trefoils are packed. Threefold centers occur in the center of each trefoil and hexagon and at the tips where three trefoils are joined. Mirror axes run along the common edge of two trefoils, bisecting the hexagons; glide axes pass between and are parallel to these mirror axes.

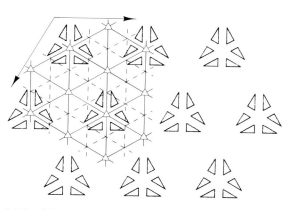

5.264   Schematic *p3m1*

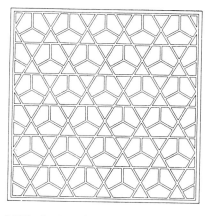

5.265   Lattice, shop front, Chengtu, Szechwan, China. From Dye 1974, pl. C12b.

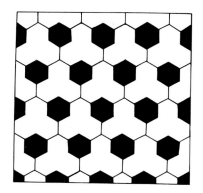

5.266   From Jones 1856, pl. 44, no. 15. Redrawn by A. Pertschuk.

p3m'

There is one coloring of *p3m1*. There are color reversals across all mirror axes and glide axes, but not about any of the threefold centers (Figure 5.267). We have constructed a pattern (Figure 5.268) where the triangular units are divided so that the mirror axes fall along the lines dividing the black and white small triangles. It should be clear that all mirror and glide reflections lead to color reversals, but no color reversals occur around the threefold centers, which are located in the middle of each patterned triangle and of each white background triangle.

p31m

In these patterns the threefold centers occur at the intersections of the three mirror reflection axes and also at other points marked by small triangles in Figure 5.269. These latter centers are neither on mirror axes nor on glide axes.

We examine two Chinese lattice patterns, the first of which appeared on a coat of mail worn by door gods on early nineteenth-century doors at Chengtu, Szechwan, China (Figure 5.270). Here the trefoil pattern is packed without spaces between (unlike the *p3m1* pattern of Figure 5.266).

The threefold centers are located in the center of each trefoil (at the intersection of the three mirror axes) and at the junction point of three trefoils (which is not on a mirror axis). Another Chinese lattice (Figure 5.271) has an open packing arrangement. Threefold centers are present in the middle of each large triangle (on the mirror

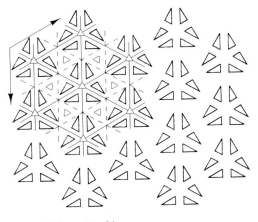

5.269   Schematic *p31m*

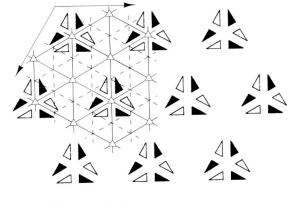

5.267   Schematic *p3m'*

5.268   Invented design. Redrawn by A. Pertschuk.

5.270   Lattice, coat of mail for door gods, A.D. 1800, Chengtu, Szechwan, China. From Dye 1974, pl. C5a.

5.271   Lattice, China. From Dye 1974, pl. C15b.

axis) and each small (background) triangle (not on the mirror axis).

Two simplified *p31m* patterns from borders of Persian manuscripts are the last examples. The first is a packing of Y-shaped units (Figure 5.272) in which the threefold centers are in the centers of the Y shapes, whose three extensions contain the mirror axes. A threefold center also occurs in the middle of each small black triangular background space between three Y-shaped units. Finally, in Figure 5.273 a three-pronged unit is centered in a six-pointed star. The threefold centers are in the tiny white circles as well as at the junctures of three points of three stars. Mirror axes pass through the three prongs.

5.272   Painting on porcelain. From Jones 1856, pl. 59, no. 34. Redrawn by A. Pertschuk.

5.273   Manuscript decoration, Persia. From Jones 1856, pl. 45, no. 19. Redrawn by A. Pertschuk.

p31m′

There is only one coloring of *p31m*. Here color reversals occur across all mirror axes and glide axes, but not about the threefold rotational centers (Figure 5.274). Our invented pattern (Figure 5.275) is based on an underlying sixfold structure, but the whole pattern admits only threefold rotations because of the threefold shape of the design elements. Consequently, all rotations preserve colors. There are threefold rotations about the center of each black and white three-pronged shape, and also about the points where six equilateral triangles meet. Rotations of 120° about these centers do not reverse colors.

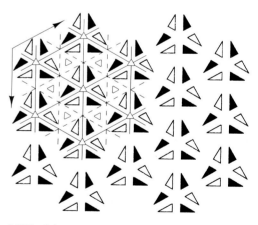

5.274   Schematic *p31m′*

5.275   Invented design. Redrawn by A. Pertschuk.

5.2.5 Patterns with 60° Rotations

p6

We now study two-dimensional patterns which allow the maximum number of rotations about a point: six 60° rotations. Remember that finite designs can, theoretically, admit any number of rotations about a single central point; two-dimensional patterns, however, can only admit two-, three-, four-, or sixfold rotations.

In *p6* patterns there are no mirror or glide reflections, but there are sixfold, threefold, and twofold rotations. In the schematic drawing in Figure 5.276 the sixfold center lies in the middle of a unit with six rotating parts. Threefold centers lie at the juncture of three such units; twofold centers lie between any two sixfold units.

A nice example is the Chinese lattice (Figure 5.277) where the *p6* structure is described by bamboo sections. Here the sixfold center lies in the middle of the hexagon formed by six rotating pairs of bamboo sections. The threefold center is in the small white triangle central to three such sixfold units, and a twofold center is in the middle of each bamboo section.

Another example is on a mosaic pavement from Ravenna (Figure 5.278). The sixfold center is in the middle of the six-petaled flower, around which rotate six rectangular units. Threefold centers lie where the corners of three rectangular units touch, and twofold centers are in the middle of the rectangle.

A large jar from Pseira, Crete (Figure 5.279), is decorated with a curvilinear *p6* pattern. The sixfold centers are at the center of the spirals. The threefold centers are in the middle of

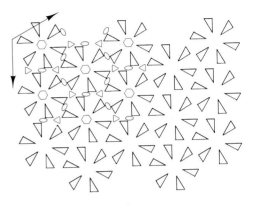

5.276   Schematic *p6*

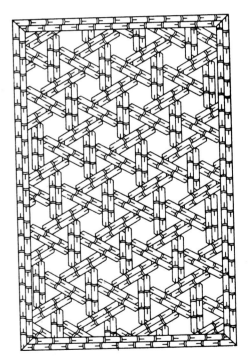

5.277   Lattice, Yünnan Guild Hall, A.D. 1900, Suifu, Szechwan, China. From Dye 1974, pl. C13.

the white triangular units. The two-fold centers lie in the black background area between the points of two triangular units. (Note that, strictly speaking, the spirals have no rotational symmetry at all; they must be replaced by concentric circles to make this a true *p6* pattern.)

5.278 Mosaic pavement, Ravenna, Italy. From Berti 1976, pl. 55.

5.279 "Pithos" (ceramic jar), Pseira, Crete. From Purce 1974, no. 48. Redrawn by A. Pertschuk.

p6'

There is only one coloring of *p6*, where color reversals occur as sections rotate around any sixfold center (Figure 5.280).

This pattern seems to have been a Moslem favorite in Agra, India. There are references to its occurrence in the Itmad-ud-Daulah, as well as in the Taj Mahal. It is redrawn in Figure 5.281. The sixfold center lies in the middle of the six-pointed star.

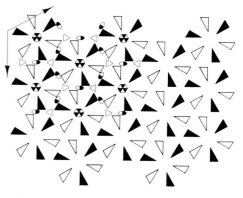

5.280   Schematic *p6'*

5.281   Tile, mausoleums Itmad-ud-Daulah and Taj Mahal, India. Drawn by D. Crowe.

p6m

This symmetry class and its colorings are the most complex of the two-dimensional patterns. In addition to the two-, three-, and sixfold centers (located in the same relative positions as in the *p6* patterns), this class has mirror and glide axes. Six mirror axes pass through each sixfold center. Glide axes also run in six directions (Figure 5.282). Patterns with *p6m* symmetry appear on an oval basket tray (Figure 5.283), on a front panel of a kimono on a Japanese netsuke (Figure 5.284), and on a section of glazed tiling from Iran (Figure 5.285). On the basket tray, the grain of the weaving technically reduces the symmetry to class *p6*, and on the glazed tiling the embossed pattern in the stars reduces the *p6m* symmetry to *cm*, but in both cases we focus on the arrangement and shape of the units.

5.282   Schematic *p6m*

5.284   Netsuke, Japan (California Academy of Sciences, San Francisco, no. 429-44). Photo by C. Thomas.

5.283   Plaited basket tray, Oceania (California Academy of Sciences, San Francisco, no. 59-23). Photo by C. Thomas.

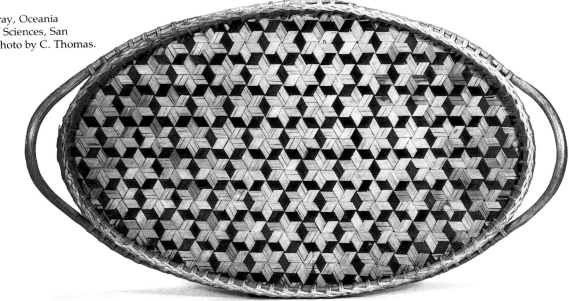

Two other examples where the close packing of regular hexagons is that of an ordinary honeycomb are a pair of silver inlaid stirrups from seventeenth-century Japan (Figure 5.286) and a Kuba enema bottle (Figure 5.287); the latter has a *p6m* hexagonal pattern within a *cmm* structure of elongated hexagons.

5.285 Glazed tile, thirteenth-fourteenth centuries, Iran (Excavations of the Metropolitan Museum of Art, 1936, no. 37.40.26.27)

5.286 Stirrups, iron with silver inlay, lacquer, seventeenth-eighteenth centuries, Edo, Japan (Asian Art Museum of San Francisco. The Avery Brundage Collection, no. B69 M51)

5.287 Wood enema bottle, Kuba, Zaire (Musée Royal de l'Afrique Centrale, Tervuren, Belgium, no. R.G.43992)

p6'm'm

This coloring of *p6m* can be distinguished from the others because no half-turn preserves colors but mirror reflections in lines through two closest sixfold centers do preserve colors (Figure 5.288).

We illustrate this with a nineteenth-century American quilt (Figure 5.289). In this orientation, colors are preserved across the vertical mirror axes, and reversed around the six- and twofold centers. Note that reflections across horizontal mirror axes do not preserve colors; these reflection axes do not pass through closest sixfold centers.

5.288   Schematic *p6'm'm*

5.289   Quilt, nineteenth century, American. Courtesy of the Shelburne Museum, Shelburne, Vermont.

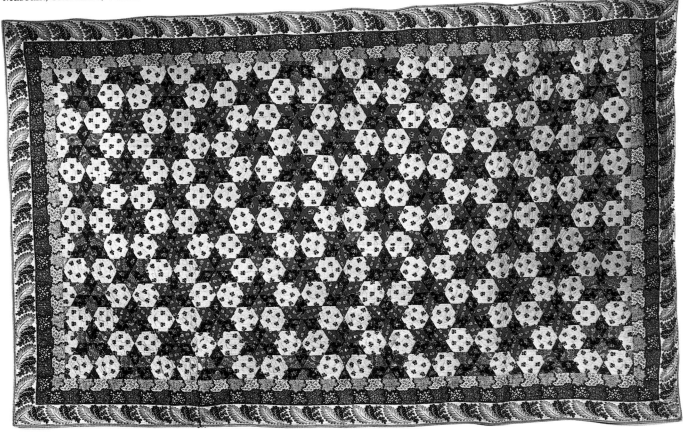

5.290 Schematic *p6'mm'*

p6'mm'

In this coloring, no half-turns preserve colors, and mirror reflections in lines through closest sixfold centers reverse colors (Figure 5.290). These two facts together distinguish this from other colorings of *p6m*.

The most common manifestation of *p6'mm'* is a grid of equilateral triangles colored alternately, checkerboard style. Our example is the carved and painted cap on a Yombe statue (Figure 5.291). All half-turns (between two triangles) reverse colors, as do all 60° rotations (about the points where six triangles meet). Reflections across mirror axes (which pass through closest sixfold centers) reverse colors; reflections across vertical mirror axes preserve colors.

Another *p6'mm'* pattern is seen in Figure 5.292, where the snowflakes alternate colors. All mirror axes through the centers of these snowflakes preserve colors.

5.293 Schematic *p6m'm'*

p6m'm'

This *p6m* coloring has color reversals across all mirror axes but all admissible rotations—sixfold, threefold, or twofold—preserve colors. (Figure 5.293). Essentially the same pattern appeared in Figure 5.63, above.

5.291 Wood figurine, Yombe (Musée Royal de l'Afrique Centrale, Tervuren, Belgium, no. R.G.37964)

5.292 Allover pattern. From Hornung 1975, pl. 12. Redrawn by A. Pertschuk.

Bowl, Flagstaff black-on-white, American
Southwest (Museum of Northern Arizona,
Flagstaff, no. 894/A.464)

6 Finite Designs

THE THIRD CATEGORY of design, along with the one-dimensional and two-dimensional, consists of finite designs. These are designs which admit no translations or glide reflections, and hence are not called "patterns." (Recall the definitions in Section 2.3.) However, they may admit one or both of the other symmetries, rotation and mirror reflection.

There can be ambiguity concerning whether some common circular designs should be called finite designs or one-dimensional designs. Examples of these are designs on the bottom interior of a pot, or within a circle on some plane surface. We find useful the criterion of Charles Amsden (1936:9) for deciding whether a design is a "band" (i.e., one-dimensional design):

> Taken as a form of pattern layout, a band must have certain characteristics. It must have definitely greater length than width, else it would be more precisely described by some term expressive of a geometric figure, as rectangle or square. It must have an upper or lower boundary line of generally parallel trend, to preserve its striplike form. It must either encircle or cross the whole field of design. . . . Banding then may be defined as a division of available decorative area by the drawing of parallel lines to create a zone of decoration.

Using this definition as a guideline, we look ahead here to explain why some of the illustrations we shall examine in this chapter are finite designs, rather than bands.

The designs of Figures 6.2–6.6 definitely do not lie within boundary lines of "generally parallel trend," and hence, are finite designs. In Figure 6.7 conceivably an inner circle (around the central black region) could be drawn which would be "generally parallel" to the outer edge of the basket. However, the inner circle covers a large black area and is thus not identical in shape to the narrow black line around the rim. Only if this inner circle were white, the background color for this basket, would it be more natural to call this a band design.

In Figure 6.11, on the other hand, although the inner region is indeed part of the white background, the fact that there are only three repetitions of the motif around the band makes us reluctant to call this a band design. In practice, a design with three or fewer repetitions is more naturally assigned to the finite design category, while a similar design with four or more repetitions might be considered to be a band design. However, the excessive width of the proposed band (relative to the small size of the central region) prevents us from doing this for the Hopi basket plaque in Figure 6.13.

We have not written a flow chart for the finite designs because, strictly speaking, there are infinitely many classes of finite designs, at least one for each positive whole number n. Nevertheless, the recognition and classification of finite designs is simpler than the classification of one-dimensional or two-dimensional patterns.

6.1a *c5* Japanese design. From Ōuchi 1977, 91.

6.1b *d6* Japanese design. From Ōuchi 1977, 31.

6.1c *c16'* Japanese design. From Ōuchi 1977, 22.

6.1d *d'4* Japanese design. From Ōuchi 1977, 49.

6.1e *d16'* Japanese design. From Ōuchi 1977, 78.

The infinity of different types of one-color finite designs falls into only two broad classes, *cn* and *dn*, as described in Section 2.5.1. The *cn* designs are those which admit rotations by 1/*n*th of a complete turn (360°/*n*), but no reflections. The *dn* designs admit these same rotations and they also admit mirror reflections. The *cn* designs appear to spin around their centers (for example, a swastika is *c4*); the *dn* designs seem more static (for example, a square is *d4*).

For the two-color finite designs, the infinity of classes falls into three broad classes, as described in Section 3.4.1. The first is *cn'* (when *n* is even), which is the only way a *cn* pattern can be colored with two colors consistent with its symmetries; rotations by 360°/*n* reverse colors. The second is *d'n*, a coloring of *dn* in which all reflections reverse colors and all rotations preserve colors. The third is *dn'* (when *n* is even), in which some reflections reverse colors and some preserve colors, while rotations by 360°/*n* reverse colors. A representative example of each of these five classes, taken from a Japanese design book, is shown in Figure 6.1.

We present a small sample of the most commonly occurring finite designs to familiarize the user with this category. After some study, it should be possible to easily identify the number of rotations and/or reflection axes as well as the color alternations.

We begin with finite designs which have rotations, but do not have reflections. A small dish by famed Acoma Pueblo potter Lucy Lewis (Figure 6.2) has twofold rotation only, class *c2*. The twofold center lies in the middle of the dish, between the two stepped triangles. The only possible two-color version of a *c2*

6.2 *c2* Ceramic dish by Lucy Lewis, Acoma Pueblo (California Academy of Sciences, San Francisco, no. 370-139). Photo by C. Thomas.

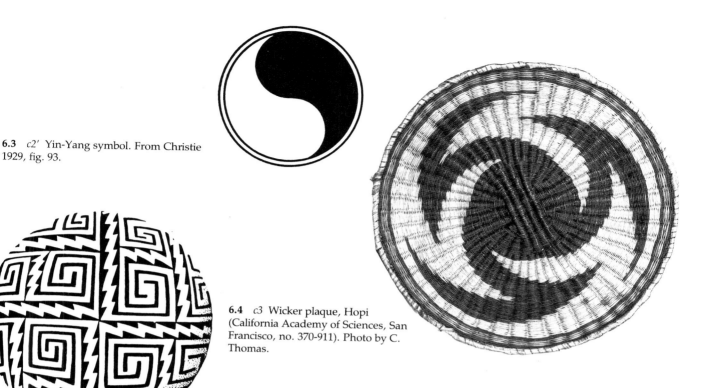

6.3   *c2'* Yin-Yang symbol. From Christie 1929, fig. 93.

6.4   *c3* Wicker plaque, Hopi (California Academy of Sciences, San Francisco, no. 370-911). Photo by C. Thomas.

6.5   *c4* Ceramic bowl, interior. Pueblo III. From Appleton 1950, pl. 35.

pattern is seen in the familiar Yin-Yang symbol, class *c2'* (Figure 6.3). A three-fold design, class *c3*, is found on a Hopi wicker plaque (Figure 6.4). A fourfold design, class *c4*, is seen on the interior of a prehistoric Anasazi bowl (Figure 6.5), and on an incised shell gorget from the Mississippian tradition of the American Southeast (Figure 6.6). A fivefold example, class *c5*, is found on a Pima coiled basket (Figure 6.7).

6.6   *c4* Shell gorget, Mississippian tradition, American Southeast (Museum of the American Indian, Heye Foundation, no. 15/855)

6.7   *c5* Coiled plaque, Pima (California Academy of Sciences, San Francisco, no. 370-836). Photo by C. Thomas.

6.8 *d1* Carved wood box lid, Gudbrandsdal, Norway. From Arneberg 1951, pl. 22, no. 2.

The other symmetry possible for finite designs is mirror reflection where the axes pass through the central point. We see a simple example of one vertical mirror axis on a lid from a Norwegian trunk (Figure 6.8). This arrangement, class *d1*, is, of course, that found on all bilaterally symmetrical masks and other similar two part designs. We show a bronze *yu* from the late Shang dynasty (Figure 6.9) where the elaborate pattern on the side of the vessel has *d1* symmetry.

We now examine finite designs having both rotations and mirror reflections. A simple example is found on a beaded pouch (Figure 6.10) which has both vertical and horizontal mirror axes and thus admits twofold rotation as well. It is class *d2*. A three-part design with mirror axes, class *d3*, is seen on a Maidu basket tray (Figure 6.11).

Four-part patterns are quite common. For example, the inner circle of the carved butter mold from Norway (Figure 6.12) has four mirror axes and fourfold rotations. It is thus class *d4*. (Here we are ignoring the unsystematic coloring of the small strips of triangles, as well as the variety of design around the outer border.) The same class is represented by a coiled Hopi basket plaque (Figure 6.13). The outer "flowers" on a birchbark container from the northeastern United States (Figure 6.14) also exhibit this symmetry. In this example, however, although the three-part flowers do not have color reversal, the inner four-pointed "star" does. Thus, the inner star, by itself, has *d4'* colored symmetry. (In fact, by assigning it to class *d4'* we are still ignoring the diagonal striations. If those are taken into account, the inner star has *c4'* symmetry.)

6.9 *d1* Bronze *yu*, Late Shang, China (Avery Brundage Collection, Asian Art Museum of San Francisco, no. B60 B336)

6.10 *d2* Beaded pouch, Plains (California Academy of Sciences, San Francisco, no. 478-14). Photo by C. Thomas.

6.11 *d3* Basket tray, Maidu (California Academy of Sciences, San Francisco, no. 541-2). Photo by C. Thomas.

6.12 *d4* Carved wood butter mold, Telemark, Norway. From Arneberg 1951, pl. 61, no. 1.

6.13 *d4* Coiled plaque, Hopi (California Academy of Sciences, San Francisco, no. 91-4). Photo by C. Thomas.

6.14 *d4, d4'* Birchbark container, porcupine quill decoration, Woodlands (Rochester Museum and Science Center, no. 70.89.110). Photo by D. Washburn.

6.15 *d'4* Calabash, Solongo, Zaire (Musée Royal de l'Afrique Centrale, Tervuren, Belgium, no. R.G.27016)

A final example of fourfold colored symmetry is on a Solongo calabash (Figure 6.15). Quarter-turns consistently preserve colors, while mirror reflections reverse colors. It is thus class *d'4*.

Other commonly occurring finite designs are composed of six parts. They may admit rotations only, as on the Chinese gate motif from A.D. 1800 (Figure 6.16) which is class *c6*. Or, they may have both rotations and reflections, as on a Ming dynasty bronze temple tablet (Figure 6.17), which is class *d6*.

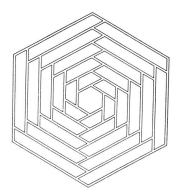

6.16 *c6* Lattice gate motif, East Suburb, Chengtu, Szechwan, A.D. 1800, China. From Dye 1974, pl. &a 10a.

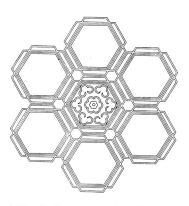

6.17 *d6* Bronze temple tablet, Mount Omei, Szechwan. Ming dynasty, China. From Dye 1974, pl. C11.

Some designs are so truncated that they appear to be finite designs but are not. For example, on a rare painted blanket (Figure 6.18) the predominant pattern appears to be an offset "swastika," but further examination reveals an underlying over-under "plaiting" of *p4g* structure. (Irregularities in the units and background area technically cancel all symmetries.)

Finally, some finite figures have neither line (axis) nor point (rotational) symmetry. That is, they are asymmetrical and their class is *c1*. The figure on the interior of a Pueblo IV ceramic bowl (Figure 6.19) is a clear example.

6.18 *p4g* Painted blanket, Hidden House, Arizona, A.D. 1250 (Arizona State Museum, no. 20511). Photo by E. B. Sayles.

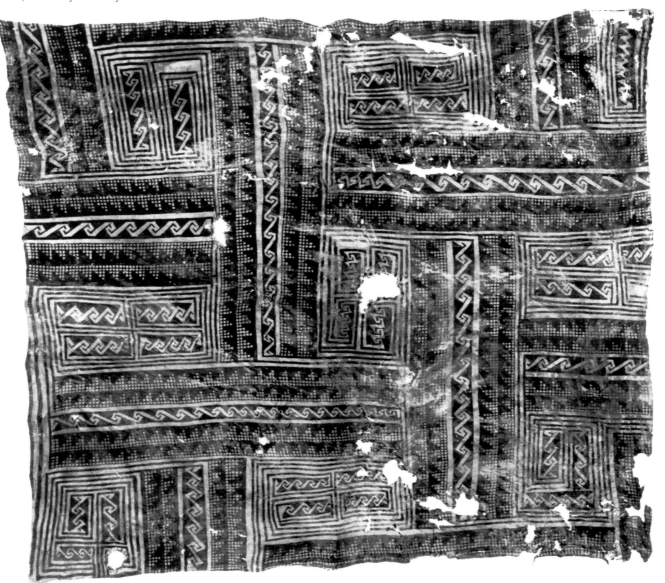

6.19   *c1* Ceramic design, Four Mile Ruin,
Arizona. From Sides 1961, pl. 3.

Spanish tiles, sixteenth century (Convento
Santo Domingo, Lima, Peru)

7 Problems in Classification

THIS CHAPTER discusses in detail some particular examples which present problems whose resolution may be of help to the reader analyzing similar cases.

7.1 Pattern Dimension

It still may be difficult to determine the dimensionality of a pattern when the shape of the design field is misleading. For example, often two-dimensional patterns are placed in narrow design fields which appear at first glance to be bands. Recall that one-dimensional patterns are often called band patterns, because they most frequently occur in narrow design fields. Nevertheless, the criterion for one-dimensionality is that there is a single translation direction, while the criterion for two-dimensionality is that there are translations in more than one direction. Further, patterns can only be called two-dimensional if there are at least two rows, each at least two units long, of the basic design unit. Thus, the shape of the design field which accommodates the pattern is not relevant as long as there are repetitions of the design in the required number of directions. For this reason it is necessary to check a design within its design field carefully to determine that a two-dimensional pattern has not been compressed into a band-shaped field.

We show here an example of a pre-Columbian Peruvian garment (Figure 7.1) that has three sections of two-dimensional patterns. The middle pattern (*cmm*) is in a band-like field, but careful inspection reveals three full rows and two other truncated rows of units along the horizontal, within this narrow field. This tells us that the pattern admits vertical as well as horizontal translation. The presence of multiple translation directions, not the shape or size of the design field, determines that this pattern is two-dimensional.

7.1 Cotton garment, Inca, A.D. 1470–1532 (Los Angeles County Museum of Art, no. M.74.151.22)

255

7.2   Ceramic design, Chile. From
Gutierrez, n.d., no. 111.

7.3   Textile, late nineteenth–early
twentieth century, Bali (The Fine Arts
Museums of San Francisco, no. 1953.42.1)

On another example from Chile (Figure 7.2) there are two horizontal bands of black hourglass units separated by a blank white space. Because there are copies of the basic hourglass unit in both horizontal and vertical directions, we can consider this pattern to be a two-dimensional *pmm* pattern.

In our third example, the Balinese textile of Figure 7.3, we are not tempted to view the whole design as a single band, because it clearly fills the entire cloth. It would be possible to analyze it as fourteen individual bands of type *pm'a2'* separated by narrow white background stripes. However, because of the perfect alignment of the individual bands with each other, our preference is to call this a two-dimensional $p_c'gg$ pattern.

Often a series of zigzags (a two-dimensional pattern, class *pmg*) is oriented vertically. For some reason many users seem to want to classify this orientation, particularly when it is confined within a band-like field, as a one-dimensional pattern. However, if the vertical bands of zigzags are turned 90°, it should be clear that the pattern is two-dimensional, as on the Guatemalan blouse in Figure 7.4.

7.4   Woman's blouse, Guatemala (Lowie Museum of Anthropology, University of California, Berkeley, no. 3-37)

7.2 Compound Patterns

The classification of designs composed of a combination of one- and two-dimensional patterns may be confusing. For example, the blocks of two-dimensional design on a tapa cloth from Samoa (Figure 7.5) are separated by bands of one-dimensional design. Each should be classified separately. The squares of alternately colored zigzags are class $p'_b mg$; the narrow vertical (in this orientation) bands of colored diamonds separating the squares are class $p'mm2$; and the narrow horizontal bands of colored hourglass figures separating the squares are class $pm'm2'$.

It may also be possible to classify the symmetry of the layout of the entire pattern if alignment of the sections is consistent enough. In the case of the Samoan tapa, one way is to consider that the two-dimensional blocks with the zigzags oriented horizontally are of one color, and the two-dimensional blocks with the zigzags oriented vertically are of another color. The design then becomes a square checkerboard, class $p'_c 4mm$. (Most if not all of the blocks are

7.5 Tapa, Samoa. Courtesy of the Field Museum of Natural History, Chicago (no. 111355).

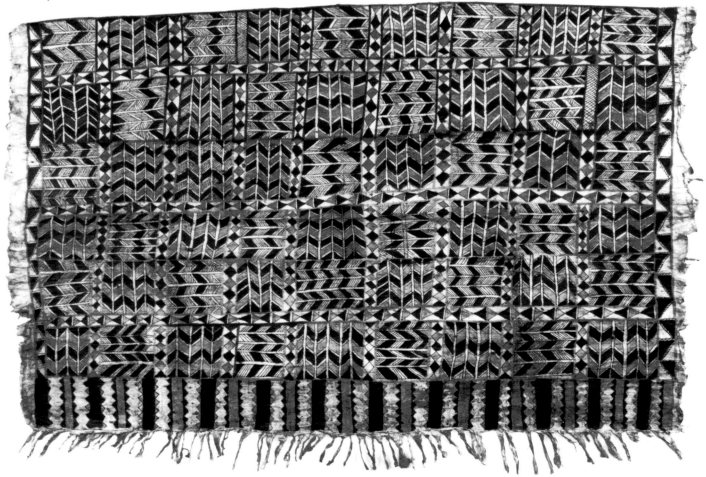

7.6 Ceramic design, San Ildefonso
Pueblo. From Chapman 1970, pl. 101j.
Redrawn by A. Pertschuk.

7.7 Ceramic design, San Ildefonso
Pueblo. From Chapman 1970, pl. 140a.
Redrawn by the University of Wisconsin
Cartographic Lab.

7.8 Ceramic design, San Ildefonso
Pueblo. From Chapman 1970, pl. 140b.
Redrawn by the University of Wisconsin
Cartographic Lab.

square. A rectangular checkerboard would be class $p'_c mm$.) Classification of areas containing different motifs as if they were shapes in a colored pattern has also been suggested by Makovicky (1986:955).

Another type of compound design has sections which are so closely juxtaposed and sometimes interlocked that it may be difficult to determine that they are composed of separate patterns, with either the same symmetries or different symmetries. An example is the San Ildefonso Pueblo ceramic pattern in Figure 7.6, where the upper row is of class $p'111$, while the lower row admits vertical reflections and is of class $p'm11$.

Meaningful classification of such patterns can only be made when the two bands are analyzed separately. Confusing and combining the two types of patterns may mask potentially interesting information inherent in the differences between layout arrangements.

Compound patterns, such as those in Figure 7.6 which are composed of one-dimensional bands with different structures, are more easily recognized than those which are composed of bands having the same structure. The pattern in Figure 7.7 exemplifies the latter type. Both parts of this San Ildefonso design are characterized by vertical reflection. However, the upper band is not colored; its class is $pm11$. The lower band is color class $pm'11$. Note also that in this case the two bands are not in exact alignment.

Slightly different is the San Ildefonso pattern in Figure 7.8, where the upper and lower bands appear to have the same symmetry since the motifs are juxtaposed. However, the upper row of stepped units is not colored, so it is a $pm11$ design, while the lower row is of the colored class $p'm11$.

In the Fijian tapa in Figure 7.9 the lowest band of design has two symmetries: the overall $pm'a2'$ symmetry of the white and black right triangles, and the $p112'$ symmetry of the narrow vertical dividing panels.

7.9 Tapa, Fiji. Courtesy of the Field
Museum of Natural History, Chicago (no.
165426).

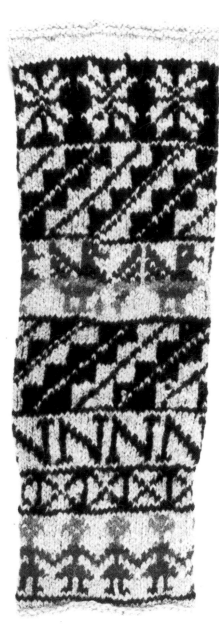

7.10 Wool leggings, twentieth century, Juliaca, Peru (California Academy of Sciences, San Francisco, no. 11-65). Photo by C. Thomas.

Often where a series of bands are juxtaposed, the bands are clearly separate entities and do not interlock, touch, or align as do the bands in the patterns discussed above. We see one such example on a twentieth-century wool legging from Juliaca, Peru (Figure 7.10), where there are seven different bands, all of which should be classified separately. The second and fourth from the top are sufficiently irregular that we cannot classify them as repeated patterns. From top to bottom, the other bands are *pmm2, p111, p112, pmm2,* and *pm11.*

7.11 Ceramic design, Chile. From Gutierrez, n.d., no. 109.

We now show a very perplexing design from Chile (Figure 7.11) that seems to confound analysis. We suggest analyzing the pattern in two parts: the outer border of black and gray triangles, and the inner design of spirals and stepped units. The outer border is *p'112,* in which some half-turns preserve colors, some reverse. The inner design, as it actually appears, has no symmetries except translation. The apparent half-turns are an illusion of perspective caused by the implied imaginary "folding" of the panels in space. If these panels were "flattened out," the inner design would be *p112'*; all half-turns would reverse colors.

The Japanese silk brocade of Figure 7.12 has a number of pattern complexities. The two superimposed hexagonal grids, each separately of class *cmm,* are immediately apparent. (Note that the hexagons are not quite regular hexagons; if they were, these grids individually would be of class *p6m.*) Although the light-colored grid conceals part of the black grid, the class of each is *cmm.*

Within this double grid are zigzag lines which separate patterned regions. Uncolored, these zigzag areas also are of class *cmm.* This consistency is broken when we look at the patterned material within the zigzags, since the upper and lower halves of the regions bounded by the zigzags contain different patterns. Note, however, that the left and right halves contain the same patterns. Hence, for the pattern consisting of the zigzags and the patterned regions bounded by them, there are reflections (across vertical lines), but no rotations. In this analysis the class is *pm.*

7.12   Detail, silk brocade, nineteenth
century, Japan (Los Angeles County
Museum of Art, no. M.39.2.530)

7.3 Pattern Irregularities

The presence of minor irregularities which technically cancel the prevailing symmetry may be unintentional or intentional. Common examples of the former are occasional insertions of differently shaped or colored units, one row of units in a long series which faces the wrong direction, or the alteration (usually diminution), in shape of a motif in order to fit one last unit in a row. These irregularities, strictly speaking, can cancel out a perfectly symmetrical pattern. However, given their infrequent occurrence, we have largely ignored them for the purposes of classifying the dominant symmetry of the pattern.

For example, in the rose quilt in Figure 7.13 we see that the flowers themselves are hexagonal, while the arrangement is not a *p6m* net, but a *pmm* net. The positioning of the flowers is not quite consistent, so that it is difficult to pass mirror reflection axes vertically and horizontally in the same position through and between the petals. This latter is an example of an irregularity that is probably due to artisan attention to the general placement (which in this case gives a *pmm* pattern) but inattention to the precise arrangement of the flower parts. For such cases, we classify according to the general intent—in this case, *pmm*.

7.13 Quilt, "American." Courtesy of the Shelburne Museum, Vermont.

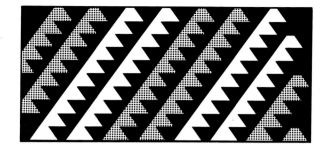

7.14 Woman's beaded loincloth, Zulu. From Bossert 1955, 9, no. 17. Redrawn by C. Sudekum.

It is often the case that the artist seems to have intended a certain pattern arrangement but exactitude in axial positioning was difficult to achieve because of the medium or decorating equipment. The $p_b'm$ pattern on a Zulu woman's loincloth is typical of such a situation (Figure 7.14). This design was produced in beaded embroidery, so irregularities are to be expected. When a mirror reflection axis is passed through the apexes of the triangles, the alignment is imperfect, but we assume that this is unintentional. This pattern is made harder to analyze because the black background color appears to be a third color. In fact, the colored rows alternate two at a time—two dotted, two white, and so forth. The overall symmetry is $p_b'm$.

Another probably unintentional irregularity can be seen in the tapa in Figure 7.15, where obvious pattern repetition has been technically cancelled by a shift in stamping angle of the diagonal, as well as a slight variation in motif, in

7.15 Tapa, Samoa (California Academy of Sciences, San Francisco, no. 519-5). Photo by C. Thomas.

the large rectangular units in the fourth horizontal row from the top. We would nevertheless classify this pattern as $p_b'2$, noting this one deviation. This classification, incidentally, depends on ignoring the narrow horizontal bands between the rectangular units. Often a rough schematic sketch will help clarify such a complex design. Once the pairs of decorated triangles are redrawn as parallelograms, the pattern is easier to see as a simple coloring of *p2*.

A particularly difficult example on a Tongan tapa cloth (Figure 7.16), which we will key out through the flow chart, shows how irregularities in motif shape and placement may reduce the classification of the whole design to asymmetry.

Let us first determine the symmetry of the overall pattern, ignoring the small black triangles. We choose the 90° section of the two-dimensional flow chart because there are fourfold centers in the centers of some squares. There are reflections consistent with color. In fact, they exist in four directions along the vertical, horizontal, and two diagonal axes, so we can answer "yes" to the next two questions.

We then answer the question, "Is there a twofold center which preserves colors?" This can be a very tricky question since we must ascertain that the twofold centers we refer to are just that—points about which there are 180° rotations, but no 90° rotations.

The twofold centers in this pattern are located between black and white triangles, and half-turns about these centers reverse colors. There are half-turns about the middles of the black and white hourglass units which do preserve colors, but because these points also admit 90° rotations, which reverse colors, these are not twofold centers and thus are not relevant to the question. We must answer "no." This leads us to the last question, "Does reflection in a line through two closest fourfold centers preserve colors?" In this pattern these lines are the dark vertical and horizontal lines; reflection across them reverses colors. This yields a classification of $p_c'4gm$ for the underlying structure of the design.

Now let us consider the classification taking into account the small black triangles. Many of these are right triangles, but others seem to be isosceles. Further, the two types of small black triangles are not placed systematically in the larger pattern. Since this irregularity makes it impossible to translate the units, the whole pattern must be considered asymmetrical.

Other types of irregularities are more intentional and they range from regularly placed "irregularities," to more arbitrary irregularities that may have some other cultural coding functions.

On the elegant textile from Paracas, Peru (Figure 7.17), winged men holding trophy heads are arranged in an obvious *cm* layout. Careful inspection of the details of their costumes, however, reveals that the staffs in their right hands end in a hanging head, while ones in their left hands end in a hanging winged unit. This difference is consistent and obvious on each figure. Thus, this is a pattern with structure class *cm* that is reduced in the final elaborated design to class *p1*.

7.16 Detail, tapa, Tonga (California Academy of Sciences, San Francisco, no. 423–107). Photo by C. Thomas.

7.17 Detail, burial mantle, Paracas, Peru, 300–200 B.C. (Ross Collection, Museum of Fine Arts, Boston, no. 16.34)

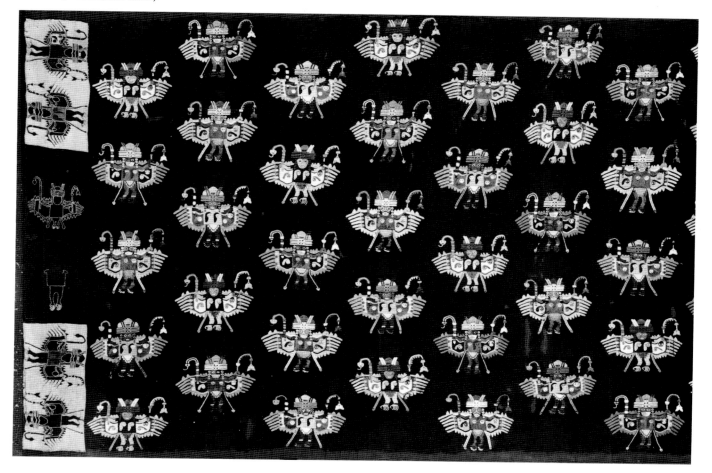

There are also well-known cases of the purposeful use of a single irregularity, such as the "spirit line" in Navajo weaving, which technically cancels the overall symmetry of a rug or blanket; it serves the crucial function of releasing any spirit which may be accidentally "trapped" inside the design as the weaving is completed. Such practices caution us not to dismiss such irregularities as mere "mistakes." Such a label reveals our Western bias for perfection, reflected and reinforced by machines which stamp and weave without fault. Any mistakes which do occur in our perfect world are sold as "seconds" or "irregulars." One reason for these variations has been advanced by Van Esterick, who has suggested (1980) that asymmetrical patterns arise from artists' feelings that perfect symmetry is boring and that deviations from symmetry allow for artistic innovations.

Our survey of patterns throughout the world has revealed a very subtle, but fairly high incidence of irregularities which have their own "consistency" in appearance. That is, the irregularities appear with a consistent rhythm different from the predominant symmetry of the pattern. We suggest that this may be yet another coded information system known only to persons within that cultural system.

For example, an elegant case where the irregularities mark important cosmological information has been reported by Morris (1987). He found that the designs on a *huipil* worn by a saint in the church at Chamula, Chiapas, Mexico, showed marked shifts in colors at what seemed to be irregular intervals. However, closer study of the periodicity of these color changes revealed that the motifs are repeated in one color and then change colors with periodicities of 3, 4, 9, 13, 18, 20, and 52. These correspond to the important temporal and spatial referents of the ancient Mayan world, which continues to be central to the world view of these Tzotzil-speaking Indians: the 3 primary layers of the universe (heaven, earth, underworld); the 4 corners of the earth; the 9 layers of the underworld; the 13 layers of the heavens; the 18 months of the agricultural calendar; the 20 days in each month; and the 52-year cycle.

A second example comes from the Bamana tribe in Mali, who produce mud-dyed cloths with geometric patterns punctuated with "irregularities" (Brett-Smith 1984). However, these deviations from the pattern are not mistakes but are intentional. The patterns contain encoded knowledge; the deviations conceal this information from all but the initiated who are permitted access to such knowledge.

Conclusion

AUTHORS RARELY feel fortunate to have taken ten years to complete a project, but in this case developments in mathematical nomenclature and psychological studies of art, as well as increasing acceptance by social scientists of the application of a closed, mathematically based classification system for the products of human activity have enhanced this book and improved the timing of its debut.

The focus of this book is on the presentation of a mathematically based classification system for nonrepresentational patterns in the plane. Such patterns, which we would normally call "geometric" or "abstract" as opposed to those which we call "figurative," are commonly found on textiles, tiling, ceramics, basketry, carved wood, or worked stone as borders or overall areas of decorative embellishment. While the explication of the principles of symmetry and the procedure of analysis has dominated this book, we would be remiss if we did not present some justifications for the value of such a classificatory approach.

We have attempted, in our introductory chapter, to respond to the proverbial question, "What makes this system any better than the systems we already have?" We have enumerated examples where the use of this classificatory approach has not only uncovered structural consistences in a stylistic system but also correlated such consistencies or discontinuities with other events in the culture's history.

In this final statement we wish to reemphasize aspects of the analytical power of systematic, objective classification systems and to suggest avenues for future research.

One of the most exciting developments in the interaction of geometry, perceptual psychology, and art is to be found in the recent work by Margaret Hagen, *Varieties of Realism: Geometries of Representational Art* (1986). Limiting her study to representational art (that is, figurative images as opposed to the geometric patterns we consider here), she works from the premise that all such art is based on geometric principles. She outlines a hierarchy of four categories of geometric transformations that can describe all representational art: Metric (Euclidean) geometry, Similarity geometry, Affine geometry, and Projective geometry. While these are only some of the many possible geometries, they effectively describe most of Western and non-Western art since the first depictions of the Upper Paleolithic. What makes this work unique is that Hagen, a perceptual psychologist, shows how such a structural classification focuses on some of the same features involved in the perceptual process.

Briefly, Hagen outlines how human perception involves picking up specific information about persistent properties in the environment: size, shape, distance, slant, color, etc. Representational pictures succeed because they have consistently structured these invariants as they are perceived from a certain station-point (that is, viewing position of the artist). Thus, each "style" represents a consistent use of these geometries and station-point options. If there is a shift in geometry, there is a change in style.

Hagen's work is directly relevant to the classification of symmetries presented here because her more global treatment of geometry puts our work in perspective. That is, while she describes the transformations and invariants present in four geometries of representational art, our work only deals with one of these geometries—Metric transformations (translations, rotations, and reflections) in the two-dimensional plane. However, since we are dealing with repeated patterns, rather than a single figural image, and we address geometric rather than representational art, we can more precisely classify the transformations through enumeration of these specific symmetry classes of the one- or two-dimensional patterns. Thus, while we address only one of the four geometric styles outlined by Hagen, we treat it in more detail.

Hagen illustrates the Metric style with wall paintings from Egyptian tombs. In these depictions, a single scene is depicted from multiple station-points; that is, each object in the scene—person, vase, animal, etc.—is depicted from a different perspective, as if the artist had moved directly in front of each object in order to draw it "face on." Of the four geometric perspectives, Hagen points out, this one gives the most precise information about the relative shapes and sizes of objects, because of its attention to symmetry and balance between shapes. She suggests that the Egyptians (and, we suggest, any other cultural group that uses this perspective) place a primary emphasis on clarity about the objects depicted. In the case of Egyptian tombs, this may have been for the benefit of the deceased, for their use in the next world. In other cultures, the importance may be for daily life.

Hagen emphasizes that in Metric transformations, as in the other three geometries, the consistencies in a given style structure within a culture occur across great spans of time, and that "there exists no style that is a hodgepodge of several geometries" (1986:117, 201).

For the culture's members, she asserts, these consistencies must have some communicative function. Representational art is created and evaluated within a specific context. Members know—although not necessarily consciously—the rules for generation of the representations, and they can sort "correct" pictures from those that violate the rules (1986:85). In this way, as we have shown more specifically with some of the studies of the use of certain symmetries by Indians in Northwestern California, cultures use these geometric structurings of the parts as tribal identifiers.

For the analyst, they make possible both reliable categorizations and systematic comparisons among styles. Although, of course, no style can be described solely in terms of geometric structures, knowledge of structural consistencies can be one framework within which to understand certain behavioral events. Examination of other features of a style, such as technique of manufacture, will reveal different consistencies which will not necessarily map precisely with those of structure.

We contend that each of the features in a style can and should be systematically described for maximal understanding of the style and how it functions within its cultural context. In the case of the metric geometries presented in this book, as with the different geometries presented by Hagen, we find that they describe invariant properties which have been shown to be fundamental to the process of information selection and categorization. What we present is a systematic way to stand outside our own Western perspective and describe objectively how different cultures differently structure their depictions of their world. Our understanding of what a style is and what it means for its users is dependent on our ability to define and study the very universal properties which are the fundamental components of the perceptual process. In concert, our knowledge of mathematics, psychology, and cultural principles behind a given style will enable us to both define its meaningful parameters and specify how they function.

In this work we have outlined how symmetry is a mathematical property which generates repeated patterns, as well as a feature used in the perception and categorization of form. Studies to date have clearly and consistently shown that a given culture preferentially uses only certain of these structural transformations and how the consistencies and changes in such structural aspects of style directly relate to cultural consistencies and changes.

There is much work left to be done—even for this small segment of art we call geometric pattern. Most consider this kind of design to be purely decorative ornament. We believe otherwise and suggest that even this nonrepresentational art has important cultural communicative value. In future research we must study differences in cross-cultural preferences for all the plane pattern symmetries associated with culturally meaningful stimuli, and we must investigate the significance of different geometries in different cultural contexts.

This approach does not mean that we want to focus more narrowly on the quantifiable aspects of culture, to the exclusion of the human factor. Quite the contrary: in seeking a theory of style we are seeking a general concept about classes of phenomena, a theory which will be more than a mere classifier of a specific body of phenomena. The pursuit of such a theory requires that we first define cultural relationships which can be indicated by classifications of invariant features—precisely so that such classifications need not be the beginning and the end of research. And even in the writings of humanistic anthropologists, we find the call to focus on systematic relationships of features:

. . . the greatest urgency [is] to establish a highly generalized language capable of identifying and describing constituent physical units and of stating their relationships. (Armstrong 1971:142)

We contend that it is necessary to gather baseline knowledge about the invariant properties perceived and used in classificatory processes and to systematize them in a classificatory scheme which allows us to see their consistent appearance in coherent bodies of data. We have systematized the property of symmetry for one- and two-dimensional patterns in the plane. We have argued that this feature informs us about things that are perceptually important to members of a culture. It is now our task to further observe how this feature is manifested and manipulated in a number of cultural systems and situations.

Patterning in human behavior lies at the heart of cultural systems. It allows both participants and observers to anticipate the future, creates predictable and comfortable daily situations, and is the basis for the observer's concepts of style, tradition, and institution. The understanding of a property essential to pattern, and the ability to map it systematically in design as well as in other domains of activity, can only heighten our insights into culture as a system.

Appendixes

1 The Four Rigid Motions of the Plane

This appendix is devoted to a proof of the fact that there are only four rigid motions of the Euclidean plane, namely *rotations, translations, reflections,* and *glide reflections.* (The "Euclidean plane" is the plane of everyday experience—the table top, the blackboard, the stretched canvas, the unrolled surface of a cylindrical pot, the flat woven fabric—imagined to extend to infinity in all directions.) The proof is not very complicated, and derives from the following sequence of propositions, whose proofs will be given in order.

Proposition 1. Three non-collinear points, ABC, and their images A'B'C', completely determine a rigid motion of their plane. More concisely: "If we know where some triangle goes, we know where everything goes."

Proposition 2. Every rigid motion of a plane is obtainable as a sequence of three (or fewer) mirror reflections. In short: "Every rigid motion is the product of three (or fewer) reflections."

Proposition 3. (a) Every product of two (mirror) reflections is a *rotation* or *translation.*

(b) Every product of three (mirror) reflections is a *reflection* or *glide reflection.*

Of the proofs of Propositions 1, 2, and 3, the first two are quite easy to understand. The proof of Proposition 3 (especially 3b) requires a somewhat more detailed analysis. For none of them is any more mathematics involved than the rudiments of high school geometry.

First, some simple notational conventions. We use A, B, C, O, P, Q, and X to denote *points* in the plane, attaching subscripts and superscripts ("primes") as needed. We reserve L_1, L_2,

and L_3, sometimes with primes attached, for *lines* in the plane. We write "AB" to mean the *distance* from A to B (or B to A). However, "L_1L_2" (where L_1 and L_2 are *lines*) means the rigid motion "reflection in line L_1 followed by reflection in line L_2." The *line* determined by A and B is called "line AB." The *segment* determined by points A and B is called "segment $\overline{AB}$," or "$\overline{AB}$."

A rigid motion *preserves distances.* That is, if a rigid motion takes points A and B to A' and B' respectively, then AB = A'B'. That is, a rigid motion is an *isometry* ("same metric" or "same distance") and is often referred to by that name. For us, "rigid motion" (or just "motion") and "isometry" are synonymous.

Sometimes a distinction between *proper motions* and *improper motions* is useful. The proper motions (rotations and translations) are those which are a product of an even number of mirror reflections; they are "orientation-preserving." The improper motions (mirror reflections and glide reflections) are those which are a product of an odd number of reflections; they are "orientation-reversing."

Proof of Proposition 1: (See Figure A.1.) Suppose we know that a rigid motion takes ABC to A'B'C'. Suppose X is any other point in the plane. Where is the point X' to which X is moved by the rigid motion? Certainly AX = A'X' (since the motion preserves distances). That is, X' is on a circle of radius AX with center at A'. Likewise, X' is on a circle of radius BX with center at B'. Hence X' is one of the two points of intersection of these two circles. Finally, the fact that X' is on a circle of radius CX with center at C' determines which of these two points is X'.

Notice that the proof actually shows how to locate X'. Just draw three circles with centers at A', B', C', having radii AX, BX, CX respectively. The only point they have in common is X'.

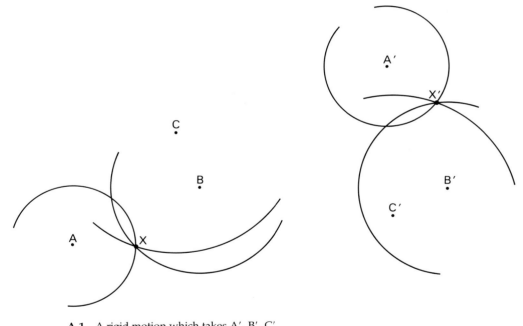

A.1   A rigid motion which takes A', B', C' to A, B, C necessarily takes X to X'.

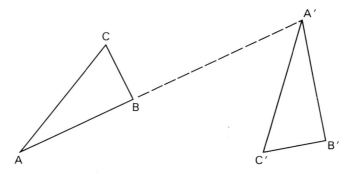

A.2   Triangle ABC moves to triangle A′B′C′ by a rigid motion.

Proof of Proposition 2: To make a convenient figure, suppose ABC are vertices of a right triangle (right angle at B), and that B lies on the line AA′, where A′B′C′ is the right triangle to which ABC moves by our isometry. (See Figure A.2.) By Proposition 1, we only need to show that the same result can be accomplished by a sequence of three (or fewer) reflections.

The proof is very simple.

(i) The first reflection is in the line L_1 which is the perpendicular bisector of segment $\overline{AA'}$. (See Figure A.3.) Let A′B_1C_1 be the triangle to which ABC goes after reflection in L_1.

(ii) The second reflection is in the line L_2, which is the perpendicular bisector of segment $\overline{B_1B'}$. Note that L_2 contains A′, because A′ is equidistant from B_1 and B′. (See Figure A.4.) Hence A′ does not move under this reflection.

Let A′B′C_2 be the triangle to which A′B_1C_1 goes after reflection in L_2.

(iii) If it happens that C_2 coincides with C′, we are done. If not, a third reflection, in the line L_3 which is the perpendicular bisector of $\overline{C_2C'}$ will take C_2 to C′. Moreover L_3 contains A′ (since A′ is equidistant from C_2 and C′) and B′ (since B′ is equidistant from C_2 and C′). Hence A′ and B′ do not move under this reflection.

The sequence of reflections: reflection in L_1 followed by reflection in L_2 followed by reflection in L_3, takes ABC to A′B′C′ and completes the proof.

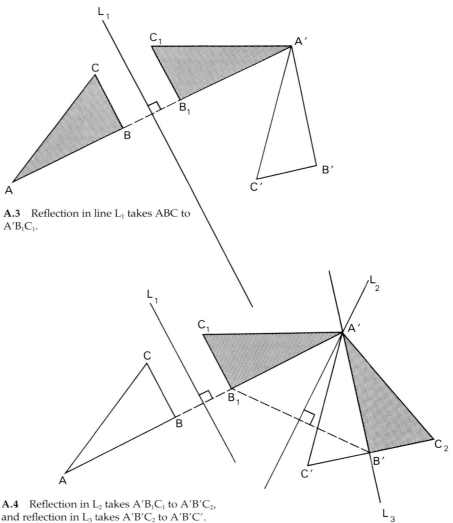

A.3   Reflection in line L_1 takes ABC to A′B_1C_1.

A.4   Reflection in L_2 takes A′B_1C_1 to A′B′C_2, and reflection in L_3 takes A′B′C_2 to A′B′C′.

Proof of Proposition 3a: If a rigid motion is the result of applying exactly two reflections, say in lines L_1 and L_2, then there are just two possibilities:

(i) L_1 and L_2 are parallel, distance d apart,

(ii) L_1 and L_2 intersect at angle α at some point O.

In case (i), reflection in L_1 takes triangle ABC to $A_1B_1C_1$, and reflection in L_2 takes triangle $A_1B_1C_1$ to $A_2B_2C_2$, as shown in Figure A.5. It is immediately seen that the result is the same as if ABC is just *translated* by distance 2d in the direction perpendicular to L_1 and L_2.

Case (ii) is exactly analogous. Reflection L_1 takes triangle ABC to $A_1B_1C_1$, and reflection in L_2 takes $A_1B_1C_1$ to $A_2B_2C_2$, as shown in Figure A.6. It is again clear that the result is the same as if ABC is just rotated by angle 2α about O. By Proposition 1 we know that if our "two reflection" isometry acts like a translation, respectively rotation, on one triangle, it acts in the same way on all points X. This completes the proof of Proposition 3a.

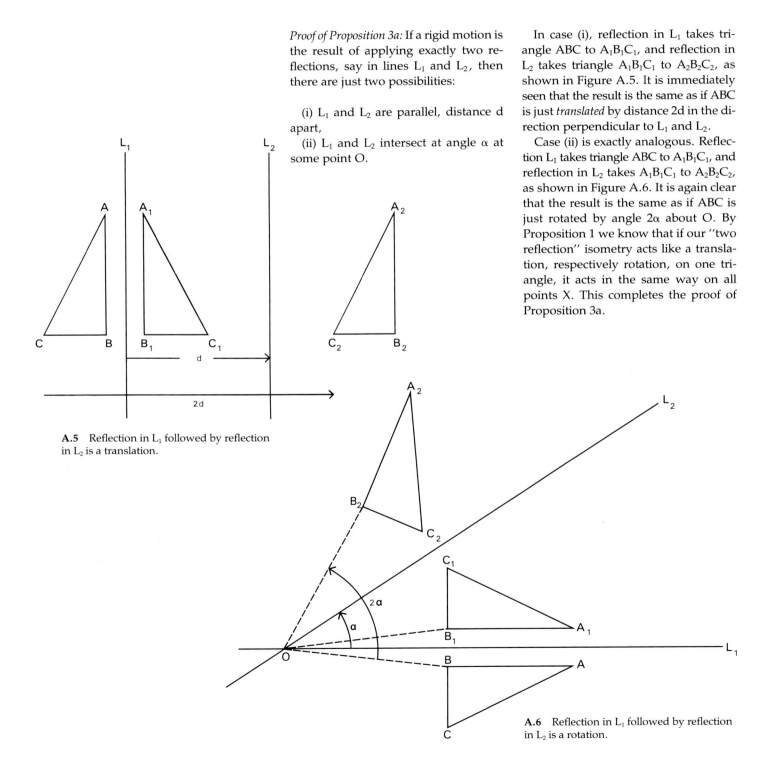

A.5   Reflection in L_1 followed by reflection in L_2 is a translation.

A.6   Reflection in L_1 followed by reflection in L_2 is a rotation.

Remark: The converse of Proposition 3a is also true. That is, any translation or rotation is the product of some two reflections. However, notice that the two reflections are not uniquely determined. In the case of a translation $t = L_1L_2$ ("reflection in L_1 followed by reflection in L_2") we could just as well write $t = L_1'L_2'$, where L_1' and L_2' are any two lines parallel to L_1 and L_2 such that the directed distance d from L_1' to L_2' is the same as the directed distance from L_1 to L_2. (See Figure A.7.)

In the case of a rotation, $r = L_1L_2$, we could just as well write $r = L_1'L_2'$, where L_1' and L_2' meet at the point O of intersection of L_1 and L_2 at the same (directed) angle α. (See Figure A.8.)

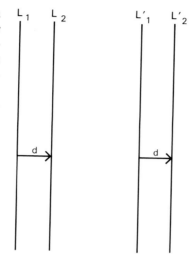
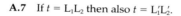

A.7 If $t = L_1L_2$ then also $t = L_1'L_2'$.

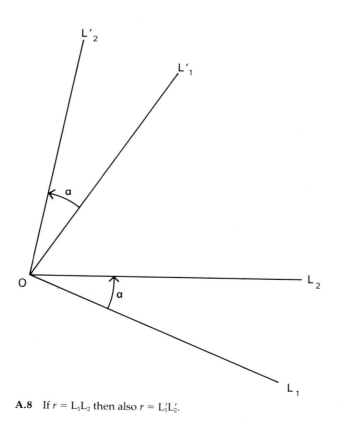

A.8 If $r = L_1L_2$ then also $r = L_1'L_2'$.

Proof of Proposition 3b: We will show that any product $L_1L_2L_3$ ("reflection in L_1, followed by reflection in L_2, followed by reflection in L_3") reduces to

(i) a single reflection if L_1, L_2, L_3 are parallel,

(ii) a single reflection if L_1, L_2, L_3 are concurrent,

(iii) a glide reflection if two of the lines are parallel, and the third meets both, and

(iv) a glide reflection if two of the lines meet at a point P and the third meets both, but does not contain P.

(i) Note that by the preceding remark any product L_1L_2 in parallel lines can be replaced by $L_1'L_2'$ where L_1' and L_2' are parallel to L_1 and L_2 and the distance, d, between L_1' and L_2' is the same as the distance between L_1 and L_2. In particular, if we take L_2' to be L_3 and L_1' to be at distance d back from L_3, then $L_1L_2 = L_1'L_3$. (See Figure A.9.)

Hence $(L_1L_2)L_3 = (L_1'L_3)L_3 = L_1'$, since L_3L_3 leaves every point fixed.

(ii) Case (ii) is exactly like case (i), except that we now replace L_1 by a line L_1' making the same angle, say α, with L_3 as L_1 makes with L_2. (See Figure A.10.) Then $(L_1L_2)L_3 = (L_1'L_3)L_3 = L_1'$, as in case (i).

(iii) This case reduces immediately to case (iv). For, if exactly two of the lines L_1, L_2, L_3 are parallel, then L_2 meets either L_1 or L_3. Without loss of generality we can assume L_2 meets L_3, say at P. (See the solid lines in Figure A.11.) Then if L_2 and L_3 are replaced by L_2' and L_3', meeting at P at the same angle as L_2 and L_3, we know $L_2L_3 = L_2'L_3'$. Hence $L_1L_2L_3 = L_1L_2'L_3'$. But L_1, L_2', L_3', are the configuration of case (iv).

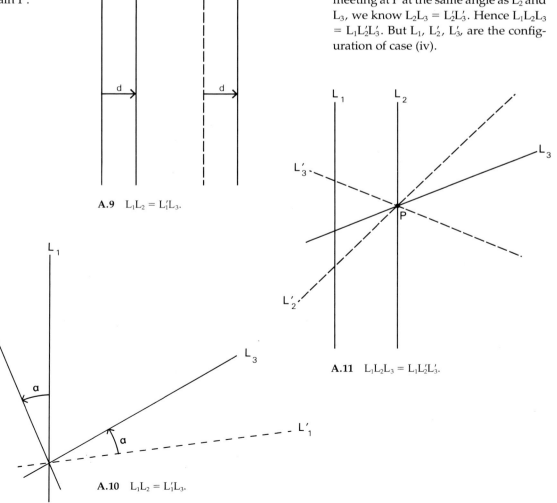

A.9 $L_1L_2 = L_1'L_3$.

A.10 $L_1L_2 = L_1'L_3$.

A.11 $L_1L_2L_3 = L_1L_2'L_3'$.

(iv) In this case L_1, L_2, L_3 are in "general position," i.e., L_2 and L_3 meet at some point P, L_1 does not. (See the solid lines of Figure A.12.) We replace L_2 and L_3 by L_2' and L_3', where L_2' is perpendicular to L_1, and L_2', L_3' meet at P at the same angle as L_2, L_3. Then $L_1L_2L_3 = L_1L_2'L_3'$.

Now we replace L_1 and L_2' by L_1' and L_2'' (meeting at the same point, Q), with L_1' perpendicular to L_3' and L_2'' perpendicular to L_1'. (See Figure A.13.) Hence $L_1'L_2'' = L_1L_2'$, so that $L_1L_2L_3 = L_1L_2'L_3' = L_1'L_2''L_3'$. Since L_2'' is parallel to L_3' (both being perpendicular to L_1'), the product $L_2''L_3'$ is a translation. Hence $L_1'(L_2''L_3')$ is a reflection (in L_1') followed by a translation ($L_2''L_3'$) in the same direction as L_1'. That is, $L_1L_2L_3$ ($=L_1'L_2''L_3'$) is a glide reflection. This completes the proof.

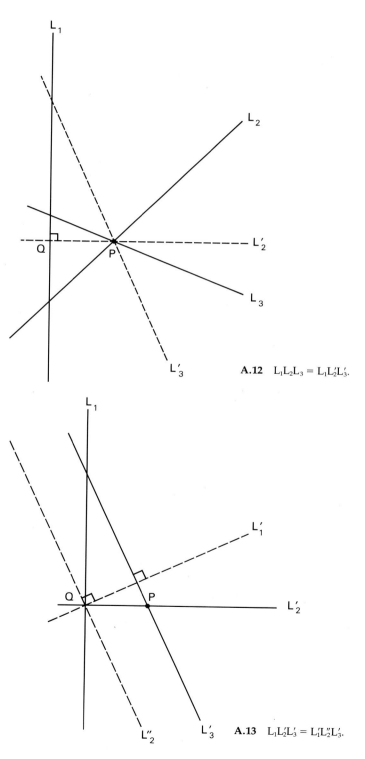

A.12 $L_1L_2L_3 = L_1L_2'L_3'$.

A.13 $L_1L_2'L_3' = L_1'L_2''L_3'$.

2 The Seven Classes of One-Dimensional Design

In this appendix we sketch a proof that there are only seven one-dimensional (discrete) repeated patterns. We thank William Fisher for this proof. In this appendix, all capital letters denote motions. We use F (for flip-flop) for horizontal reflection, R for vertical reflection, and T for translation. A juxtaposition, such as "FR," means "motion F followed by motion R."

A figure is called a "one-dimensional pattern" if it admits translations in exactly one direction (including the "opposite" or "inverse" of that direction) and, moreover, there is some minimal translation in that direction. We call this minimal translation T_m, where m is the minimal distance.

From Appendix 1, we know that the only other possible rigid motions are:

(a) *Reflections*, which can only be vertical reflections, R, or horizontal reflections, F.

(b) *Rotations*, which can only be half-turns (180°). In Appendix 1 it was shown that every rotation by angle α is the product of reflections in two lines, making angle $\alpha/2$ with each other. So any (180°) rotation can be written FR (or RF).

(c) *Glide reflections*, which can be written TF ($= FT$). Since T_m is the minimal "glide," the minimal glide reflection which is not just T_m followed by a horizontal reflection F will be $T_{m/2}F$. (If the minimal glide reflection were not $T_{m/2}F$ then some combination of it with suitable translations would yield a translation by a distance less than the minimal distance m.)

From Appendix 1 we know that a translation by distance d is the product of two reflections in parallel lines at distance $d/2$ apart. Hence, $T_{m/2}F = RR^*F$, where R, R^* are reflections in parallel lines at distance $m/4$ apart.

Table A.1 shows all conceivable combinations of T_m with the other four types of rigid motions: F, R, FR, $T_{m/2}F$. We will show first that nine of these sixteen "possibilities" are, in fact, not possible; and second, that each of the remaining seven actually occurs. This will complete the enumeration.

The proof that nine of the table entries are impossible is in six short steps:

(i) If F and R occur, then FR must occur. This rules out cases 3 and 6.

(ii) If F and FR occur, then $F(FR) = R$ must occur. This rules out cases 4 and 7.

(iii) $T_{m/2}F$ and F cannot both occur, since their product is $T_{m/2}$, which contradicts the fact that T_m is the minimal translation. This rules out the two further cases 1 and 9.

(iv) If R and $T_{m/2}F$ both occur, then some half-turn ("FR") must occur. This follows from the fact (mentioned just after (c) above) that $T_{m/2}F = RR^*F$. For then, if both R and $T_{m/2}F$ occur, we have $RT_{m/2}F = R(RR^*F) = R^*F$. But R^*F ($= FR^*$) is a half-turn. This rules out the further case 10, since it has no half-turn.

(v) If $T_{m/2}F$ and FR both occur, then $(T_{m/2}F)(FR) = T_{m/2}R$ occurs also. But $T_{m/2}R = (R^*R)R = R^*$ is a reflection. This rules out case 11, which has no such reflection.

(vi) The final impossible case is 8, which has "R" and "FR," say R^* and FR. Then $FRR^* = FT_k = T_kF$ is a glide reflection (or possibly just F, if $R^* = R$). Combining T_kF with suitable translations yields either F or $T_{m/2}F$. This rules out case 8, since neither F nor $T_{m/2}F$ occurs there.

Only seven cases remain. Each of these can, in fact, occur and each is illustrated, with its notation, in the last two columns of Table A.1.

Table A.1

Combinations of Motions Producing One-Dimensional Patterns

Here are the sixteen possible combinations of T_m with the four other motions for one-dimensional patterns, as explained in Appendix 2. A check mark indicates occurrence of the motion.

The last two columns illustrate the symmetry classes resulting from these combinations of motions (where they are possible) along with the notation for the resulting patterns.

	T_m	F	R	FR	$T_{m/2}F$	Patterns	Notation
1	√	√	√	√	√		
2	√	√	√	√			*pmm2*
3	√	√	√		√		
4	√	√		√	√		
5	√		√	√	√		*pma2*
6	√	√	√				
7	√	√		√			
8	√		√	√			
9	√	√			√		
10	√		√		√		
11	√			√	√		
12	√	√					*p1m1*
13	√		√				*pm11*
14	√			√			*p112*
15	√				√		*p1a1*
16	√						*p111*

3 Comparative Notation for the Two-Color, Two-Dimensional Patterns

Table A.2 compares five notations for the forty-six two-color, two-dimensional repeated patterns.

The first column is the basic notation used in this book, which is that of Table II and Figure 141 in Belov and Tarkhova 1964. (Their table contains three misprints, the primes having been omitted from $p'_c gg$, $p'_c 4$, and $p'_c 4mm$. Our table restores the primes.)

The second column is the type/subtype notation recently suggested by Coxeter (1986) and described in our Section 3.4. It is particularly convenient because it can be determined by use of the one-color flow chart of Table 5.1 instead of the more extensive Table 5.2.

The third column is the notation of Grünbaum and Shephard (1987).

The fourth column is the notation of Woods (1936).

The fifth column is the notation of Washburn. In a monograph (1977a) distinctions were sometimes made between various versions of a pattern, depending on orientation and spacing of the motifs. Consequently for some of the forty-six patterns there are several symbols.

We have not included the notation of Loeb because he has adequately done that (1971:97–98, Table 8). The notation we use is referred to there as "Shubnikov/Belov notation," and our $p'_c 4gm$ is called $p'4gm$.

We have also omitted the notation of Lockwood and Macmillan (1978:200–201, Fig. 27.09). It is very similar to the one we use, though a 1 or 2 is often inserted to indicate the absence or presence of a twofold rotation.

Table A.2
Comparative Notations for Two-Color, Two-Dimensional Repeated Patterns

Belov and Tarkhova (1964)	Coxeter type/subtype (1986)	Grünbaum and Shephard (1987)	Woods (1936)	Washburn (1977a)
$p'_b 1$	$p1/p1$	$p1[2]$	$b11$	$2\text{-}1_1 00 = 2\text{-}1_2 00 = 2\text{-}1_3 00$
pg'	$pg/p1$	$pg[2]_1$	$112'_1$	$2\text{-}100x_2^2 = 2\text{-}100y_2^2$
$p'_b 1g$	pg/pg	$pg[2]_2$	$b2_1 1$	$2\text{-}100x_1^2 = 2\text{-}100x_2^1 = 2\text{-}100y_1^2 = 2\text{-}100y_2^1$
$p'_b m$	$pm/pm(m)$	$pm[2]_3$	$b12$	$2\text{-}1_2 10 = 2\text{-}1_1 01$
$p'_b 1m$	$pm/pm(m')$	$pm[2]_5$	$a12$	$2\text{-}11_2 0 = 2\text{-}11^2 0 = 2\text{-}101_2 = 2\text{-}101^2$
$c'm$	pm/cm	$pm[2]_2$	$ca12$	$2\text{-}1_2 1_2 0 = 2\text{-}1_2 1^2 0 = 2\text{-}1_1 01_2 = 2\text{-}1_1 01^2$
pm'	$pm/p1$	$pm[2]_4$	$12'1$	$2\text{-}11_2^2 0 = 2\text{-}101_2^2$
$p'_b g$	pm/pg	$pm[2]_1$	$b12_1$	$2\text{-}1_2 1_2^2 0 = 2\text{-}1_1 01_2^2$
$p'_c m$	cm/pm	$cm[2]_3$	$n12$	$2\text{-}110x_2 = 2\text{-}101y_2$
cm'	$cm/p1$	$cm[\ddot{2}]_1$	$c112'$	$2\text{-}11^2 0x_2 = 2\text{-}101^2 y_2$
$p'_c g$	cm/pg	$cm[2]_2$	$n12_1$	$2\text{-}11^2 0x_1 = 2\text{-}101^2 y_1$
$p'_b 2$	$p2/p2$	$p2[2]_2$	$2/b11$	$2\text{-}2_1 00 = 2\text{-}2_2 00 = 2\text{-}2_3 00 = 2\text{-}2_1^2 00 = 2\text{-}2_2^2 00 = 2\text{-}2^2 00$
$p2'$	$p2/p1$	$p2[2]_1$	$2'11$	$2\text{-}2_3^2 00$

Table A.2—*Continued*

Belov and Tarkhova (1964)	Coxeter type/subtype (1986)	Grünbaum and Shephard (1987)	Woods (1936)	Washburn (1977a)
pgg'	pgg/pg	$pgg[2]_1$	$2'2'_1 2_1$	$2\text{-}2_3^2 00 x_2 y_1 = 2\text{-}2_3^2 00 x_1 y_2$
$pg'g'$	$pgg/p2$	$pgg[2]_2$	$22'_1 2'_1$	$2\text{-}200 x_2 y_2$
$pm'g'$	$pmg/p2$	$pmg[2]_5$	$22'2'_1$	$2\text{-}201_2 x_2^2 = 2\text{-}21_2 0 y_2^2$
$pm'g$	pmg/pg	$pmg[2]_2$	$2'2_1 2'$	$2\text{-}2_1^2 01_2 x_1^1 = 2\text{-}2_2^2 1_2 0 y_1^1$
$p'_b gg$	pmg/pgg	$pmg[2]_3$	$a2_1 2_1$	$2\text{-}2_1 01_2 x_1^2 = 2\text{-}2^0 01_2 x_2^1 = 2\text{-}2_2 1_2 0 y_1^2 = 2\text{-}2^2 1_2 0 y_2^1$
pmg'	pmg/pm	$pmg[2]_4$	$2'2'_1 2$	$2\text{-}2_1^2 01 x_2^2 = 2\text{-}2_3^2 10 y_2^2$
$p'_b mg$	pmg/pmg	$pmg[2]_1$	$b2_1 2$	$2\text{-}2_1 01 x_2^1 = 2\text{-}2_2 10 y_1^2 = 2\text{-}2^2 01 x_1^2 = 2\text{-}2^2 10 y_1^2$
$c'mm$	pmm/cmm	$pmm[2]_3$	$ca22$	$2\text{-}2_3 1_2 1_2 = 2\text{-}2^2 1^2 1_2 = 2\text{-}2^2 1_2 1^2 = 2\text{-}2_3 1^2 1^2$
$p'_b mm$	pmm/pmm	$pmm[2]_1$	$a22$	$2\text{-}2_1^2 1^2 1 = 2\text{-}2_1^2 11^2$
pmm'	pmm/pm	$pmm[2]_2$	$2'2'2$	$2\text{-}2_3^2 1_2^2 1 = 2\text{-}2_3^2 11_2^2$
$p'_b gm$	pmm/pmg	$pmm[2]_4$	$a2_1 2$	$2\text{-}2_1^2 1_2^2 1_2 = 2\text{-}2_2^2 1_2 1_2^2 = 2\text{-}2_1 1^2 1_2^2 = 2\text{-}2_2 1_2^2 1^2$
$pm'm'$	$pmm/p2$	$pmm[2]_5$	$22'2'$	$2\text{-}21_2^2 1_2^2$
$p'_c mm$	cmm/pmm	$cmm[2]_5$	$n22$	$2\text{-}211 x_2 y_2$
$p'_c mg$	cmm/pmg	$cmm[2]_3$	$n22_1$	$2\text{-}2_3^2 11_2^2 x_2 y_1 = 2\text{-}2_3^2 1_2^2 1 x_1 y_2$
cmm'	cmm/cm	$cmm[2]_2$	$c2'22'$	$2\text{-}2_3^2 11_2^2 x_1 y_2 = 2\text{-}2_3 1_2^2 1 x_2 y_1$
$cm'm'$	$cmm/p2$	$cmm[2]_4$	$c22'2'$	$2\text{-}21_2^2 1_2^2 x_2 y_2$
$p'_c gg$	cmm/pgg	$cmm[2]_1$	$n2_1 2_1$	$2\text{-}21_2^2 1_2^2 x_1 y_1$
$p4'$	$p4/p2$	$p4[2]_2$	$4'11$	$2\text{-}4^2 00$
$p'_c 4$	$p4/p4$	$p4[2]_1$	$4/n11$	$2\text{-}4_3 00 = 2\text{-}4_3^2 00$
$p'_c 4mm$	$p4m/p4m$	$p4m[2]_5$	$4/n22$	$2\text{-}4_3 1_2 1_2 = 2\text{-}4_3^2 1^2 1^2$
$p4'mm'$	$p4m/pmm$	$p4m[2]_4$	$4'22'$	$2\text{-}4^2 11$
$p4'm'm$	$p4m/cmm$	$p4m[2]_3$	$4'2'2$	$2\text{-}4^2 1_2^2 1_2^2$
$p4m'm'$	$p4m/p4$	$p4m[2]_2$	$42'2'$	$2\text{-}41_2^2 1_2^2$
$p'_c 4gm$	$p4m/p4g$	$p4m[2]_1$	$4/n2_1 2$	$2\text{-}4_3^2 1_2 1_2 = 2\text{-}4_3 1^2 1^2$
$p4g'm'$	$p4g/p4$	$p4g[2]_1$	$42'_1 2'$	$2\text{-}400 x_2 y_2$
$p4'g'm$	$p4g/cmm$	$p4g[2]_2$	$4'2'_1 2$	$2\text{-}4^2 00 x_2 y_2$
$p4'gm'$	$p4g/pgg$	$p4g[2]_3$	$4'2_1 2'$	$2\text{-}4^2 00 x_1 y_1$
$p3m'$	$p3m1/p3$	$p3m1[2]$	$312'$	$2\text{-}31^2 0 x_2 = 2\text{-}301^2 y_2$
$p31m'$	$p31m/p3$	$p31m[2]$	$32'1$	$2\text{-}30^2 1 x_2 = 2\text{-}310^2 y_2$
$p6'$	$p6/p3$	$p6[2]$	$6'$	$2\text{-}6^2 00$
$p6'm'm$	$p6m/p31m$	$p6m[2]_1$	$6'22'$	$2\text{-}6^2 1_2^2 1 x_2 y_1$
$p6'mm'$	$p6m/p3m1$	$p6m[2]_2$	$6'2'2$	$2\text{-}6^2 11_2^2 x_1 y_2$
$p6m'm'$	$p6m/p6$	$p6m[2]_3$	$62'2'$	$2\text{-}61_2^2 1_2^2 x_2 y_2$

Bibliography

Adams, Marie Jeanne. 1973. Structural Aspects of a Village Art. *American Anthropologist* 75(1):265–79.

Alexander, E., and K. Herrmann. 1929. Die 80 zweidimensionalen Raumgruppen. *Zeitschrift für Kristallographie* 70:328–45.

Amsden, Charles. 1936. *An Analysis of Hohokam Pottery Design*. Medallion Paper 23. Globe, Ariz.: Gila Pueblo.

Appleton, Le Roy H. 1950. *Indian Art of the Americas*. New York: Charles Scribner's Sons. (Reprinted in 1971, with some changes in design colors, as *American Indian Design and Decoration* New York: Dover.)

Armstrong, Robert P. 1971. *The Affecting Presence: An Essay in Humanistic Anthropology*. Urbana: University of Illinois Press.

Arneberg, Halfdan. 1951. *Norwegian Peasant Art: Men's Handicrafts*. Oslo: Fabritius & Sonner.

Arnheim, Rudolf. 1974. *Art and Visual Perception*. Berkeley: University of California Press.

Arnold, Dean E. 1983. Design Structure and Community Organization in Quinua, Peru. In *Structure and Cognition in Art*, edited by D. K. Washburn, 56–73. Cambridge: Cambridge University Press.

Ascher, Marcia, and Robert Ascher. 1981. *Code of the Quipu: A Study in Media, Mathematics, and Culture*. Ann Arbor: University of Michigan Press.

Attneave, F. 1954. Some Informational Aspects of Visual Perception. *Psychological Review* 61(3):183–93.

———. 1955. Symmetry, Information, and Memory for Pattern. *The American Journal of Psychology* 68(2):209–22.

Audsley, W., and G. Audsley. 1882. *Outlines of Ornament in the Leading Styles*. London: Scribner & Welford. (Reprinted in 1968 as *Designs and Patterns from Historic Ornament* [unabridged]. New York: Dover.)

Belov, N. V. 1964. On One-Dimensional Infinite Crystallographic Groups. In *Colored Symmetry*, edited by A. V. Shubnikov, N. V. Belov and others, 222–27. New York: Pergamon. (Originally published in *Kristallografia* 1[1956]:474–76.)

Belov, N. V., and E. N. Belova. 1964. Mosaics for the Dichromatic Plane Groups. In *Colored Symmetry*, edited by A. V. Shubnikov, N. V. Belov, and others, 220–21. New York: Pergamon. (Originally part of the paper "Mosaics for 46 Plane [Shubnikov] Antisymmetry Groups and for 15 [Federov] Color Groups," *Kristallografia* 2[1957]:21–22.)

Belov, N. V., and T. N. Tarkhova. 1964. Dichromatic Plane Groups. In *Colored Symmetry*, edited by A. V. Shubnikov, N. V. Belov, and others, 211–19. New York: Pergamon. (Originally part of the paper "Groups of Colored Symmetry," *Kristallografia* 1[1956]:4–9.)

Belov, N. V., E. N. Belova, and T. N. Tarkhova. 1964. Polychromatic Plane Groups. In *Colored Symmetry*, edited by A. V. Shubnikov, N. V. Belov, and others, 228–37. New York: Pergamon. (Originally part of the paper "Groups of Colored Symmetry," *Kristallografia* 1[1956]:10–13, with addenda in 1[1956]:615, 619–21; 2[1957]:21–22; 3[1958]: 618–20.)

Bentley, A. M. 1977. Symmetry in Pattern Reproduction by Scottish and Kenyan Children. *Journal of Cross-Cultural Psychology* 8(4):415–24.

———. 1980. Pattern Reproduction in Two Cultures. *International Journal of Psychology* 15:1–9.

Berlin, Brent, and Paul Kay. 1969. *Basic Color Terms: Their Universality and Evolution*. Berkeley: University of California Press.

Berti, Fede. 1976. *Mosaici Antichi in Italia.* Vol. 1, *Regione Ottava, Ravenna.* Rome: Istituto Poligrafico dello Stato, Libreria Dello Stato.

Birkhoff, George D. 1933. *Aesthetic Measure.* Cambridge: Harvard University Press.

Boas, Franz. 1927. *Primitive Art.* Oslo: Aschehoug. (Reprint, 1955. New York: Dover.)

Bossert, Helmuth. 1955. *Folk Art of Primitive Peoples.* New York: Praeger.

Brainerd, George W. 1942. Symmetry in Primitive Conventional Design. *American Antiquity* 8(2):164–66.

Brett-Smith, Sarah Catharine. 1984. Speech Made Visible: The Irregular as a System of Meaning. *Empirical Studies of the Arts* 2(2):127–47.

Brew, John O. 1946. *Archaeology of Alkali Ridge, Southeastern Utah.* Papers of the Peabody Museum of Archaeology and Ethnology, Vol. 21. Cambridge: Harvard University.

Brown, Harold, Rolf Bülow, Joachim Neubüser, Hans Wondratschek, and Hans Zassenhaus. 1978. *Crystallographic Groups of Four-Dimensional Space.* New York: John Wiley & Sons.

Bruce, V. G., and M. J. Morgan. 1975. Violations of Symmetry and Repetition in Visual Patterns. *Perception* 4:239–49.

Bruner, J. 1957. On Perceptual Readiness. *Psychological Review* 64:123–52.

Buerger, M. 1963. *Elementary Crystallography.* New York: John Wiley & Sons.

Buerger, M. J., and J. S. Lukesh. 1937. Wallpaper and Atoms: How a Study of Nature's Crystal Patterns Aids Scientist and Artist. *Technology Review* 39(8):338–42.

Burckhardt, J. J. 1966. *Die Bewegungsgruppen der Kristallographie.* 2d ed. Basel: Birkhäuser.

Burckhardt, J. J., and B. L. van der Waerden. 1961. Farbgruppen. *Zeitschrift für Kristallographie* 115:231–34. (Reprinted in Burckhardt 1966:200–203.)

Burnside, W. 1911. *Theory of Groups of Finite Order.* 2d ed. Cambridge: Cambridge University Press.

Cadwell, J. H. 1966. *Topics in Recreational Mathematics.* Cambridge: Cambridge University Press.

Chapman, Kenneth M. 1970. *The Pottery of San Ildefonso Pueblo.* School of American Research Monograph no. 28. Albuquerque: University of New Mexico Press.

Christie, Archibald H. 1929. *Pattern Design: An Introduction to the Study of Formal Ornament.* 2d ed. Oxford: Clarendon Press. (Reprinted 1969. New York: Dover. Originally published in 1910 under the title *Traditional Methods of Pattern Designing.* Oxford: Clarendon Press.)

Clement, D. E., F. Sistrunk, and Z. C. Guenther. 1970. Pattern Perception Among Brazilians As a Function of Pattern Uncertainty and Age. *Journal of Cross-Cultural Psychology* 1(4):305–13.

Clouzot, Henri. n.d. Introduction. In *Tissus Nègres.* Paris: Libraire Des Arts Decoratifs.

Cole, M., J. Gay, and J. Glick. 1968. A Cross-Cultural Investigation of Information Processing. *International Journal of Psychology* 3(2):93–102.

Corballis, M. C., and C. E. Roldan. 1974. On the Perception of Symmetrical and Repeated Patterns. *Perception and Psychophysics* 16(1):136–42.

———. 1975. Detection of Symmetry as a Function of Angular Orientation. *Journal of Experimental Psychology* 1(3):221–30.

Coxeter, H. S. M. 1961. *Introduction to Geometry.* New York: John Wiley & Sons.

———. 1974. *Regular Complex Polytopes.* Cambridge: Cambridge University Press.

———. 1985. The Seventeen Black and White Frieze Figures. *Mathematical Reports of the Academy of Science, The Royal Society of Canada* 7(5):327–31.

————. 1986. Coloured Symmetry. In *M. C. Escher: Art and Science,* edited by H. S. M. Coxeter et al., 15–33. Amsterdam and New York: Elsevier.

Coxeter, H. S. M., and W. O. J. Moser. 1972. *Generators and Relations for Discrete Groups.* 3d ed. Berlin: Springer.

Coxeter, H. S. M., M. Emmer, R. Penrose, and M. L. Teuber, editors. 1986. *M. C. Escher: Art and Science.* Amsterdam and New York: Elsevier.

Critchlow, Keith. 1976. *Islamic Patterns: An Analytical and Cosmological Approach.* New York: Schocken.

Crowe, Donald W. 1971. The Geometry of African Art. Part 1. Bakuba Art. *Journal of Geometry* 1:169–82.

————. 1975. The Geometry of African Art. Part 2. A Catalog of Benin Patterns. *Historia Mathematica* 2:253–71.

————. 1980. Symmetry in African Art. *Ba Shiru* 11(1):57–71.

————. 1982. The Geometry of African Art. Part 3. The Smoking Pipes of Begho. In *The Geometric Vein: The Coxeter Festschrift,* edited by C. Davis, B. Grünbaum, and F. A. Sherk, 177–89. New York: Springer.

————. 1986. The Mosaic Patterns of H. J. Woods. In *Symmetry: Unifying Human Understanding,* edited by Istvan Hargittai, 407–11. New York: Pergamon.

Crowe, Donald W., and Dorothy K. Washburn. 1985. Groups and Geometry in the Ceramic Art of San Ildefonso. *Algebras, Groups and Geometries* 3(2):263–77.

————. 1987. Flow Charts as an Aid to the Symmetry Classification of Patterned Design. In *Material Anthropology: Contemporary Approaches to Material Culture,* edited by B. Reynolds and M. Stott, 69–101. Lanham, Maryland: University Press of America.

Cunningham, Clark E. 1973. Order in the Atoni House. In *Right and Left: Essays on Dual Symbolic Classification,* edited by Rodney Needham, 204–38. Chicago: University of Chicago Press.

Day, Lewis F. 1904. *Ornament and its Application.* London: B. T. Batsford.

de Jong, W. F. 1959. *General Crystallography: A Brief Compendium.* San Francisco: Freeman.

Deregowski, J. B. 1972. The Role of Symmetry in Pattern Reproduction by Zambian Children. *Journal of Cross-Cultural Psychology* 3(3):303–7.

————. 1974. Effects of Symmetry Upon Reproduction of Kohs-Type Figures: An African Study. *British Journal of Psychology* 65(1):93–102.

Dolmetsch, H. 1889. *Der Ornamentenschatz.* Stuttgart: Julius Hoffmann. (English edition, 1912, London.)

Donnay, J. D. H., and G. Donnay. 1985. Symmetry and Antisymmetry in Maori Rafter Designs. *Empirical Studies of the Arts* 3(1):23–45.

Dowlatshahi, Ali. 1979. *Persian Designs and Motifs for Artists and Craftsmen.* New York: Dover.

Dunnell, Robert C. 1971. *Systematics in Prehistory.* New York: Free Press.

Dürer, Albrecht. 1525. *Underweysung der Messung.* Nuremberg. (Reissued in 1972. Portland, Oregon: Collegium Graphicum.)

Dye, Daniel Sheets. 1937. *A Grammar of Chinese Lattice,* Vols. 1, 2. Harvard-Yenching Institute Monograph Series, vol. 5. Cambridge: Harvard University Press. (Reprint, 1974. New York: Dover.)

Edwards, Phoebe. 1975. *Anyone Can Quilt.* Elmsford, New York: Benjamin.

Eisenman, R., and J. Rappaport. 1967. Complexity Preference and Semantic Differential Ratings of Complexity-Simplicity and Symmetry-Asymmetry. *Psychonomic Science* 7(4):147–48.

El-Said, Issam, and Ayse Parman. 1976. *Geometric Concepts in Islamic Art*. London: World of Islam Festival Publishing Company.

Enciso, Jorge. 1953. *Design Motifs of Ancient Mexico*. New York: Dover.

Engelbrecht, William. 1974. The Iroquois: Archaeological Patterning on the Tribal Level. *World Archaeology* 6:52–65.

Faris, James C. 1972. *Nuba Personal Art*. Toronto: University of Toronto Press.

Federov, E. S. 1891. Symmetry of Regular Systems of Figures. *Proceedings of the Imperial Saint Petersburg Society, Series 2*, 28:1–146.

———. 1891. Symmetry in the Plane. *Proceedings of the Imperial Saint Petersburg Society, Series 2*, 28:345–89.

Fejes Tóth, L. *Regular Figures*. International Series of Monographs on Pure and Applied Mathematics, vol. 48. New York: Macmillan.

Fischer, Joseph. 1979. *Threads of Tradition: Textiles of Indonesia and Sarawak*. Berkeley: Lowie Museum of Anthropology, University of California.

Fischer, J. L. 1961. Art Styles as Cultural Cognitive Maps. *American Anthropologist* 63(1):79–93.

Flemming, Ernst. n.d. Introduction. In *An Encyclopaedia of Textiles of the Earliest Times to the Beginning of the Nineteenth Century*. Berlin: Ernst Wasmuth.

Foster, David H. 1984. Local and Global Computational Factors in Visual Pattern Recognition. In *Figural Synthesis*, edited by P. J. Dodwell and T. Caelli, 83–115. Hillsdale, New Jersey: Lawrence Erlbaum Associates.

Fox, John. 1975. The Use of Structural Diagnostics in Recognition. *Journal of Experimental Psychology* 1(1):57–67.

Freyd, J., and B. Tversky. 1984. Force of Symmetry in Form Perception. *American Journal of Psychology* 97(1):109–26.

Friedrich, Margaret Hardin. 1970. Design Structure and Social Interaction: Archaeological Implications of an Ethnographic Analysis. *American Antiquity* 35(3):332–43.

Gans, David. 1969. *Transformations and Geometries*. New York: Appleton-Century Crofts.

Gardner, Howard. 1981. *The Quest for Mind*. 2d ed. New York: Knopf.

Germain, Suzanne. 1969. *Les Mosaïques de Timgad: Étude Descriptive et Analytique*. Paris: Éditions du Centre National de la Recherche Scientifique.

Gerspach, M. 1975. *Coptic Textile Designs*. New York: Dover.

Glassie, Henry. 1975. *Folk Housing in Middle Virginia: Structural Analysis of Historic Artifacts*. Knoxville: University of Tennessee Press.

Gombrich, E. H. 1979. *The Sense of Order*. Oxford: Phaidon Press Ltd.; Ithaca: Cornell University Press.

Grabar, Oleg. 1978. *The Alhambra*. Cambridge: Harvard University Press.

Grafton, C. G. 1975. *Geometric Patchwork Quilts*. New York: Dover.

Grünbaum, Branko. 1984. The Emperor's New Clothes: Full Regalia, G-String, or Nothing? *Mathematical Intelligencer* 6(4):47–53.

Grünbaum, Branko, and G. C. Shephard. 1977. Classification of Plane Patterns. Paper presented at summer meeting of the American Mathematical Society, Seattle.

———. 1981. A Hierarchy of Classification Methods for Patterns. *Zeitschrift für Kristallographie* 154:163–87.

———. 1983. Tilings, Patterns, Fabrics and Related Topics in Discrete Geometry. *Jahresbericht der deutschen Mathematiker-Vereinigung* 85:1–32.

———. 1987. *Tilings and Patterns*. San Francisco: Freeman.

Grünbaum, Branko, Zdenka Grünbaum, and G. C. Shephard. 1986. Symmetry in Moorish and Other Ornaments. In *Symmetry: Unifying Human Understanding*, edited by Istvan Hargittai, 641–53. New York: Pergamon.

Guggenheimer, Heinrich W. 1967. *Plane Geometry and its Groups*. San Francisco: Holden-Day.

Gumerman, George J., and David A. Phillips, Jr. 1978. Archaeology Beyond Anthropology. *American Antiquity* 43(2):184–91.

Gutierrez, Abel A. n.d. *Dibujos Indigenas de Chile*. Santiago: Imprenta Universitaria.

Hagen, Margaret A. 1986. *Varieties of Realism: Geometries of Representational Art*. Cambridge: Cambridge University Press.

Hamlin, A. D. F. 1916. *A History of Ornament: Ancient and Medieval*. New York: Century.

Hamilton, Augustus. 1896. *The Art Workmanship of the Maori Race in New Zealand*. Wellington: New Zealand Institute.

Hanneman, E. F. 1969. *Grass Roots Art of New Guinea*. Sidney: Pacific Publications.

Hanson, F. Allan. 1983. When the Map is the Territory: Art in Maori Culture. In *Structure and Cognition in Art*, edited by D. K. Washburn, 74–89. Cambridge: Cambridge University Press.

———. 1985. From Symmetry to Anthropophagy: The Cultural Context of Maori Art. *Empirical Studies of the Arts* 3(1):47–62.

Hardin, Margaret Ann. 1977. Individual Style in San José Pottery Painting: The Role of Deliberate Choice. In *The Individual in Prehistory*, edited by J. Hill and J. Gunn, 109–36. New York: Academic Press.

Hargittai, Istvan, ed. 1986. *Symmetry: Unifying Human Understanding*. New York: Pergamon. (Reprinted from the journal *Computers and Mathematics with Applications*. Part 1, vol. 12B[1–2]; part 2, vol. 12B[3–4].)

Hargittai, Istvan, and Györgyi Lengyel. 1984. The Seven One-Dimensional Space-Group Symmetries in Hungarian Folk Needlework. *Journal of Chemical Education* 61:1033.

———. 1985. The Seventeen Two-Dimensional Space-Group Symmetries in Hungarian Needlework. *Journal of Chemical Education* 62:35–36.

Harris, Marvin. 1968. *The Rise of Anthropological Theory*. New York: Crowell.

Hatcher, Evelyn Payne. 1974. *Visual Metaphors: A Formal Analysis of Navajo Art*. American Ethnological Society Monograph no. 58. St. Paul: West.

Hawkes, Terence. 1977. *Structuralism and Semiotics*. Berkeley: University of California Press.

Heesch, H. 1929. Zur systematischen Strukturtheorie, I. *Zeitschrift für Kristallographie* 71:95–102.

Henry, N. F. M., and K. Lonsdale. 1952. *International Tables for X-Ray Crystallography*. Vol. 1. Birmingham: Kynoch Press, for the International Union of Crystallography.

Hermann, C. 1929. Zur systematischen Strukturtheorie III Ketten-und Netzgruppen. *Zeitschrift für Kristallographie* 69:250–60.

Hershenson, M., and J. Ryder. 1982. Perceived Symmetry and Visual Matching. *The American Journal of Psychology* 95(4):669–80.

Hodder, Ian. 1977. The Distribution of Material Culture Items in the Baringo District, Western Kenya. *Man*, n.s., 12:239–69.

———. 1982. *Symbols in Action: Ethnoarchaeological Studies of Material Culture*. Cambridge: Cambridge University Press.

Hofstadter, Douglas R. 1980. *Gödel, Escher, Bach: An Eternal Golden Braid*. New York: Vintage.

Holm, Bill. 1965. *Northwest Coast Indian Art: An Analysis of Form*. Seattle: University of Washington Press.

Holser, W. T. 1961. Classification of Symmetry Groups. *Acta Crystallographica* 14:1236–42.

Hornung, Clarence P. 1975. *Allover Patterns for Designers and Craftsmen*. New York: Dover.

Howe, E. S. 1980. Effects of Partial Symmetry, Exposure Time, and Backward Masking on Judged Goodness and Reproduction of Visual Pattern. *Quarterly Journal of Experimental Psychology* 32:27–55.

Humbert, Claude. 1980. *Islamic Ornamental Design*. New York: Hastings House.

Jaeger, Frans Maurits. 1917. *Lectures on the Principle of Symmetry and its Application in all Natural Sciences*. Amsterdam: Elsevier.

Jahoda, G. 1956. Assessment of Abstract Behavior in a Non-Western Society. *Journal of Abnormal Social Psychology* 53:237–43.

———. 1976. Reproduction of Kohs-Type Figures by Ghanaian Children: Orientation Errors Revisited. *British Journal of Psychology* 67(2):203–11.

Jarratt, J. D., and R. L. E. Schwarzenberger. 1980. Coloured Plane Groups. *Acta Crystallographica* A36:884–88.

———. 1981. Coloured Frieze Groups. *Utilitas Mathematica* 19:295–303.

Johnston, Susan. 1979. *Patchwork Quilt Coloring Book*. New York: Dover.

Jones, Owen. 1856. *The Grammar of Ornament*. (Reprint 1982. New York: Van Nostrand Reinhold.)

Julesz, Bela. 1975. Experiments in the Visual Perception of Texture. *Scientific American* 232(4):34–43.

Kaeppler, Adrienne L. 1978. Melody, Drone and Decoration: Underlying Structures and Surface Manifestations in Tongan Art and Society. In *Art in Society*, edited by M. Greenhalgh and V. Megaw, 261–74. New York: St. Martin's Press.

Kent, Kate P. 1972. West African Decorative Weaving. *African Arts* (Autumn):22–27, 67–70.

———. 1983. Temporal Shifts in the Structure of Tradition: Southwestern Textile Design. In *Structure and Cognition in Art*, edited by D. K. Washburn, 113–37. Cambridge: Cambridge University Press.

Kepler, J., trans. 1966. *The Six-Cornered Snowflake* [1611]. Oxford: Clarendon Press.

Kim, Scott. 1981. *Inversions: A Catalog of Calligraphic Cartwheels*. Peterborough: BYTE Books.

Klarner, David A., ed. 1981. *The Mathematical Gardner*. Boston: Prindle, Weber & Schmidt.

Knight, G. H. 1984. The Geometry of Maori Art. Part 1: Rafter Patterns. *New Zealand Mathematics Magazine* 21(3):36–40. Part 2: Weaving Patterns. *New Zealand Mathematics Magazine* 21(3):80–86.

Korn, Sheila M. 1978. The Formal Analysis of Visual Systems as Exemplified by a Study of Abelam Painting. In *Art in Society*, edited by M. Greenhalgh and V. Megaw, 161–73. New York: St. Martin's Press.

Kroeber, A. L. 1957. *Style and Civilization*. Ithaca: Cornell University Press.

Lechtman, Heather. 1977. Style in Technology—Some Early Thoughts. In *Material Culture: Styles, Organization, and Dynamics of Technology*. Edited by H. Lechtman and R. Merrill, 3–20. St. Paul: West.

Levi, Doro. 1947. *Antioch Mosaic Pavements*, Vol. 2. Princeton: Princeton University Press.

Lewis, Albert Buell. 1924. *Block Prints from India for Textiles.* Anthropology Design Series, no. 1. Chicago: Field Museum of Natural History.

———. 1925. *Decorative Art of New Guinea.* Anthropology Design Series, no. 4. Chicago: Field Museum of Natural History. (Reprint, 1973. New York: Dover.)

Locher, J. L., ed. 1982. *M. C. Escher: His Life and Complete Graphic Work.* New York: Abrams.

Locher, P. J., and C. F. Nodine. 1973. Influence of Stimulus Symmetry on Visual Scanning Patterns. *Perception and Psychophysics* 13(3):408–12.

Lockwood, E. H., and R. H. Macmillan. 1978. *Geometric Symmetry.* Cambridge: Cambridge University Press.

Loeb, Arthur L. 1971. *Color and Symmetry.* New York: Wiley-Interscience.

Lyford, Carrie A. 1953. *Ojibwa Crafts.* Indian Handcrafts Series, no. 5. Washington, D.C.: Branch of Education, Bureau of Indian Affairs, Department of the Interior.

Maccoby, E. E. 1968. What Copying Requires. *Ontario Journal of Educational Research* 10:163–70.

Macdonald, Sheila Oates, and Anne Penfold Street. 1976. On Crystallographic Colour Groups. *Lecture Notes in Mathematics* 560:149–57. Berlin: Springer.

———. 1978a. The Analysis of Colour Symmetry. *Lecture Notes in Mathematics* 686:210–22. Berlin: Springer.

———. 1978b. The Seven Friezes and How to Colour Them. *Utilitas Mathematica* 13:271–92.

MacGillavry, Caroline H. 1976. *Fantasy and Symmetry: The Periodic Drawings of M. C. Escher.* New York: Abrams. (Reprint of *Symmetry Aspects of M. C. Escher's Periodic Drawings,* published in 1965 for the International Union of Crystallography. Utrecht: A. Oosthoek's Uitgeversmaatschappij.)

Makovicky, Emil. 1986. Symmetrology of Art: Coloured and Generalized Symmetries. In *Symmetry: Unifying Human Understanding,* edited by Istvan Hargittai, 949–80. New York: Pergamon.

Maranda, Pierre. 1972. Structuralism in Cultural Anthropology. In *Annual Review of Anthropology,* Vol. 1, edited by B. J. Siegel and others, 329–48. Palo Alto, Calif.: Annual Reviews.

March, Lionel, and Philip Steadman. 1971. *The Geometry of Environment: An Introduction to Spatial Organization in Design.* London: RIBA Publications. (Reprint, 1974. Cambridge: MIT Press.)

Martin, George E. 1982. *Transformation Geometry: An Introduction to Symmetry.* New York: Springer.

Menzel, Dorothy. 1976. *Pottery Style and Society in Ancient Peru.* Berkeley: University of California Press.

Mera, H. P. 1937. *The "Rain Bird": A Study in Pueblo Design.* Memoirs of the Laboratory of Anthropology, vol. 2. Santa Fe.

Meyer, Franz Sales. 1894. *Handbook of Ornament: A Grammar of Art Industrial and Architectural Designing in all its branches for practical as well as theoretical use.* 4th ed. New York: Hessling & Spielmeyer.

Mills, George. 1959. *Navajo Art and Culture.* Colorado Springs: The Taylor Museum of the Colorado Springs Fine Arts Center.

Morris, Walter F., Jr. 1987. Symbolism of a Ceremonial Huipil of the Highland Tzotil Maya Community of Magdalenas, Chiapas. *Notes of the New World Archaeological Foundation* 4:1–24. Provo, Utah: Brigham Young University.

Müller, Edith. 1944. *Gruppentheoretische und Strukturanalytische Untersuchungen der Maurischen Ornamente aus der Alhambra in Granada.* Ph.D. diss., University of Zürich, Rüschlikon.

Muller, Jon D. 1977. Individual Variation in Art Styles. In *The Individual in Prehistory,* edited by J. Hill and J. Gunn, 23–39. New York: Academic Press.

————. 1979. Structural Studies of Art Styles. In *The Visual Arts: Plastic and Graphic,* edited by J. Cordwell, 139–211. The Hague.

Munari, Bruno. 1966. *Discovery of the Circle.* New York: George Wittenborn.

Munn, Nancy D. 1973. *Walbiri Iconography.* Ithaca: Cornell University Press.

Naylor, Maria, ed. 1975. *Authentic Indian Designs: 2500 Illustrations from the First forty-four Annual Reports of the Bureau of American Ethnology.* New York: Dover.

Niggli, P. 1924. Die Flächensymmetrien homogener Diskontinuen. *Zeitschrift für Kristallographie* 60:283–98.

————. 1926. Die regelmässige Punktverteilung längs einer Geraden in einer Ebene. *Zeitschrift für Kristallographie* 63:255–74.

Niman, John, and Jane Norman. 1978. Mathematics and Islamic Art. *American Mathematical Monthly* 85:489–90.

O'Daffer, Phares G., and Stanley R. Clemens. 1976. *Geometry: An Investigative Approach.* Menlo Park: Addison-Wesley.

O'Neale, Lila M. 1932. *Yurok-Karok Basket Weavers.* University of California Publications in American Archaeology and Ethnology, Vol. 32, no. 1. Berkeley.

Ōuchi, Hajime. 1977. *Japanese Optical and Geometrical Art.* New York: Dover.

Palmer, S. E., and K. Henenway. 1978. Orientation and Symmetry: Effects of Multiple, Rotational, and Near Symmetries. *Journal of Experimental Psychology* 4(4):691–702.

Paraskevopoulos, I. 1968. Symmetry, Recall, and Preference in Relation to Chronological Age. *Journal of Experimental Child Psychology* 6:254–64.

Perleberg, H. C. n.d. *Peruvian Textiles.* New York: H. C. Perleberg.

Persoz, J. 1846. *Traité Théorique et Pratique de l'Impression des Tissus,* Vol. 4. Paris: Victor Masson.

Petrie, Flinders. 1930. *Decorative Patterns of the Ancient World.* British School of Archaeology in Egypt. (Reprinted in 1974 as *Decorative Patterns of the Ancient World for Craftsmen.* New York: Dover.)

Pettit, Philip. 1975. *The Concept of Structuralism.* Berkeley: University of California Press.

Pick, Anne D. 1980. Cognition: Psychological Perspectives. In *Handbook of Cross-Cultural Psychology,* Vol. 3, edited by H. C. Triandis and W. Lonner, 117–53. Boston: Allyn & Bacon, Inc.

Plog, Fred. 1977. Archaeology and the Individual. In *The Individual in Prehistory,* edited by J. Hill and J. Gunn, 13–21. New York: Academic Press.

Plog, Stephen. 1980. *Stylistic Variation in Prehistoric Ceramics.* Cambridge: Cambridge University Press.

Pólya, G. 1924. Über die Analogie der Kristallsymmetrie in der Ebene. *Zeitschrift für Kristallographie* 60:278–82.

Prisse d'Avennes, Achille. 1978. *Arabic Art in Color.* New York: Dover. (Reprint. Originally published as *La Décoration Arabe,* by Prisse d'Avesnes [sic]. Paris: André Daly Fils, n.d.)

Purce, Jill. 1974. *The Mystic Spiral.* London: Thames and Hudson.

Racinet, A. 1869. *L'Ornement Polychrome.* Paris: Firmin Didot frères.

Redman, Charles L. 1977. The Analytical Individual and Prehistoric Style Variability. In *The Individual in Prehistory,* edited by J. Hill and J. Gunn, 41–53. New York: Academic Press.

Reed, Stephen K. 1973. *Psychological Processes in Pattern Recognition.* New York: Academic Press.

Reichel-Dolmatoff, Gerardo. 1971. *Amazonian Cosmos.* Chicago: University of Chicago Press.

Roaf, Michael. 1978. A Mathematical Analysis of the Styles of the Persepolis Reliefs. In *Art in Society,* edited by M. Greenhalgh and V. Megaw, 133–45. New York: St. Martin's Press.

Roby, David, ed. 1973. *Structuralism: An Introduction.* Oxford: Clarendon Press.

Rock, I. 1973. *Orientation and Form.* New York: Academic Press.

Rock, I., and R. Leaman. 1963. An Experimental Analysis of Visual Symmetry. *Acta Psychologica* 21:171–83.

Roe, Peter G. 1980. Art and Residence among the Shipibo Indians of Peru: A Study in Microacculturation. *American Anthropologist* 82(1):42–71.

Rose, Bruce I., and Robert D. Stafford. 1981. An Elementary Course in Mathematical Symmetry. *American Mathematical Monthly* 88:59–64.

Rosen, Joe. 1975. *Symmetry Discovered: Concepts and Application in Nature and Science.* Cambridge: Cambridge University Press.

Sackett, James R. 1985. Style and Ethnicity in the Kalahari: A Reply to Wiessner. *American Antiquity* 50(1):154–59.

Salvador, Mari Lyn. 1978. *Yer Dailege! Kuna Women's Art.* Albuquerque: Maxwell Museum of Anthropology.

Schapiro, Meyer. 1962. Style. In *Anthropology Today: Selections,* edited by Sol Tax, 278–303. Chicago: University of Chicago Press.

Schattschneider, Doris. 1978. The Plane Symmetry Groups: Their Recognition and Notation. *American Mathematical Monthly* 85(6):439–50.

———. 1986. In Black and White: How to Create Perfectly Colored Symmetric Patterns. In *Symmetry: Unifying Human Understanding,* edited by Istvan Hargittai, 673–95. New York: Pergamon.

Schleifer, Leopold. 1968. *Dekor-Muster-Struktur.* Ulm-Donau: Karl Grömer.

Schwarzenberger, R. L. E. 1974. The Seventeen Plane Symmetry Groups. *The Mathematical Gazette* 58:123–31.

———. 1980. *N-Dimensional Crystallography.* San Francisco: Pitman.

———. 1984. Colour Symmetry. *Bulletin of the London Mathematical Society* 16:209–40.

Senechal, Marjorie. 1975. Point Groups and Color Symmetry. *Zeitschrift für Kristallographie* 142:1–23.

———. 1979. Color Groups. *Discrete Applied Mathematics* 1:51–73.

———. 1983. Coloring Symmetrical Objects Symmetrically. *Mathematics Magazine* 56:3–16.

Senechal, Marjorie, and George Fleck, eds. 1977. *Patterns of Symmetry.* Amherst: University of Massachusetts Press.

Serpell, R. 1971. Preference for Specific Orientation of Abstract Shapes Among Zambian Children. *Journal of Cross-Cultural Psychology* 2(3):225–39.

Shapiro, M. B. 1960. The Rotation of Drawings by Illiterate Africans. *Journal of Social Psychology* 52:17–30.

Shepard, Anna O. 1948. *The Symmetry of Abstract Design with Special Reference to Ceramic Decoration.* Contribution no. 47, Carnegie Institution of Washington Publication no. 574.

————. 1956. *Ceramics for the Archaeologist.* Carnegie Institution of Washington Publication no. 609.

Shepard, R. N., and J. Metzler. 1971. Mental Rotation of Three-Dimensional Objects. *Science* 171(3972):701–3.

Shubnikov, A. V. 1962. Symmetry and Antisymmetry Groups (classes) of Finite Strips. *Soviet Physics-Crystallography* 7(1):1–4.

————. 1962. Black-White Groups of Infinite Ribbons. *Soviet Physics-Crystallography* 7(2):145–49.

Shubnikov, A. V., N. V. Belov, and others. 1964. *Colored Symmetry.* New York: Pergamon.

Shubnikov, A. V., and V. A. Koptsik. 1974. *Symmetry in Science and Art.* New York: Plenum.

Sides, Dorothy Smith. 1961. *Decorative Art of the Southwestern Indians.* New York: Dover.

Speiser, A. 1927. *Theorie der Gruppen von endlicher Ordnung.* 2d ed. Berlin: Springer.

Speltz, Alexander. 1915. *The Coloured Ornament of All Historical Styles. Part 1: Antiquity.* Leipzig: K. F. Koehlers Antiquarium.

————. 1914. *The Coloured Ornament of All Historical Styles. Part 2: Middle Ages.* Leipzig: A. Schumann.

————. n.d. *The Coloured Ornament of All Historical Styles. Part 3: Modern Times.* Leipzig: K. F. Koehlers Antiquarium.

Stephenson, Charles, and F. Suddards. 1897. *A Text Book Dealing with Ornamental Design for Woven Fabrics.* London: Methuen.

Stevens, Peter S. 1974. *Patterns in Nature.* Boston: Atlantic-Little, Brown.

————. 1980. *Handbook of Regular Patterns: An Introduction to Symmetry in Two Dimensions.* Cambridge: MIT Press.

Stewart, Joe D. 1979. The Formal Definition of Decorative Traditions in the Jornada Area: A Case Study of Lincoln Black-on-Red Designs. In *Jornada Mogollon Archaeology: Proceedings of the First Jornada Conference*, edited by P. H. Beckett and R. N. Wiseman, 295–344. Las Cruces: Cultural Resources Management Division, New Mexico State University.

————. 1980. Further Suggestions on the Analysis of Nubian Ceramic Decoration. *Current Anthropology* 21(4):539–40.

————. 1983. Structural Analysis of Three Rivers Redware Designs. *Kiva* 49(1–2):39–65.

Szilagyi, P. G., and J. C. Baird. 1977. A Quantitative Approach to the Study of Visual Symmetry. *Perception & Psychophysics* 22(3):287–92.

Tana, Pradummna, and Rosalba Tana. 1981. *Traditional Designs from India for Artists and Craftsmen.* New York: Dover.

Tanner, Clara Lee. 1976. *Prehistoric Southwestern Craft Arts.* Tucson: University of Arizona Press.

Tekane, I. 1963. Symmetrical Pattern Completions by Illiterate and Literate Bantu. *Psychologia Africana* 10:63–68.

Thompson, Laura. 1945. Logico-Aesthetic Integration in Hopi Culture. *American Anthropologist* 47(4):540–53.

Van Esterik, Penny. 1979. Symmetry and Symbolism in Ban Chiang Painted Pottery. *Journal of Anthropological Research* 35(4):495–508.

————. 1981. *Cognition and Design Production in Ban Chiang Painted Pottery.* Papers in International Studies, Southeast Asia Series, no. 58. Athens: Ohio University Center for International Studies.

Vastokas, Joan M. 1978. Cognitive Aspects of Northwest Coast Art. In *Art in Society*, edited by M. Greenhalgh and V. Megaw, 243–59. New York: St. Martin's Press.

Wade, David. 1982. *Geometric Patterns and Borders.* New York: Van Nostrand Reinhold.

Washburn, Dorothy Koster. 1977a. *A Symmetry Analysis of Upper Gila Area Ceramic Design.* Papers of the Peabody Museum of Archaeology and Ethnology, vol. 68. Cambridge: Harvard University.

———. 1977b. A Symmetry Classification of Pueblo Ceramic Design. In *Discovering Past Behavior: Experiments in the Archaeology of the American Southwest*, edited by Paul Grebinger, 101–21. New York: Gordon Breach.

———. 1980. The Mexican Connection: Cylinder Jars from the Valley of Oaxaca. In *New Frontiers in the Archaeology and Ethnohistory of the Greater Southwest*, edited by Carroll L. Riley and Basil C. Hedrick 70–84. Transactions of the Illinois State Academy of Science, vol. 72, no. 4.

———. 1983a. Toward a Theory of Structural Style in Art. In *Structure and Cognition in Art*, edited by D. Washburn, 1–7. Cambridge: Cambridge University Press.

———. 1983b. Symmetry Analysis of Ceramic Design: Two Tests of the Method on Neolithic Material from Greece and the Aegean. In *Structure and Cognition in Art*, edited by D. Washburn, 138–64. Cambridge: Cambridge University Press.

———. 1984. The Usefulness of Typological Analysis for Understanding Aspects of Southwestern Prehistory: Some Conflicting Returns from Design Analysis. In *Regional Analysis of Prehistoric Ceramic Variation: Contemporary Studies of the Cibola Whitewares*, edited by A. Sullivan and J. Hantman, 120–34. Anthropological Research Papers, no. 31. Tempe: Arizona State University.

———. 1986a. Symmetry Analysis of Yurok, Karok and Hupa Indian Basket Designs. *Empirical Studies of the Arts* 4(1):19–45.

———. 1986b. Pattern Symmetry and Colored Repetition in Cultural Contexts. In *Symmetry: Unifying Human Understanding*, edited by Istvan Hargittai, 767–81. New York: Pergamon.

Washburn, Dorothy K., and R. G. Matson. 1985. Use of Multidimensional Scaling to Display Sensitivity of Symmetry Analysis of Patterned Design to Spatial and Chronological Change: Examples from Anasazi Prehistory. In *Decoding Prehistoric Ceramics*, edited by B. Nelson, 75–101. Carbondale: Southern Illinois University Press.

Washburn, Dorothy K., and Andrea Petitto. 1985. Informant Criteria for Judging Traditional Designs. Manuscript.

Watt, Matthew Digby. 1848. *Specimens of the Geometrical Mosaic of the Middle Ages.* London: Day & Sons, for The Royal Society of Arts and The Archaeological Institute of Great Britain and Ireland.

Watt, William C. 1966. Morphology of the Nevada Cattlebrands and their Blazons. National Bureau of Standards Report no. 9050. Washington, D.C.: U.S. Department of Commerce.

Weber, L. 1929. Die Symmetrie homogener ebener Punktsysteme. *Zeitschrift für Kristallographie* 70:309–27.

Weyl, Hermann. 1952. *Symmetry.* Princeton: Princeton University Press.

Wiessner, Polly. 1983. Style and Social Information in Kalahari San Projectile Points. *American Antiquity* 48(2):253–76.

Wieting, Thomas W. 1982. *The Mathematical Theory of Chromatic Plane Ornaments.* New York: Marcel Dekker.

Williams, Geoffrey. 1971. *African Designs from Traditional Sources.* New York: Dover.

Witherspoon, Gary. 1977. *Language and Art in the Navajo Universe.* Ann Arbor: University of Michigan Press.

Wobst, Martin. 1977. Stylistic Behavior and Information Exchange. In *For the Director: Research Essays in Honor of James B. Griffin,* edited by C. Cleland, 317–42. Anthropological Papers, no. 61. Ann Arbor: University of Michigan.

Wood, Denis. 1975. Making Seen: The Perception and Generation of Patterns in the Clothing of the Highlands of Chiapas, Mexico. In *Patterns.* Raleigh: School of Design, North Carolina State University.

Woods, H. J. 1935. The Geometrical Basis of Pattern Design. Part 1: Point and Line Symmetry in Simple Figures and Borders. *Journal of the Textile Institute,* Transactions 26:T197–210. Part 2: Nets and Sateens. *Journal of the Textile Institute,* Transactions 26:T293–308. Part 3: Geometrical Symmetry in Plane Patterns. *Journal of the Textile Institute,* Transactions 26:T341–57.

———. 1936. The Geometrical Basis of Pattern Design. Part 4: Counterchange Symmetry in Plane Patterns. *Journal of the Textile Institute,* Transactions 27:T305–20.

Yale, Paul B. 1968. *Geometry and Symmetry.* San Francisco: Holden-Day.

Zaslavsky, Claudia. 1973. *Africa Counts: Number and Pattern in African Culture.* Boston: Prindle, Weber & Schmidt.

Zaslow, Bert. 1977. A Guide to Analyzing Prehistoric Ceramic Decorations by Symmetry and Pattern Mathematics. In *Pattern Mathematics and Archaeology.* Anthropological Research Papers, no. 2. Tempe: Arizona State University.

———. 1980. Mirror Orientation in Hohokam Designs and the Chronology of Early Hohokam Phases. *The Kiva* 45(3):211–25.

———. 1981. *Pattern Dissemination in the Prehistoric Southwest and Mesoamerica: A Comparison of Hohokam Decorative Patterns with Patterns from the Upper Gila Area and from the Valley of Oaxaca.* Anthropological Research Papers, no. 25. Tempe: Arizona State University.

Zaslow, Bert, and Alfred E. Dittert. 1977a. Pattern Theory Used as an Archaeological Tool: A Preliminary Statement. *Southwestern Lore* 43(1):18–24.

———. 1977b. *Pattern Mathematics and Archaeology.* Anthropological Research Papers, no. 2. Tempe: Arizona State University.

Index

General Index

Notation Index

This index is divided into sections for finite designs, one-dimensional patterns, and two-dimensional patterns in the plane. Page numbers refer to the passages where each symmetry class is defined, "keyed out," and illustrated by a schematic drawing and examples. Boldface numbers refer to the flow chart or branch of a flow chart where the symmetry class appears. (There are no flow charts for finite designs.)

Credits

THE FOLLOWING granted permission to reprint photographs and drawings. Numbers indicate figures in this book. Sources may be found in the captions.

Arizona State Museum, University of Arizona: 6.18. *Asian Art Museum of San Francisco:* 4.35, Chapter 5 frontispiece, 5.69, 5.106, 5.253, 5.286, 6.9. BEELDRECHT: 5.216. *Bernice P. Bishop Museum, Honolulu:* 5.117, 5.158. *Beverly Latin Collection:* 5.128. *Brooklyn Museum:* 5.65. *California Academy of Sciences, San Francisco:* 2.16, Chapter 4 frontispiece, 4.30, 4.38, 4.44, 4.45, 4.61, 4.66, 4.80, 4.87, 4.97, 4.100, 4.101, 4.106, 4.113, 4.116, 4.122, 4.123, 4.131, 4.145, 4.146, 4.150, 5.18, 5.22, 5.24, 5.31, 5.43, 5.61, 5.83, 5.93a, 5.107, 5.123, 5.124, 5.126, 5.129, 5.136, 5.146, 5.148, 5.161, 5.166, 5.167, 5.169, 5.170, 5.177, 5.192, 5.206, 5.208, 5.221, 5.223, 5.224, 5.227, 5.229, 5.230, 5.283, 5.284, 6.2, 6.4, 6.7, 6.10, 6.11, 6.13, 7.10, 7.15, 7.16. *Centre National de la Recherche Scientifique (Paris):* 5.14, 5.202, 5.244, 5.249. *College Museum, Hampton University, Hampton, Virginia:* 5.12, 5.34, 5.133, 5.138, 5.149. *Colorado Historical Society, Denver:* 4.32, 4.77. *Fabritius and Sonners Forlag:* 4.29, 4.33, 4.82, 4.144, 6.8, 6.12. *Dennis Penley Collection:* 5.80. *Field Museum of Natural History, Chicago:* 4.139, 5.66, 5.86a, 5.89, 7.5, 7.9. *Fine Arts Museums of San Francisco (The M. H. de Young Memorial Museum):* Chapter 1 frontispiece, 4.88, 5.5a, 5.20, 5.71, 5.165, 5.172, 7.3. *Haffenreffer Museum of Anthropology, Brown University:* 2.18, 5.168. *Heard Museum, Phoenix:* 5.27. *Helen L. Allen Textile Collection, University of Wisconsin, Madison:* 5.13, 5.19, 5.38, 5.99, 5.115, 5.190, 5.201, 5.246. *Institut de Folklore, Skopje:* 5.2 *Istituto Poligrafico e Zecca dello Stato (Rome):* 5.74, 5.147, 5.258, 5.278. *Laurence Moss Collection:* 4.62. *Los Angeles County Museum of Art:* 5.79, 7.1, 7.12. *Los Angeles County Museum of Natural History:* 5.75. *Lowie Museum of Anthropology, University of California, Berkeley:* Chapter 2 frontispiece, 4.48, 4.76, 5.90, 5.127, 5.225, 7.4. *Margaret Woodbury Strong Museum, Rochester:* 5.112. *Metropolitan Museum of Art, New York:* 5.187, 5.213, 5.285. *MIT Press:* 5.9, 5.45, 5.48. *Musée Royal de l'Afrique Centrale (Tervuren, Belgium):* 2.2, 4.52, 4.119, 5.37, 5.67, 5.68, 5.78, 5.109, 5.122, 5.134, 5.145, 5.154, 5.157, 5.184, 5.186, 5.197, 5.222, 5.236, 5.250–52, 5.287, 5.291, 6.15. *Museum of Fine Arts, Boston:* 4.39, 5.88, 7.17. *Museum of New Mexico for the School of American Research:* 5.17, 5.102. *Museum of New Mexico:* 4.51, 5.131. *Museum of Northern Arizona, Flagstaff:* 5.135, Chapter 6 frontispiece. *Museum of the American Indian, Heye Foundation:* 5.185, 6.6. *Oxford University Press:* 2.8c, 3.2, 3.5, 3.6a–c, 5.40, 5.42, 5.49, 5.51, 5.53, 5.55, 5.73, 5.84, 5.111, 5.163, 5.189, 5.195, 5.212, 6.3. *Peabody Museum, Salem, Mass.:* 5.179. *Phaidon Press:* 4.133, 5.59. *Pitt Rivers Museum, Oxford:* 4.55. *Portland Art Museum:* 5.198. *Princeton University Press:* 4.134, 5.210, 5.211, 5.226, 5.248, 5.259. *R. Martin Smith Collection:* 5.218. *Rijksmuseum Kroller-Muller, Otterlo, The Netherlands:* 5.96. *Rochester Museum and Science Center, Rochester:* 4.59, 4.69, 4.98, 4.107, 5.199, 6.14. *Royal Society of New Zealand:* 3.17, 4.43, 4.81, 4.89, 4.94a–c, 4.99, 4.105, 4.132, 4.137, 4.151, 5.44. *School of American Research:* 2.5b, 2.5d, 2.7b, 2.9c, 2.11e, 2.13, 2.15, 2.19a–b, 2.20–23, 3.12a, 3.14, 4.2a, 4.3a, 4.4, 4.5a, 4.7, 4.8, 4.10–20, 4.22–25, 4.27, 4.28, 4.31, 4.37, 4.41a–e, 4.42a–b, 4.47, 4.54, 4.58a–d, 4.64, 4.65, 4.68, 4.73–75, 4.86, 4.91, 4.96a–e, 4.103, 4.104, 4.109, 4.112, 4.115, 4.121, 4.125, 4.126, 4.129, 4.136, 4.142, 4.148, 4.149. *Shelburne Museum, Shelburne, Vermont:* 5.289, 7.13. *State Historical Society of Wisconsin:* 5.72. *The Textile Museum, Washington, D.C.:* 5.1, 5.3, 5.104, 5.203. *Trustees of the British Museum:* 4.79, 4.110 *University Museum, University of Pennsylvania:* Chapter 3 frontispiece. *University of Arizona Press:* 4.70, 4.71, 4.83, 5.95. *University of California Press:* 4.130. *Victoria and Albert Museum:* 5.108.

Illustrations redrawn by Amy Pertschuk: 2.11a, 3.12a, 4.2a, 4.3a, 4.5a, 4.6, 4.7, 4.9, 4.10, 4.16, 4.19, 4.20, 4.21, 4.23, 4.25, 4.37, 4.47, 4.49, 4.54, 4.56, 4.112, 4.115, 4.127, 4.136, 5.7, 5.10, 5.21, 5.30, 5.56, 5.82, 5.92, 5.93b, 5.113, 5.116, 5.119, 5.152, 5.173, 5.181, 5.182, 5.215, 5.219, 5.232, 5.234, 5.237, 5.238, 5.240, 5.255, 5.263, 5.266, 5.268, 5.272, 5.273, 5.275, 5.279, 5.292, 7.6.

Illustrations redrawn by Colleen Sudekum: 4.92, 4.140, 5.39, 5.98, 5.143, 5.175, 5.205, 5.209, 5.241, 7.14.

Computer drawings by Mike Case: 5.64, 5.70, 5.76, 5.81, 5.85, 5.87, 5.91, 5.94, 5.97, 5.100, 5.103, 5.105, 5.110, 5.114, 5.118, 5.120, 5.125, 5.130, 5.132, 5.137, 5.141, 5.144, 5.150, 5.153, 5.156, 5.160, 5.162, 5.164, 5.171, 5.174, 5.176, 5.178, 5.180, 5.183, 5.188, 5.193, 5.196, 5.200, 5.204, 5.207, 5.214, 5.217, 5.220, 5.228, 5.233, 5.235, 5.239, 5.243, 5.247, 5.254, 5.256, 5.260, 5.262, 5.264, 5.267, 5.269, 5.274, 5.276, 5.280, 5.282, 5.288, 5.290, 5.293.